Alpena Co. Library
211 N. 1st Ave.
Alpena, MI 49707

Alpena Co. Library
211 N. 1st Ave.
Alpena, MI 49707

THE HOCKEY METHOD

BEGINNER SKATING - BEGINNER PUCK CONTROL

BOB DE LA SALLE

Order this book online at www.trafford.com
or email orders@trafford.com

Most Trafford titles are also available at major online book retailers.

© Copyright 2014 Bob de la Salle.

All rights reserved. No part of this publication may be reproduced, stored in a retrieval system, or transmitted, in any form or by any means, electronic, mechanical, photocopying, recording, or otherwise, without the written prior permission of the author.

Printed in the United States of America.

ISBN: 978-1-4907-2693-9 (sc)
ISBN: 978-1-4907-2692-2 (hc)
ISBN: 978-1-4907-2694-6 (e)

Library of Congress Control Number: 2014902517

Because of the dynamic nature of the Internet, any web addresses or links contained in this book may have changed since publication and may no longer be valid. The views expressed in this work are solely those of the author and do not necessarily reflect the views of the publisher, and the publisher hereby disclaims any responsibility for them.

Any people depicted in stock imagery provided by Thinkstock are models, and such images are being used for illustrative purposes only.
Certain stock imagery © Thinkstock.

Trafford rev. 02/25/2014

 www.trafford.com

North America & international
toll-free: 1 888 232 4444 (USA & Canada)
fax: 812 355 4082

For all first time skaters especially to Julie, Chantal, Erin and Lucas who demonstrated most of the drills in this book.

The Hockey Method

Volume 1

Book 1 Beginner Skating
(For Parents and Instructors)

Book 2 Beginner Puck Control
(For Parents and Instructors)

Contents

Preface xv
Introduction 1
Background 5

The Hockey Method 9
   1. Assessment 11
   2. Problem 12
   3. Analysis 13
      Concepts 13
      Drill Properties 14
      Skill-Level Breakdown and Progression 15
   4. Solution (Drills) 16
   5. Troubleshooting Skill Problems 17

Backdrop 19
   Swimming Analogy 19
      Problem 21
      Beginner Development Problems
         Not as Evident in Swimming 22
      Solution 23
      Rationale 23
   Ability of Kids (Myth of Ability) 24
   January—December Birthday Syndrome 26

How to Use This Book 31
   The Hockey Method Drill Matrix 31
   Parent Instant Recipe 33
   Mastering Drills 34
   Grading 36

Book 1:   Beginner Skating 39
   Why Beginner Skating? 39

No Time for Basics.. 40
First—Beginner Basics 41
Second—Team Play 41
    When is a beginner ready for team play?............................... 42
Can we Learn both Beginner Basics and Team Play
at the Same Time? 44
Instructing Beginner Skaters 45
    Beginner Skaters 45
    Age Considerations... 47
    Adult Beginners.. 48
    Communicating with the Beginner 50
    Exaggeration Technique 50
    Beginner Confidence 51
Parents 53
    Parents as First Instructors 53
    Lone Ranger Hockey for Kids (Keep-Away) 55
    Beginner Hockey Equipment Considerations for Parents........ 57
        General 57
        Skates 57
        Helmet 59
        Hockey Stick 59
The Four Major Skating Problems for Beginner Skaters............ 60
1—Skate-Feel Concepts 63
    Problem 63
    Analysis 63
    Solution 64
Skate-Feel Drill Description 65
    Walk—Concept 1 65
    Run—Concept 2... 79
    Glide—Concept 3 83
    Jump—Concept 4 90
    Rock—Concept 5 98
2—Toe-Heel Concepts 104
    Problem 104
    Analysis 104
    Solution 105
Toe-Heel Drill Description.. 106
    Toes Out—Concept 6 106

    Toes In—Concept 7 125
    Edges—Concept 8 132
    Heel—Concept 9 148
3—Knee Concepts 159
  Problem 159
  Analysis 160
  Solution 161
Knee Concepts Drill Description 162
    Knee Bend—Concept 10..162
    Knee Extension—Concept 11... 177
    Lateral—Concept 12 188
    Drop—Concept 13 196
    Kick—Concept 14... 201
    Advanced Jump—Concept 15 206
4—Balance Concepts... 209
  Problem 209
  Analysis 210
  Solution 210
Balance Drill Description 211
    Agility—Concept 16 211
    Flexibility—Concept 17 222
    Pivot—Concept 18 232
    Power—Concept 19 241
Special Combination Drills without the Puck 250
  Combo 5 250
  Magic 6 250

Book 1: Beginner Skating Drill List (Book 1) 252

Book 2:   Beginner Puck Control 261
  Why Beginner Puck Control?... 261
  The Five Major Problems
  for Beginner Puck Control.. 262
  1—Hands Concepts.. 264
    Problem 264
    Analysis 264
    Solution 265
  Hands Drill Description... 265
    Grip—Concept 20 265

    Wrist—Concept 21 270
    Puck Repeat—Concept 22 274
2—Eyes Concepts (Eyes Off the Puck) 275
    Problem 275
    Analysis 275
    Solution 276
Eyes (Off the Puck) Drill Description.. 277
    Dribble—Concept 23.. 277
    Balance—Concept 24 287
3—Puck Concepts 290
    Problem 290
    Analysis 291
    Solution 291
Puck Concepts Drill Description... 292
    Soft Hands—Concept 25 292
    Agility—Concept 26 301
4—Stick Concepts 312
    Problem 312
    Analysis 313
    Solution 313
Stick Drill Description 314
    Manipulate—Concept 27..314
    Stick Length—Concept 28..319
    Stick Reach—Concept 29 333
    Stick Blade—Concept 30 340
5—Puck-Control Balance Concepts.. 346
    Problem 346
    Analysis 346
    Solution 346
Puck-Control Balance Drill Description.. 347
    Puck-Control Balance—Concept 31....................................... 347
Special Combination drills with the Puck 353
    Combo 5 (with pucks) 353
    Magic 6 (with pucks) 353

Book 2: Beginner Puck-Control Drills (Book 2) 355

Conclusion...355

Epilogue **361**
  Body Contact 361
    Body Contact for Kids..361
    Hit-Line Proposal 363
    Troubleshooting Skill Problems................................... 364
      Example 1—Crossovers 366
        Problem—Crossovers (Agility skating problem—book 3).... 366
        Analysis—Crossovers.. 366
        Solution—Crossovers 367
      Example 2—Stopping 369
        Problem—Stopping (Agility skating problem—book 3) 369
        Analysis—Stopping 370
        Solution—Stopping 370
      Example 3—Weak Stride... 371
        Problems—Weak Stride
          (Forward skating problem—book 3)...................... 372
        Analysis—Weak Stride 372
        Solution—Weak Stride 372

Acknowledgments **375**

Bibliography...**377**
  Drill Sources and References 377

Appendices **379**

Appendix A: Concept List (31 Levels) **381**
Appendix B: Elementary (E) Drill List................................ **383**
Appendix C: Medium (M) Drill List................................... **389**
Appendix D: Advanced (A) Drill List **395**
Appendix E: Ultimate (U) Drill List................................... **401**
Appendix F: Fun Drill List **405**
Appendix G: Grading Checklist E and M drills **407**
Appendix H: Grading Checklist—Skill Concepts
             (Concepts/Levels 1-31)..................................**419**
Appendix I: General Contents Volume 2 .... **421**

Preface

I was a typical youth who grew up in a small town on the Canadian prairies. In those days there were no trained hockey coaches that I knew of. Like most hockey players, skating did not come easy for me at first. I never played organized minor hockey.

As a kid, I was on a minor hockey team that played a total of two games each year. Those two games were in the Alberta bantam provincial playoffs. Our bantam minor hockey team had only two practices each year. They were to prepare us for the provincial playoff games. We had barely enough players who could skate well enough to make the team. Of course, we never won. I never did wear the correct size of skates, and my parents never saw me skate. They didn't have the time or interest to see me on the ice. This was typical for most kids in the 1950s.

My minor hockey career lasted only two years for a grand total of four games, and the team collected zero points. I don't remember winning. Only one of the players on our team went to a higher level of hockey. He had an opportunity to go to college in grade nine where he practiced and learned to play at a more competitive level. However, I believe I am a good person to teach hockey basics because skating did not come easy to me and I know what it is like to not be able to do it.

Wanting to learn how to play hockey despite my failures as a beginner skater, I was persistent and tried to analyze my skating problems. If I was ever going to learn how to skate, I knew I had to find solutions to my skating problems. They were numerous, and I had to do it by myself. At the time, having no idea what I was doing, I had to somehow figure out how to skate. I didn't realize it then, but what I did was break hockey skills down into small parts, then practice those small parts. Years later, I translated those small parts into elementary, achievable skill concepts needed by all beginners.

I learned to skate as a beginner through trial and error and by myself because there was no one else around. At first it was usually in the dark of night with no lights on those icy streets of our small town, St. Paul, Alberta. I spent most of my early hockey life learning in two primary ways: firstly, without skates playing shinny on icy streets and, secondly, without a stick skating on a large lake. I either played on the street without skates, or I skated without a stick on one of two lakes close enough to walk to from our town.

My actual beginner skating was on streets, where numerous sparks flew from my skate blades as they touched rocks from the gravel seeping through the ice and hard snow on those icy streets. Of course, there was no pavement. This was the tail end of the horse and buggy days, and yes, we did use frozen horse manure for pucks when we needed to. You learn to develop great balance when suddenly, one or sometimes both skates, come to a sudden halt in mid stride, as the skate blade hits a rock or touches the ground underneath the ice and hard snow.

I learned advanced skating (skating fast) on a lake, about one mile across in size. Often, with weather permitting, we skated farther out toward the middle of the lake. Unbeknownst to us kids, often the ice would get thinner in the middle of the lake and eventually too thin to support our weight. As ice started to crack beneath us, we would turn back and head to shore as fast as we could go. I heard the cracking of ice following right behind me. I felt ice go up and down by waves of water underneath the ice. In order to stay ahead of the cracking of ice behind me, I had to skate as fast as I could until I reached thicker ice closer to shore. I knew if I slowed down or stopped, I would have gone through the ice. This was especially a problem in spring when there was no ice in the middle of the lake at all, only water.

Oftentimes, closer to shore, we learned to jump when we skated over muskrat runs as ice beneath us gave way. Learning to jump in midair with nothing to support your weight, as ice disintegrated into a muskrat run underneath our skates, was a true balancing act. Those who skated slow or could not make a sudden jump into midair without pushing down went through the ice. It was not uncommon for kids to go home soaking wet from the waist down. By the time they got home, their pant legs were solid ice.

Three neighbor kids from the same family had recently drowned while skating on the same lake. There is nothing like fear in your mind, having to skate for your life, to learn how to skate fast. That was when I realized the importance of long strides with hard pushes into the ice with fast foot recovery. To this day, like most, I skate faster without the puck than while carrying it, and despite my age, I still have a strong stride.

Even though this may sound like it, this preface is not a memoir; it's just background reference. A good deal of thinking for the elementary drills in this book originated from my recollection of learning how to skate in those days.

Now my grandchildren have started skating, so I decided to pull documentation from my old hockey school, de la Salle School of Hockey Basics, out of mothballs. I probably would not be writing this book if it had not been for interest shown by my grandchildren, Julie, Chantal, Erin, and her twin brother, Lucas, who is now a novice hockey player.

Introduction

A beginner is one who wants to learn how to skate for the first time. Teaching skating skills at an early age is not a new idea. Hockey Canada has been leading the development of hockey skills for many years. They have done an exceptional job covering the basics of hockey. This is what Hockey Canada is about—early skill development. Minor hockey programs and organizations have been trying to follow the Hockey Canada program, but something is missing. Everyone seems to be in a hurry to start playing scheduled hockey games. Why is that? Does it have anything to do with wanting to win, win, win? Consequently, kids are pushed too early into drills too difficult for them to handle. Every healthy kid has the ability to learn to skate well. They can achieve the drills in this book, provided they are taught in a logical sequence, slowly building each simple skill upon each other in a defined process. With interest and determination to practice, all kids possess the ability to gain a much higher skill level than is being achieved today.

Starting complex team drills too early removes all confidence from kids. They must gain confidence at the very beginning. Simple and easy drills give confidence to beginners. We must let kids take their time learning simple skills, one easy step at a time. The number of hockey drills out there in the hockey world is unlimited. The current problem is there is no structure to lay out what drill should be done when. This book alone identifies approximately three hundred basic drills beginners should practice, and they should learn most of them before starting team play. Why so many drills? There are thirty-one different basic beginner skill concepts (levels) indentified in this volume, and they require approximately eight to ten drills to master each concept. How is a beginner supposed to gain confidence with this number of drills, especially when these drills are thrown at them randomly and with no thought when kids are starting out? Even when presented in a logical sequence, it takes a lot of effort and time by everyone involved—kids, parents, and trainers. It can't be rushed and there is no shortcut. You must practice the drills involved and complete each concept (or level), one at a time, before going on to the next concept (level). In order to learn skills properly, drills should be done slowly and deliberately. Learn to improve a little bit each day and over time it will become huge. Beginners learn the best at their own pace. Learning to skate is complex, and learning to control the puck is even more difficult. You will realize from this book that what beginners have to go through to learn how to skate is horrendous for them at first, and they need time to absorb it slowly. Most important, they need confidence from the very first day.

Parents expect their kids to play hockey games as soon as possible. It doesn't matter whether kids are prepared for team play or not, as long as their team wins. Of course they want to win; otherwise why have to schedule games? Consequently, in order for coaches to start team play and teach the rules of the game so they can win, basic skills are sacrificed. Adult expectation for kids starting out in hockey is far too great. Parents are just in too much of a hurry to start their kids playing and winning hockey games. Adults need much more patience teaching beginner skaters. The game of hockey is too complex to rush through the learning process just to start playing organized hockey games. Like swimming, kids must learn simple skills slowly, and they should not move forward to the next skill level until the previous level is successfully achieved. There is no swimming competition in the first or second years for swimming, but there is in hockey. It takes years to develop swimming to a competitive level, so should hockey. Kids need to learn the basics skills before playing organized hockey games. There is no better feeling than being able to comfortably carry a puck on a stick while moving fast on skates and being able to put the puck into the net. This is all kids expect, and the sooner they learn the basic skills, the sooner they will be able to do it.

Considering the number of skills and drills needed by beginners, we can't afford to waste the early development time on team play. We need to focus more on early skill development first. Unfortunately, within the current minor hockey paradigm, there is no time left for kids to master basic skills. In most cases, minor hockey programs start playing games before basic skills have been taught. In fact, today's way of thinking effectively forces coaches to teach systems before most kids have had any chance to learn the skills needed to execute them. Most kids today are simply not ready for team play. There needs to be a better *transition* from the first time a player puts on a pair of skates to when he/she plays the first hockey game. Kids need an environment where basic skills can be learned first. A situation where skills can be practiced until they become automatic and where kids don't need to think about them when they are playing the game.

This beginner transition phase is critical, and it is not being addressed today. Basic skating, passing and shooting is the foundation of hockey development. However, beginner hockey is the footing that supports this foundation because every hockey player was a beginner once. Today's beginners are tomorrow's hockey players. AA, AAA, Junior A, College and NHL players are a direct reflection of the level of skills initially learnt at the beginning. The final level of the skills that all players will eventually reach, is a direct result of how strong the foundation and the footing it's built on is, at the very beginning. The higher the level of skills initially developed, the stronger the final skills will be. The weaker the foundation is, the weaker the ultimate skill level will be. The surprisingly weak level of hockey skills in Canada compared to Europeans is alarming. *The Hockey Method* is in response to this adverse skill level. It is a solution that builds a strong footing for the foundation for minor hockey development. It breaks basic skills down into the thirty-one different conceptual movements the human body must make during skating and puck control. Each concept is organized into numerous simple drills. The thirty-one concepts or skill levels in this book define the structure needed for this early transition phase in hockey development.

The peculiar thing that makes this thesis even more surprising is that drills are so simple parents who have never skated can teach beginner skating with success. In fact, at this early stage with kids, team coaches are not needed. What kids need is someone to lead and direct them through various simple drills that are easy to follow. In other words, an instructor. Instructors can be any adult or older kid who is able to read the descriptions and directions of the drill. This book is not about coaching; it is about instructing. Coaching involves systems of positional team play and how to read, recognize, and react to the play. Instruction means direction and guidance. The drill sequence in this book will allow anyone to direct drills from the sidelines, over the boards, or on the ice wearing shoes, instead of having to wear skates, if they choose. At this early stage, you don't need to know how to skate, and you don't need to demonstrate the drill. Read the drill description, then simply show the picture of the drill to the beginner. Kids are smart; you will be surprised at how quickly they pick it up, with only a little direction and a picture of the actual drill.

To make the idea of this transition phase even more astonishing, many of these drills can be introduced by practicing them off the ice (OI), in the dressing room, at home, or anywhere else on any hard surface. So the very young kids can start without having any access to the ice rink at all. Since most of these concepts are simple movements of the human body (feet, knees, legs, and hips), many drills can be introduced before kids actually go on the ice. These simple movements of the body don't need a sheet of slippery ice for kids to be on in order to start. Practicing off the ice is an option to enhance the introduction to drills on the ice later.

Let's face it, North Americans are falling behind Europeans in the development of ice hockey fundamentals. Just look at our international record. There is something missing. The objective of this book is to fill in this missing gap in hockey development. It consists of two books (or two parts) concerning beginner skating (book 1) and beginner puck control (book 2) for ice hockey. The volume begins by explaining *The Hockey Method*, which is an analytical process to teach anyone how to skate and play hockey starting at the beginner level and to progress on to an elite skill level. It defines a method of instructing beginners in that transitional phase from the first time a kid puts on a pair of skates until he or she is ready to start playing team games. Then ideas and concerns regarding beginner hockey are discussed. The two parts, book 1 and book 2, follow that, with the concepts and drills involved. Book 1 puts forward the idea of parents getting actively involved with beginner skating, then it indentifies the four major problems involved with beginner skating and finally shows parents how to instruct beginners how to skate for the first time. Then it provides solutions for these four problems in the form of drills for the skill concepts or levels involved. Book 2 starts by discussing the connection between puck control and body contact. It shows parents how to teach puck control by indentifying the five major problems involving puck control for beginners. Finally, book 2 provides solutions for these five problems in the form of drills for the skill concepts or levels involved.

Background

As a technology instructor, I did some research in computers and telecommunications. In order to instruct my three kids how to skate and my two boys how to play minor hockey, I applied my technical analysis to the game of ice hockey.

The coaching of hockey at that time was totally unplanned. Hockey skills had not been studied or analyzed in much detail, except for Lloyd Percival, then followed by Howie Meeker. I studied hockey by taking coach training levels 1 to 5 through the original Canadian Amateur Hockey Association National Coaching Certification Program (CAHA NCCP) in the 1970s. After learning and becoming certified by experienced coaches, including Clare Drake and Billy Moores, I became a coaching instructor for the AAHA. I taught coaching clinics for levels 1, 2, and 3 to many minor hockey coaches throughout the province of Alberta. I am a level 5 NCCP coach and coached most minor hockey age groups for approximately twenty years. I have been influenced mostly by those two hockey coaching innovators, Lloyd Percival with *The Hockey Handbook* (1960) and Howie Meeker with his *Hockey Basics* (1972) (see the bibliography at the back of this book, "Drill Sources and References")

My professional hockey school operated for several years. The de la Salle School of Hockey Basics was one of the first hockey schools to implement skating timing and speed calculations (after Lloyd Percival's hockey college several years earlier). My school was also a pioneer using video technology to analyze skating. After each hockey school session, we would analyze each player's skating, with the players in a dressing room set up specifically to watch video of previous training sessions. This was in the early 1970s, prior to VCRs and camcorders, when we used reel-to-reel video equipment. Every player's skill level for each fundamental skill was graded and recorded on a report card and given to them upon completion of their five—or six-day session. The simple skating and puck-control concepts in this book have proven to be very successful for me after years of coaching beginners.

Most of these ideas were conceived in my mind during the 1970s. However, one of my first elementary skating concepts was much earlier. As a kid, when I started out, I could not figure out why other kids could handle the puck better than I could. Particularly, as I watched my cousin in the city of Edmonton, who was very good at it, I decided I had to learn how to stickhandle without looking at the puck. I got an idea to try to stickhandle with my eyes closed. I started by playing hockey by myself in the dark, often on the streets where, in those days, there were few outdoor lights. Then I graduated to the rink, where I ran into the boards several times with my eyes closed. It was unbelievable how well I could handle the puck after that. It was then when I realized how effective simple drills could be.

I also observed how my cousin Hugh Ingram, an AA hockey player, seemed to take very long strides. He told me, "Bob, your stride is too short." I could run faster than him, but he could skate faster than me. I didn't realize it, but while my feet were moving very fast, my stride was very short, and I was going nowhere fast. I learned that just because you think you are doing something right, it doesn't necessarily mean you are. Sometimes, for some things, you need to either see for yourself through your own eyes or have the confidence to believe in seeing it through someone else's eyes. At first I did not believe what Hughie told me, but I tried it anyway and it worked. I simply concentrated on longer strides and pushed hard into the ice, then eventually I could skate as fast as him. Of course, skating for my life on a lake helped as well. I realized how I must have looked like a fool the previous two years, going around the ice, moving my feet faster than everyone else and going the slowest. I learned the hard way to see through another set of eyes. At times, some kids need to see for themselves by looking into a mirror or at a video recording of themselves in order to learn some skills. Kids can learn a great deal through another set of eyes, like a parent or another player. On the other hand, in return, the instructor must keep the beginner's point of view in mind by looking through the beginner's eyes.

Since then my analysis has developed through experience coaching kids and instructing other coaches. For most of us, skating doesn't come easy. When confronted with skating for the first time, subconsciously a beginner has to go through a thought process something like this. He or she would, first of all, need to think about what it is he or she can't do. Then they need to figure out why they could not do it. Only then would they have any chance of figuring out how to do it correctly and properly. This is difficult for a kid to do unless an adult can help figure it out for them. Otherwise, the beginner will have no confidence in themselves at all.

The first time we are on skates, we ask, why are we falling? Why are others not falling? Why can't I get up off the ice? How do I get up off the ice? And on and on. This is not unlike the first time one tries to swim and tries not to sink to the bottom of the water. In order to realize what is really involved in trying to accomplish any skill in any sport, one has to use some ingenuity to figure out why you can't do it. Can you imagine throwing a first-time swimmer into the water on the very first day? We do this every day in hockey, except the water is frozen. Through trial and error and with practice, kids are smart enough to eventually figure out how to skate without any instruction at all. However, it takes a long time, and in most cases, kids would not learn all the basic skills. Not only can an adult or mentor make learning easier for beginners, they can make it fun. Most anyone is capable of teaching any kid to learn how to skate. I said anyone, not only coaches. Believe it or not, parents and older youths can teach beginners how to skate, even if they don't skate themselves. This book shows you how.

The Hockey Method

Today many skills are being missed early by minor hockey programs. Team skills are introduced too early, consequently basic skills are sacrificed for more complex team drills. Proof is kids can't do most drills at practices now. Basic skills often become forgotten and are missed even though they are very critical for skill development. These missed skills will take years of development to overcome and may even be lost forever. A great deal of time, effort, and money is wasted on team skills for beginners who are not ready. Those resources would be better spent on an early transition plan to provide basic skills to beginners first.

The Hockey Method is a methodology to teach anyone how to skate and play hockey, starting at the beginner level and progressing on to an elite skill level. This is an analytical approach to hockey skill development. It is a process that starts with skill assessment and analysis, creates elementary skill breakdown, helps resolve skill problems, and provides troubleshooting methods to correct skill weaknesses. It is a method of breaking hockey skills down more granularly than is done now. *The Hockey Method* is a proactive set of skill concepts that build upon each other in a predesigned sequence. The drills are so simple you don't even need to be a coach to teach them. It prepares kids early by giving them the confidence needed to successfully complete difficult hockey team drills later. *The Hockey Method* is a progressive path of drills that can be followed easily by parents and other instructors. It may be considered an instructor aid or guide. In fact it is a practice plan for beginners. The drills are rated into four different levels of difficulty with specific drill properties to further enhance their distinctiveness. This progressive path or plan is proactive because it anticipates problems before they are encountered. The process is simple, hence a simple name. I refer to this proactive progressive path or list of hockey concepts and drills as *The Hockey Method*.

I attempt to analyze basic hockey skills through the eyes of the beginner. This book provides specific solutions in the form of simple drills based on the simple concepts involving the movement of human body during skating. The drills are broken down further than they are done now. Many of these basic drills are sourced from Hockey Canada and other elite hockey programs such as the Serdachny Elite Power Skating Program (see the bibliography at the back of this book, "Drill Sources and References"). By exaggerating each element of the skill, I develop a set of concepts and organize them into sets of drills with an easy path to follow and that are simple to grade. Book 1 is for first-time beginner skaters, and book 2 is for first-time beginner puck control. The drills are organized so they can be utilized again and again for reference and reviewed later for skill maintenance and solving complex skill problems. The hockey method is progressively designed with a precise path of skills to follow. The basic idea is you should walk before you run, run before you glide, be able to turn toes in and out before you are able to use edges, bend knees before you do laterals, be able to do balances before you do pivots, be able to have a feel for the stick before you can feel the puck, and be able to move the stick before you can control the puck.

The Hockey Method is based on my original hockey school, de la Salle School of Hockey Basics, from the 1970s. That hockey school identified and immediately corrected weaknesses before they became bad habits. This is different from most of today's hockey schools of excellence, which tend to lead difficult drills with high-level demonstrators at high speed. Due to their high-intensity approach, these camps have less time to concentrate on individual weaknesses for those who can't do it properly.

Keeping in mind the learning limits of beginners, we must slow down the process. To learn how to execute, kids must do it slow at first then later increase the speed of execution. *The Hockey Method* is actually a process for hockey development where you stop and correct before you continue to practice skills incorrectly. Correcting major errors immediately is common sense not criticism. The following model makes up *The Hockey Method* methodology:

1. Assessment
2. Problem

3. Analysis
    Concepts
    Drill properties
    Skill-level breakdown
4. Solution (drills)
5. Troubleshooting skill problems

1. Assessment

Individual skill assessment is simple for a beginner. You observe a player then decide if he or she can skate or not. If they can't skate, then start at the first concept with drill 1 and continue through the drills on the list. Grade and record whether beginners are able to do each drill or concept (level). Give a grade, such as "needs improvement," "good," or "excellent." If they can't do it, then practice it. Keep the record and review later as needed.

For more complex skills later (when a player has a problem such as, can't stop left), you must identify the elements of the weakness, then go back to the appropriate concept and elementary drills in this book that make up that skill. These concepts can become part of future evaluations. However, more complex drills are usually chosen for evaluation later for specific purposes, including team tryouts.

The thirty-one basic skill concepts in this volume can be considered as thirty-one different levels and, therefore, each skill level can be used for grading in sequence as done with swimming lessons.

Beginner Skating Concepts
Skate Feel Concepts
    Walk—Concept 1
    Run—Concept 2
    Glide—Concept 3
    Jump—Concept 4
    Rock—Concept 5
Toe-Heel Concepts
    Toes out—Concept 6
    Toes in—Concept 7
    Edges—Concept 8
    Heel—Concept 9
Knee Concepts
    Knee bend—Concept 10
    Knee extension—Concept 11
    Lateral—Concept 12
    Drop—Concept 13
    Kick—Concept 14
    Advanced jump—Concept 15
Balance Concepts
    Agility—Concept 16
    Flexibility—Concept 17
    Pivot—Concept 18
    Power—Concept 19

Beginner Puck-Control Concepts
Hands Concepts
    Grip—Concept 20
    Wrist—Concept 21
    Puck repeat—Concept 22
Eyes Concepts
    Dribble—Concept 23
    Balance—Concept 24
Puck Concepts
    Soft hands—Concept 25
    Agility—Concept 26
Stick Concepts
    Manipulate—Concept 27
    Stick length—Concept 28
    Stick reach—Concept 29
    Stick blade—Concept 30
Puck-Control Balance Concepts
    Puck control—Concept 31

2. Problem

Identifying a problem during skating drills can be difficult. How do you determine and describe the problem? There are many ways to do it, and sometimes it requires a good deal of experience and intuition. This book makes it easier. Try any drill, and if it can't be completed successfully, then that is the problem; for example, if a skater can't turn toes out ninety degrees, try and then complete the drills described in concept 6, "Toes Out." Later in this book, *The Hockey Method* identifies and discusses the major problems encountered by beginners with the concepts and subsequent drills involved.

3. Analysis

Concepts

The Hockey Method goes through an analysis for each major problem encountered by the beginner skater. *The Hockey Method* tries to look through the eyes of the beginner to understand their situation. What does the beginner see as the obstacle in the way to completing a drill correctly? Problems are broken down by analyzing the basic movements that the human body must make during skating. Each skeletal move made by the human body is defined as a concept. These concepts make up the core fundamentals of what the human brain needs to nurture, in order to teach the human body (bones, muscles, tendons and nerves) how to learn to skate and play ice hockey.

Each drill in this book is rated with the level of difficulty. There are four levels of difficulty: E (elementary), M (medium), A (advanced), and U (ultimate drill for skill maintenance).

Unlike drills which are limitless in number, concepts are finite. The human body has a fixed number of bones, muscles, and tendons, etc. The number of concepts are fixed and don't change, whereas the drills that are practiced can change and are enormous in number. That is why concepts are actual skill levels; whereas drills can be different and can vary in numbers in order to learn each specific skill concept. Both are measurable and can be monitored and graded. Each concept consists of several simple drills. These concepts are listed above in section 1, "Assessment." Each of these thirty-one concepts or levels, identify and explain the drills required to practice and learn each skill. With sufficient ice time most kids should be able to complete all 31 levels before the atom age. Unfortunately, today most pee wee's and bantam's can't do them.

Drill Properties

Drills can be practiced in many ways; for example, they can be done off the ice, with the puck, forward, backward, to the left, to the right, and on one foot. Drills can be practiced at various speeds. Beside the level of difficulty, *The Hockey Method* assigns specific attributes to each drill to identify these properties; i.e., these properties specify drills that can be practiced off the ice (OI), drills that can be practiced while carrying a puck on the stick blade (P), and drills that can be done at a faster speed (F). *The Hockey Method* is an accumulation of drills specifically selected primarily from four hockey resources: Hockey Canada, Serdachny Elite Hockey Camps, NCCP, and de la Salle School of Hockey Basics. Other than from the de la Salle School of Hockey Basics, the origin of where I first observed the drill is identified at the end of each drill name (i.e., drill 34):

34M: Hop one foot stationary OI P HC F

This is drill 34 and is medium in difficulty (M), can be done off the ice (OI), can be done while controlling a puck on the stick (P), is sourced from Hockey Canada (HC), and can be done slow and fast when you blow the whistle (F).

Drill Property List

- **OI** (Off Ice)—OI identifies drills that can be done off-ice. Numerous drills can be practiced off of the ice rink on any hard flat surface, at home, in the arena dressing room or hallway. This is a good way to introduce drills that will be done later on the ice at the rink. When ice time is expensive or difficult to obtain, then this is a good option. Any drill practiced off the ice will save time when they do get on the ice. When kids get on the ice, they know the drill, and therefore, this will save explanation time on the ice. This will also make the drill easier than trying it on the ice for the first time.
- **P** (Puck)—Drills that can be practiced while keeping the puck on the stick. This is a very good method of practicing puck control at the same time as practicing and mastering skating drills. Kids must get used to keeping their head up and not looking down at the puck

all the time. They will inherently learn to keep their head up by carrying a puck during as many drills as possible.

F (Fast)—The concept of various speeds are introduced into these drills. This identifies drills that should be practiced at three different speeds: slow, fast, and superfast. That is, start these drills at a slow pace, then when they successfully complete the drill, increase the speed to a faster pace. Some drills can be increased even more into a sort of third gear to what I call a superfast. How fast? As fast as you can move your feet or hands!

HC (Hockey Canada)—Drills from the Hockey Canada library of drills and DVDs. If the description and picture of any drill is not clear enough for the instructor, then refer to the DVD video from Hockey Canada. See the bibliography at the back of this book, "Drill Sources and References."

S (Elite Series Camps)—Drills from the Serdachny Elite Hockey Camps and DVDs. If the description and picture of any drill is not clear enough for the instructor, then refer to the DVD video available from the Serdachny Elite Hockey Camps. See the bibliography at the back of this book, "Drill Sources and References."

F&B—A reminder for drills that should be practiced forward and backward.

L&R—A reminder for drills that should be done to the left and right or on the left then right foot an equal number of times.

Combo 5—A special combination of drills to efficiently cover the basic introduction of the main aspects of the forward stride in the shortest period of time.

Magic 6—A special combination of drills to cover the most agility skating skills within the shortest period of time. You can practice all of these skills within a few minutes.

Skill-Level Breakdown and Progression

In order to create appropriate drill solutions to resolve skill problems, an analysis must be done by going through minute details of the skill. To understand hockey in detail, hockey must first be broken down into the fundamental mechanical parts of the game. For skating, those fundamentals must be broken down into every basic mechanical movement of the human body. Skills must be practiced one concept at a time. Each concept should progressively build upon each other, as building blocks, to develop into the more difficult or complex skating and hockey skills. In other words work from the simple to the difficult.

The Hockey Method has done the skill breakdown for you. It breaks skating down into skill concepts. Book 1 identifies four major problems concerning the beginner skater. These four main problems are identified as groups of concepts. These concept groups are further broken down into more refined concepts and refined even further into numerous simple drills. Book 2 breaks puck control down in a similar manner by identifying the five major problems involving puck control. Those five main groups of concepts are further broken down into more refined concepts. Each concept identifies several elementary drills to help learn the skill involved. The concepts and drills build upon each other to prepare a beginner for skating and for puck control. In other words, book 1 and book 2 is an introduction only, to regular skating, passing and shooting. *The Hockey Method* introduces beginners to that strange new feeling of wearing skates for the first time, then provides the balance needed for proper skating. It introduces beginners to the weird feeling of the puck on the stick blade at the end of the long stick shaft.

4. Solution (Drills)

The analysis should identify the basic parts of a skill a beginner must learn. The question then becomes, what is the solution? This is where this book comes in again. After identifying the different skill concepts involved, this method provides solutions in the form of simple drills. The drills should be explained and demonstrated then practiced and corrected. The question then becomes, which drill do I use for which problem? With *The Hockey Method*, there is one easy answer—follow the drills sequentially. The solution is a set of concepts that are simple and easy to practice and learn. The concept groups are broken down further into thirty-one separate concepts or levels, which are again broken further down into approximately three hundred easy drills, which are building blocks that build upon each other.

The Hockey Method attempts to teach beginners by working through the drills starting with the first drill, then progresses into more complexity until the skill is learned. With the number of drills involved, the challenge becomes finding sufficient ice time to practice these drills. This can be helped by starting off-ice at home, using outdoor rinks, and sharing ice with other teams on the rink at the same time. The drills shown in this book are demonstrated by those who can do them the best, the beginners themselves. When kids see other beginners doing drills, they know they can do them as well.

Instructing a skill is not as simple as it may seem. Practicing one drill once every month would be a waste of time because the brain would not have sufficient time to learn the skill. In order to learn a skill and how to do any drill properly requires repetition for the body to learn. A drill must be done at least at five or six consecutive practices for the brain and body to learn any skill. In other words keep coming back and practicing a drill until it is successful.

The Hockey Method also introduces three different speeds into many drills. This is like three different gears. The first gear is to go slow and is to allow you to concentrate on balance. The second gear is to go faster and is to concentrate on lifting the knees higher. The third gear or high gear is to move your feet as fast as possible. I refer to this high gear as superfast and it is used in many drills throughout this book and means move the feet as fast as you can. This is the method used to create acceleration for many skills.

5. Troubleshooting Skill Problems

The Hockey Method has been developed to help identify, then correct skill problems. Once a problem has been identified, *The Hockey Method* will assist in troubleshooting these problems by identifying and correcting the basic hockey skills involved. When a beginner cannot complete a drill correctly, what do you do? How do you analyze, then identify, and determine the reason for the problem? This is where *The Hockey Method* works well because it has drilled the basic skills down into the simple identifiable concepts of the movement of the human body. It is designed to assist you in identifying the concept and then provides drills to correct the skill problem involving the concept. In other words, it allows a method of troubleshooting skill problems with complex skills, especially for the advanced drills used later in team play.

The Hockey Method is a problem-solving tool for hockey skills. The software version for this coaching aid will be available on this book's website soon. Three examples from book 3 of how complex skill problems are handled are discussed later in this book in the epilogue. These examples are very common for complex team drills, which are often attempted before players have been properly prepared. The analysis and troubleshooting method is explained for each of these three examples. There are an unlimited number of such examples in the game of hockey.

Backdrop

Before we embark on a journey through this transitional stage for beginners (thirty-one concepts or levels with approximately three hundred drills), there are a few issues to discuss. These are behind the scene concerns that have major impact in minor hockey. I start with an analogy between swimming and skating, then I discuss the potential of the ability of our kids, followed by the concern and impact of the month in which our kids are born. These opinions make compelling reasons why this hockey development transitional phase for beginners is so important. Defining and implementing an early skill development program into our hockey paradigm will benefit all hockey players in the future.

Swimming Analogy

Let's step back and look at hockey from thirty thousand feet above. It's amazing sometimes how things work out in life. Swimming is introduced and taught to beginners by breaking swimming concepts down into simple basic skills, which beginner swimmers are able to achieve. They are graded and tested on those basic skill levels. Then they must pass each one before going to the next level. This is forced upon swimming programs, not because swimming thinkers are superior to hockey people, but because, of course, the alternative would be for kids to drown in the pool. In minor hockey there is no such concern. You would never throw a beginner, who can't swim, into a pool of water to try out for a swim club. However, we throw beginners on the ice to play on teams all the time in hockey.

Hockey like swimming, is a lifelong process. Beginner swimmers cannot swim the first time they are in a pool. Beginner hockey players are not ready to play on a team the first time either. Swimmers are graded on simple achievable and structured skill levels, whereas hockey players are taught skills randomly without any structure. Beginner swimmers do not compete until they know how to swim. Beginner hockey players start competing in games immediately, when they are completely unprepared. Something is missing in hockey. The transition from a first time skater to playing on the first team is completely overlooked today.

Just because beginner hockey players cannot drown on the frozen ice, it does not mean basic skills of the game of hockey are less important. Swimming and skating are similar because they are both physically very complex for the body and difficult to learn at any age. The amazing thing is, since we do not want kids to drown while learning to swim, for their safety, we are forced to assign skill levels and grade each individual on each basic beginner skill. To be certain they won't drown, they must pass a test before they go on to the next level. However, in hockey, we make no such effort to do anything similar. Kids in hockey go directly, unprepared, into difficult team drills, with no consideration whether they can do the basic skills or not. No skill level assessment, no grading, and no testing done. No monitoring is done whatsoever, resulting in coaches having no idea which kids can do what skills. As a result, in hockey, coaches resort to selecting the tallest and strongest kids for teams because they have no idea what skills players actually have or lack. The best athletes and the smartest players are not always the biggest. The result of this selection process is some players do not get equal opportunity to make a team. Consequently, teams do not reach the maximum potential skill level in hockey.

Hockey can be and should be organized like swimming, where kids are graded. If they pass, they get credit for that level of skill and move on. If hockey was organized like swimming, older kids could mentor younger kids. Older kids can definitely teach younger kids the very basic skills. Like swimming instructors, older kids could be taught and given instructor certificates to teach certain basic concepts for specific skills levels. Older kids love to teach and give out grades to younger kids. This can be implemented at specific skill levels the same way they do in swimming. In fact, I think these youths should be paid the same as young swimming instructors. Let's spend some of that wasted money on expensive early team play, on our youths who can skate well and who are very capable of instructing younger kids. We don't need adult team coaches to teach kids how to skate any more than we need adult swimming coaches to teach kids to swim. What we need are skating and puck-control instructors. Youths are teaching swimming, and those same youths can teach skating as well. We need to adjust our minor hockey paradigm to grade the levels of achievement. The thirty-one concepts described in book 1 and book 2 could very well make up the levels needed. If this were to happen, like with swimming coaches, hockey coaches would be able to start with a team knowing which players passed the basic skills before starting team play. All we need is the will and leadership at the program level. I believe some proactive organizations are indeed looking at reassessing their current evaluation process today.

Problem

As stated several times, first-time skaters are not ready for team drills because drills are too difficult. Systems are beyond the capability of most kids because they did not complete prerequisite basic fundamentals of skating and puck control first. Team play requires a great deal of thinking. In order to free up the mind to think about system play on the ice, kids must do basic skills automatically, without having to think about them. Basic swimming skills become automatic after continual grading, testing, and practicing. Consequently, swimming basics become automatic without kids having to think about what they are doing. Swimmers don't have to think about when to kick in the water or move their head from side to side in order to breath. Their basic skills are repeating until they become automatic, then graded and passed. Consequently, swimming instructors don't need to teach prerequisite elementary skills because the kids passed the previous swimming levels. Club swimming coaches don't need to worry about kids surviving in water because the swimmer has been graded and passed all the basic skill levels long before the student reaches the swimming coach.

On the other hand, every day on the ice, most beginner hockey players are drowning mentally and lose confidence while trying to complete difficult drills with little or no hope of achieving. They do not possess the fundamental background needed when joining their first team. Hockey coaches then must endure trying to teach team play to players who have not been properly prepared for games scheduled by the minor hockey program.

Beginner Development Problems Not as Evident in Swimming

This is a list of hockey development problems that do not seem to be evident in swimming programs:

1. Drills are too difficult for beginners.
2. Basic skills are missed and replaced with complex drills too soon.
3. The number of skills presented to beginners. Beginner skaters are confronted with a horrendous number of unstructured drills, whereas beginner swimmers may face about five or six basic drills in their first level. Beginner swimmers need to only learn these five or six drills to get a passing grade then move on to the next level. It takes many basic skills to cover the complete human skeletal movement involved in the skating process, even more than in swimming. Remember there is not as much balance required for swimming.
4. Lack of time left to develop basic skills. There are too many basic skills for a team coach to cover at the beginning of the season because these skills have been completely overlooked up to that point. Immediately after being assigned to the job as coach, most of his or her time is needed to prepare the team for the imminent schedule of games, which usually start in the first or second week of the season. The number of drills required to prepare a player for team play virtually takes up all the time the coach has available. Therefore, there is no time left for basic skills.

In swimming, if kids can't swim, they are not ready, so of course they can't try out for a swim team. Hockey should be the same. If you can't pass the basic skills, you are not ready, so you shouldn't be invited to try out for a team of skilled players. The problem is, without grading and testing skills, we don't know what skills a player actually has. So there is no alternative except to pick the tallest and strongest kid.

Solution

The Hockey Method attempts to address these problems with the following solutions:

1. Simple achievable drills covering all beginner concepts, with early one-on-one instruction that is being missed by the today's traditional hockey model. A personal or private instructor can be involved, similar to swimming; it can be a parent or older youth or sibling.
2. Complete beginner skills before starting team play, hence better preparation of players for team coaches and elite programs.
3. Arrange drills to build upon each other into a progressive path that is easy to follow.
4. Test and grade **each level** before moving on to the next level.

Rationale

Develop a beginner transition phase for first timers. Organize simple short-duration drills kids can enjoy and succeed with, starting on the first day they put on a pair of skates. The game is 70 percent mental, so practice these basic skills one-on-one with a parent or another instructor until basic skills become automatic, similar to basic skills in swimming. Beginner skills should be completed before attempting more difficult team drills. Even some professional players can't do some of these beginner drills because they have never had reason to try them.

It is more valuable and less costly to invest in beginner fundamentals rather than wasting time and money on drills kids can't do. Grade and test simple drills that build upon each other to build the more difficult skills as, they do in swimming. The rationale for this book is to develop a transition stage between first-time skaters and team play, currently the missing link in hockey development. This book developed the program. Now the minor hockey associations need to implement it.

Use swimming lessons as a model for teaching basic hockey skills. The thirty-one concepts in this volume should be considered as skill levels for a level-oriented program similar to swimming.

Ability of Kids (Myth of Ability)

"Not only are no two kids the same but they have a great more ability than is attributed to them. Kids are not given credit for the great potential of their ability." John Mighton points out in his book *The Myth of Ability* (see the bibliography at the back of this book, "Drill Sources and References") that mathematic students can achieve much more than teachers believed possible. "At an early age many students are lead to believe that they just can't do math." He shows with his JUMP (Junior Undiscovered Math Prodigies) program that students not only have the ability to understand mathematics better than they think they can, but they can reach higher levels at an earlier age.

"With proper coaching and leadership, students can learn math beyond what they were told they could. Students thought they did not have the ability to do it." He shows how students can learn earlier and reach a higher limit than was thought by most educators. "They thought they just did not have the ability." John Mighton shows that the lack of ability is a myth.

John Mighton's approach in math is to break down the task of learning into very small parts and teach those parts and use them as building blocks to learn specific skills. It turns out this is exactly what this book does with hockey. Without realizing it, through trial and error, I have been using this same method throughout my coaching and teaching careers as a technology instructor and a hockey coach. Not only does it make sense, it is logical. I found that kids have much more ability and can learn at a much earlier age than given credit for. Any kid can learn sufficient skills to play hockey at a tier 1 or 2 team level. This doesn't mean they will be selected for tier 1 or tier 2, but it does mean most kids have the ability to learn the same skill level as any tier 1 player; therefore, they are capable of playing hockey with any tier 1 player. Coaches may not select them because of their height or size, but it need not be because of lack of ability.

Kids can go much further with hockey skills than parents realize. The only requirement is desire; they must *want* to do it enough to work and practice at it themselves. In other words, with proper direction and with proper instruction, all kids have the ability to be very good skaters and very good hockey players. It may not be easy, and it may require a great deal of dedication and work; however, any kid with desire can learn to skate and play with the best players in the highest tier.

John Mighton's statements from *The Myth of Ability* seem to be made for minor hockey. I can't say it any better. His observations can be applied to hockey generally and specifically to beginner skating and puck control. In his book he was thinking about math but I believe his observations apply to minor hockey as well. In my view, instead of math you can read kids and hockey into his statements. Here are relevant quotes from his book.

"Students have fallen behind to struggle with difficult skills without guidance."

"Few students survive long enough to gain the confidence and background they needed to do well."

"Ability is not determined only by genetics."

"Why do we tolerate this vast loss of potential, this great neglect of our children."

"There are concepts that only become clear after a great deal of use."

"Students are always allowed to master the simpler instances of an operation before they are taught the more complicated ones."

"Once students learn a step, it is important to allow them to repeat it until they have mastered it."

"By introducing new information in mechanical steps, and by allowing enough repetition, I was able to cover more material than if I had omitted steps."

"When a teacher introduces several pieces of information at the same time, students will often, in trying to comprehend the final item, lose all memory and understanding of the material that came before."

"Whenever I demonstrated a step I make sure these students could repeat the step."

You can Google John Mighton on the Internet—or see the bibliography at the back of this book, "Drill Sources and References,"—to order his book. I strongly recommend the reading of his book.

Beginners have the ability to achieve a much higher skill level than most people believe. *The Hockey Method* can give them that chance with this transitional phase for beginners.

January—December Birthday Syndrome

Malcolm Gladwell's book *Outliers* (see the bibliography at the back of this book, "Drill Sources and References") makes several interesting statements about success. "If you have ability the vast network of hockey scouts and talent spotters will find you, and if you are willing to work to develop that ability, the system will reward you. Success in hockey is based on individual merits. Or are they? It is those who are successful that are most likely to be given the kinds of special opportunities that lead to further success. Because we so profoundly personalize success, we *miss opportunities to lift others onto the top rung (emphasis mine)*. We are too much in awe of those who succeed and we make rules that frustrate achievement. We prematurely write off people as failures."

As stated earlier, kids have much more ability than people think. Unfortunately, many never reach their capability because they miss out with the extra coaching, training, and competition needed to fulfill their potential. They don't make it onto higher-tiered teams because they are written off too early and have not been given a fair chance to obtain the sufficient basic skills needed.

Gladwell points out another interesting phenomenon specifically regarding hockey. "More junior A players are born in January than in February, more are born in February than in March and so on until the fewest are born in December. This is not a chance occurrence but an iron law in Canadian hockey: in any elite group of hockey players—the very best of the best—40% of the players will have been born between

January and March, 30% between April and June, 20 % between July and September, and 10 % between October and December. It is worse in other countries." As stated in Gladwell's book, In Czechoslovakia those born in the last quarter of the year may as well give up hockey because they will never be selected for a team. "It's outlandish that our arbitrary choice of cutoff dates is causing long lasting effects."

I call this phenomenon the January—December syndrome. This seems strange. I just can't believe all the best athletes were born between January and April. Is that possible? One of the goals of this book is to help overcome this syndrome. We should not remove the opportunities for kids who were born in December only because they are smaller than a January-born player.

A twelve-month gap in age represents an enormous difference in physical growth, strength, and maturity, especially at an early age. Twelve months make up 25 percent of a four-year-old's life and probably 100 percent of a four-year-old's hockey life. The maximum difference between the age of a first-year novice and second-year novice can be 23 or 23.9 months. This could represent nearly half of a four—or five-year-old's life on this earth.

The way elite teams work in Canada today, a 2000 rep team (all-star team) consists of players all born in 2000, a 2002 rep team members are all born in 2002, and so on. All minor hockey programs including novice, atom, peewee, and bantam are not one-year programs but two-year programs. The cutoff date for qualification is January 1. Players selected to a traveling rep team are viewed to be more talented if they are bigger, stronger, and have had the benefit of critical extra months of maturity.

One statement in *The Outliers* from a successful junior A hockey player's parent goes as follows: "You know, he was always a bigger kid for his age. He was strong and he had a knack for scoring goals at an early age. And he was always kind of a standout for his age, a captain of his teams. When was he born—January 4th." Today it's the biggest nine—and ten-year-olds who get the most coaching and practice. Many professional hockey players started out a little bit better than their peers because they were a little older, bigger, and stronger. And that little difference led to more opportunity that made the difference a little bit bigger each year, then that edge in turn leads to another opportunity, which makes the initially small difference even bigger. It is compounded and grows by being repeated year after year.

When a player is chosen for a rep team, he gets better coaching, his teammates are better, he gets to play many more games in a season, plus he practices two or three times as often. Probably he plays all year around as well. A December-born beginner is a little smaller, has less strength in his smaller legs, has smaller arms and smaller shoulders. He has shorter reach and tends to play with less confidence. On the other hand, the January-born kid will have great confidence because of size only. So a December-born player is usually overlooked, and as the theory goes, a January-born player will be selected for a tiered team first. However, because the January-born player is bigger and stronger, it doesn't mean he or she is a better or more skilled athlete. Note, there is no January—December syndrome in swimming because basic swimming skills are enforced for all swimmers regardless of their size or the month they were born; they must be graded and are required to pass each level before moving on to the next level. Basic skills become automatic for swimmers, and kids don't have to think about it when they swim. Selecting teams primarily based on size and speed deprives many kids from reaching a level of excellence. Consequently, the potential of that body of work minor hockey organizations are striving for is never fully reached.

Generally speaking, the December-born player will eventually reach the same size as the January-born player. However, many will have missed the opportunity of higher competition, more practice time, and better coaching. Even if the younger player could potentially be a better athlete, he or she is not given the chance. Therefore, the selected December-born player, potentially a better athlete, will get a less experienced coach, his teammates will be weaker, he will play fewer games in a season, plus he will practice less. In the beginning, the advantage is not so much that the January-born kid is better, but he is a little older and stronger. By the age of thirteen or fourteen, with the benefit of better coaching and with all the extra practice under his belt, repeated year after year, any kid born from January to May now really is better, so he's the one most likely to make it to the major junior A league. In the process, many better athletes miss out, resulting in weaker overall programs.

Again from Malcolm Gladwell's book, "Obviously a January-born player has a much better chance for success than a December born player." With today's Canadian minor hockey rules and regulations, it is impossible to overcome this January—December syndrome without some type of intervention. This is part of what this book is about. It helps to overcome this syndrome by making certain basic skills are learned by all players and not only January-born players.

If we can't change Canadian national minor hockey regulations, at least we can help overcome this "iron law of arbitrary choice of cutoff dates" (from Malcolm Gladwell's book) by making sure basics are well taught to all players equally and early. It is not a player's good fortune or fault that he or she is born in January rather than December. For the December-born player, the intervention needed is a more concerted effort to provide basic skills at this earlier age.

If players, regardless of which month they were born in, are given an equal opportunity to learn from the very beginning, there is a much better chance that the skill-level gap between a January-born player and a December-born player will be greatly reduced. It all starts with the beginners. December-born kids must learn the basics immediately, or they will be bypassed before they even start playing their first game.

Currently, a good number of tier 1 team members seem to be selected primarily by the player's height and strength, which gives them much more confidence than younger, smaller players. Consequently, it becomes critical that all players be given the opportunity to gain that confidence. Beginners should be taught to achieve all the basics described in this and other books as early as possible. The later in the year your birthday happens to be, the more important it becomes to focus on all the fundamentals early.

If December-born beginners miss out on skating fundamentals, they have little or no chance of staying up with the January-born beginners. The earlier they master the basics described in this book, the better. As stated, if this syndrome is not overcome immediately, the problem multiplies itself year after year.

Of note, there is no intention to slight the January-born player in this book. Basic skills are paramount for all beginners, regardless of birth month. In some cases, bigger and stronger kids tend to be less coordinated. Often they reach a stage of less body coordination because they reached a growth spurt before the younger December-born player. This quicker body growth spurt may result in awkwardness for a period of time. Mastering basic skills before attempting system play, by all kids, will help overcome the January—December syndrome. An early transitional phase for all beginners will help minimize this situation.

If (he or she) can do 75% of the drills involving the concepts while skating backwards while carrying a puck

Book 1 – Beginner Skating Levels

Name: Lucas

Date:	Sept. 15	Oct. 15	Nov. 15
Basic Skills	Grade	Grade	Grade
Skate Feel Concepts			
1 Walk	40%	50%	70%
2 Run	40	50	60
3 Glide	30	40	50
4 Jump	40	40	40
5 Rock	10	20	30
Toe Heel Concepts			
6 Toes Out		20	30
7 Toes In		30	40
8 Edges		20	30
9 Heel		30	40
Knee Concepts			
10 Knee Bend			20
11 Knee Drag			30

How to Use This Book

This book provides a step-by-step progression of drills to follow for beginners in hockey. In fact, *The Hockey Method* goes beyond that; it defines levels of difficulty, which allows further preparation for the more advanced skating and puck-control skills for team play later in volume 2.

The Hockey Method assigns four levels of difficulty for each drill.

> E (Elementary)—The easiest and, therefore, the first drills to practice.
> M (Medium)—Medium in difficulty and can be attempted after E drills.
> A (Advanced)—The most difficult drills that may be done later if too difficult at first.
> U (Ultimate)—Although these drills are not the ultimate drills, they are a good summary or combination of the drills for that skill concept or level. Its purpose it to maintain the skill as needed later. If you can do the U drill, you probably can do all the other drills in that drill group or concept.

You can start at drill 1 and progress through all the drills. Alternatively, you can do all the E drills first, then all the M drills before attempting the more difficult A and U drills.

These levels of difficulty (E, M, A, U) also make up part of the drill identification or number (i.e., drill 1E or 25M or 36A). The letter indicates the level of difficulty.

The Hockey Method Drill Matrix

There are actually three options or ways of implementing the sequence of drills.

1. **All drills in sequence consecutively**—Start at drill 1, then proceed through each drill consecutively until you reach the final

drill. Logistically, this is the easiest path to follow. This involves completing all the drills in numerical order from 1 to the final drill. That means doing the E drills followed by the M drills, then the A drills and then the U drill within each skill concept or level. Then continue on to the next drill group.

2. **All E then all M drills**—Going directly from E drills to M, then A and U drills within the same drill group (or concept) may be too big of a step for some individuals, so an alternative path to follow is to do all E drills in the book first, then do all M drills in the book. This is the path shown below in the "Parent Instant Recipe." After doing all the E and M drills, you can either go directly to the A and U drills or wait and start the more advanced second volume of *The Hockey Method*, then come back to the A and U drills later.

3. **U drills**—Try the U drills, if beginners can do the U drill, they may be able to skip the previous drills in that skill level or concept because they probably can do all the drills in that group. Then they just need to use the drills later to maintain the skill level.

Later in volume 2, during skating, passing, and shooting, you will come back and use these drills again for skill refinement, skill maintenance, and troubleshooting other skill problems.

Which method should beginners follow? When should they use only E drills, or use E drills and M drills together? The answer is, it depends on the individual. Each player has a different level of interest, desire, and capability. Depending on the effort and cooperation provided by the beginner, the parent or instructor must decide which drills the beginner can handle. As you go through the drills, you must decide whether the beginner can move from E drills to M drills. At any point, if a kid is having difficulty with the M drills, skip the M drills and continue on to the next set of E drills instead. So when an individual is not able to or doesn't want to do the M drills, then do only the E drills. There is a list of E drills only and M drills only at the back of the book in appendixes B and C. Often as you progress partially down the list of E drills, you find suddenly the beginner can do some M or A drills. Then you can go back and complete as many of the M or A drills as you or the beginner wants or can handle. This is where the record of the grade of each drill is important. It allows you to proceed ahead at the beginner's pace and at the same time allows you to go back later and complete the drills kids did not complete based on their recorded grades.

Matrix—Another way of saying all of this is, depending on the individual capability and interest, you can follow the following matrix. There are several options. Mainly you can go across the matrix below, row by row (E then M then A and U, then to the next row, E then M, then A and U and continue to the next group, and so on), or go down the matrix, column by column (doing all E drills first, then all M drills followed by all A and then all U drills).

Concept	Drills			
Walk	E	M	A	U
Run	E	M	A	U
Glide	E	M	A	U
Jump	E	M	A	U
etc.				

A and U drills can also be done sometime later or in volume 2 when they are too difficult for the beginner.

Parent Instant Recipe

If parents don't have enough time, they don't need to read this whole book. Just read this short section. Here is the quickest and easiest formula to follow if you don't have time to read the complete book:

1. Follow the sequence of the E and M drills on the grading checklist at the back of this volume in appendix G. Consider appendix G as the practice plan. First, follow the list, practice and grade all the E (Elementary or Easy) drills, then all the M (Medium) drills. Kids can either do the drills or not. Give them a grade of Needs Improvement (NI), good (G) or Excellent (E). If kids can't do them, continue to practice the drills until they can do them.

2. Explain each drill and/or show a picture of the drill to the beginner. The drill's detailed explanations and pictures are numbered sequentially throughout the book and are highlighted for ease of use.
3. Start at home off the ice. Let the beginner do all the work by practicing drills on his or her own, under your direction. At first kids can practice most of the drills on any hard surface at home or in the dressing room or hallway at the arena. These drills are identified with OI for off-ice. To direct kids on the ice you don't' need to wear skates, you may stand off the ice surface or along the boards or in the player box if you wish.
4. Let the beginner help you record his or her accomplishments by checking off each drill on the checklist as you go through the list. Kids can give their own opinion of their grade, and they will get very enthusiastic recording their own achievements. Often you will find them to be more honest than most adults. Let each beginner be the demonstrator for at least one drill.

To explain the details of a drill to the beginner, all a parent needs to do is to read the description of the drill in the book. Then show the picture and direct the child to do the rest. The parent will understand many of the drills because most are self-explanatory, like "Drill 1, take small steps" or "Drill 2, take long steps." For drills not as intuitive, it is easy to find the explanation in the book. All drills are in numerical order and are easy to find because they are in bold type throughout the book and can be found easily by thumbing through the book.

Mastering Drills

You will find that once beginners are able to do drills on the ice, they start having fun and no longer will want to do them on hard off-ice surfaces. The drills in this book are built to be achieved progressively from drill 1 through to the last drill. Once beginners know how to do the drill, they will remember many of them by name. They will even adopt their favorites. Then they will need to practice on their own until they become very good at it. Remember you must practice any drill at least five or six times at consecutive practices, for the brain and body to learn the skill. Since the drills are simple, they can be mastered over time with practice until beginners can do them automatically without thinking about them. Parents can record the grade for beginners on the grading checklists at the back of the book, eventually mastering all the drills with a rating of "excellent."

You can indicate whether players need improvement, did good, or did excellent for each drill. As a general guide (although it does not always apply), when they can do the drill going forward, grade it as "needs improvement" (NI); when they can do it backward, grade it as "good" (G); when they can do it backward with a puck on the stick, grade it as "excellent" (E). However, you can make your own rules. This gives the beginner a challenge to work toward a goal of practicing until all the drills are mastered or graded as "excellent." I have seen kids mark their own grade on a checklist. It was amazing how honest they are with their own grades. Kids are innocent but smart; they know when their drill needs improvement or when it is good or excellent. Some kids look forward to giving themselves a rating, then going on to the next drill. They can keep practicing a drill on their own. They will be the first one to come to you and proudly say, "I can do it now, look at me, give me and excellent."

Every drill doesn't need to be excellent before you go forward with the next drill. You can work on several drills at the same time and follow the sequence of the drill numbering as much as possible, then go back and repeat drills that have not been mastered. Actually you need to work on several drills at once because you should spend only about thirty seconds on one drill at a time. This is discussed in more detail later in "Communicating with the Beginner." Work on several drills at the same time but in sequence of the drill numbers. Attempt the drills in the sequence of the drill numbers, then go back to them again and practice those not yet completed.

Although the parent is not a coach, he or she can lead the beginner in the right direction. By completing these basic drills, led by any adult or older skater, the player will achieve early skating success. Since these drills are simple and easy to complete, they will give immediate skating confidence to the player. Player confidence greatly enhances the skater's capability and interest level while raising his or her early skill level. Early player confidence can also lead to a very good and successful relationship between the player and his or her current or future team coach. You can pass this record on to the team coach for reference. A proactive coach will welcome it. This parental support will enable a coach to delve right into more complex hockey drills with much more success, knowing which basic skills have been completed and passed. *If there are specific skill problems, most coaches would be very happy to help correct.*

There are many very good elite hockey programs out there and many outstanding team initiatives in minor hockey today, such as three-on-three leagues in the spring and other summer hockey programs. Volume 1 is preparation for these higher-level programs. This book is a transition to make it easier for beginners to succeed in hockey. After successfully mastering all the drills, with a grade of "excellent," beginners will be well prepared to meet the challenge of elite hockey camps and other advanced programs led by good coaches and instructors.

Grading

As in swimming, although not historically done in hockey, testing and grading hockey skills is imperative. You must record the grade of a skill to know whether the beginner is progressing in his or her development. If the instructor doesn't know where the student is at, then the instructor is flying by the seat of his pants and will have no idea what should be done next. The instructor could be practicing the strengths the kid already has and miss out on the weaknesses the kid really needs to eliminate.

At the end of this book, in appendix G, is the grading checklist for E (Elementary) and M (Medium) drills. You can use this checklist to document the skill level of each beginner. Observe the player's skill level for each drill and record it. This will allow you to keep a record of the weaknesses, then come back and continue working on these weaknesses later. You can use the drill or set of drills to strengthen the weakness and correct the problems. Keep going back to a drill and practice it until the problem is remedied and it can be done automatically without involving any thinking by the beginner.

If the drills are so numerous, logistically, how is it possible to grade each individual for every drill? Well, first of all, they do it in swimming and other sports. Secondly, it takes a great deal of effort. It would be great to have the time to grade all the drills, but you don't necessarily need to record the grade for all three hundred drills individually. If there is not enough time and resources available, then try grading only the thirty-one concepts instead of all three hundred drills. This is a quicker alternative only for when you don't have resources or sufficient time. In this case, instead, grade only the thirty-one basic levels or skill concepts in this book. Grade each concept as a group for the drills involved. In fact, you could consider these thirty-one skill concepts as skill levels. At the end of this book, in appendix A, is a list for the thirty-one basic skill concepts or levels (also a grading checklist in appendix G). Each skill concept involves numerous elementary drills. You can add to this list of drills by creating your own drills, or you may know of others. In this alternative approach for grading purposes, just count the number of drills successfully completed to give a grade for each basic concept or level. A percentage grade can be given depending on the number of drills successfully completed; for example, 50 percent means half of the drills on the concept drill list have been completed correctly, and so on. The skill concept checklist is a fundamentals checklist of all the skill levels involved.

The recording of the grades of skills in hockey is as important as it is in swimming. Although it requires work on the part of the parent or instructor, it is worth the effort in the long run. This record can be used for further planning. In fact this checklist is a practice plan for beginners. Like in swimming, team coaches and parents should know where the level of each of the player's skill is at and whether there has been improvement or not. More important, they need to know which skill should be practiced next. A coach must know which drills need work and which drills were successful and therefore only require periodic maintenance. Beginners must learn a skill, then maintain that skill level and improve on it as he or she gets older, which means at a higher speed and with a puck. Once drills are mastered, the player's skill can be maintained by periodically revisiting the completed drills. Skills can be maintained by practicing them during warm-ups and warm-downs at team practices.

Grading general guide (appropriate for most drills)

> NI (needs improvement)—Able to do the drill forward and continuing to learn.
> Good—Able to do a drill backward
> Excellent—Able to do a drill backward with a puck

Keeping track of skill grades, like team stats, is time-consuming. This is a good task to assign to parents who are probably always there anyway and usually are willing to help. In fact, they can do more; they can do the actual grading. Parents just need direction from this book or from a team coach. All they need to do is follow through with the checklist and mark each drill with NI, G, or E.

Book 1

Beginner Skating

Lloyd Percival's *The Hockey Handbook* (see the bibliography at the back of this book, "Drill Sources and References") states, "Skating is to hockey what throwing is to baseball, what tackling is to football, or what footwork is to tennis. It is the most important fundamental. It is the foundation on which everything else in hockey is built. It must be developed. Any normal person, provided he works hard and uses the correct methods, can develop top level skating efficiency. A player with lesser skills can surpass those of greater natural ability with a well developed skating program."

If skating was easy, everyone could do it the first time they tried it. Kids can't do skating drills right off the bat. First-time skaters can't do regular skating drills. There is something missing between the time kids put skates on for the first time and the time kids are actually *ready* to skate and play a hockey game. No one can perform skating drills without a great deal of preparation first. Book 1 attempts to address this overlooked component in hockey skating skill development.

Why Beginner Skating?

The first question that comes up is, why beginner skating and not simply skating? Traditionally, kids go directly into regular skating and immediately attempt drills beyond their capability. There is definitely a significant *transitional phase*, from the first day of skating to the day a kid is able to skate well enough to start team play. A beginner skater is a first time skater. This book is actually an introduction to skating. It is preparation for the basic body manipulations and balances needed for skating. As you go through the drills, you may think some drills are only normal skating drills. In fact, they are, and you will even find that some of them seem to be advanced. The difference is they are arranged in a specific sequence. The drills are arranged proactively to provide actual solutions to the basic concepts involving the human body during skating. The number of drills that can be used to learn each basic skating concept is unlimited, but the drills chosen here have proven to be very successful.

When a youngster is introduced to skating for the first time, it is similar to an adult trying to walk on stilts for the first time. Getting to know the feel of the space between your feet (in the skate) and a floor surface is of primary importance; it is like walking on two-inch stilts. When youngsters are introduced to skating, a key to their success is their initial acceptance of the weird feeling that occurs because of that vague distance between their feet and the ice surface. Their first impression of the sport, whether good or bad, could stay with them for a long time. The sooner they gain confidence, the better. If their initial impression is not positive, they may never want to put on a pair of skates again. If a hopeful parent forces a kid when he or she is not ready, the beginner may never reach the potential of the skating ability all kids have.

Unfortunately, in the real world, most regular skating drills are too difficult for kids at the beginning. What is missed is a *transition* program for the beginner to get to where he or she is comfortable with the actual skating process sufficient for team play. Instructors need to build kids' confidence first even when kids want to play a hockey game immediately. There are too many early failures today where kids lose interest and quit before they get a good start. Kids need more preparation and fun drills, such as races and shooting on the net. This book will give them the confidence needed to get them to the point where they can really start to enjoy being on skates right from the beginning.

No Time for Basics

The conglomeration of drills in the hockey world tends to camouflage beginner skills. The number of drills is limited only by the human imagination. Consequently, there is a mass accumulation of drills out there. Also, there are even more drills being created every day to solve various skill problems in the hockey world. There are so many drills that there seems to be no time left for basic beginner drills. It takes a good number of drills just to teach beginners the basic skills of skating and puck control. This is the reason for breaking skating skills into concepts or levels. The drills chosen in this book are selected because they have proven to be very effective for beginners during this early transition phase. Beginner skills alone require a great deal of dedication, time, and effort by both instructors and skaters.

First—Beginner Basics

It is imperative that basic skills be taught before team play because beginners are not able to handle complex team drills. When beginners start skating for the first time, they are not ready for team play. The transition period between the first time a beginner puts on a pair of skates and when he or she is ready for team play is critical. Beginners must learn basic skills **first**, before team play. That is what this book is about.

Second—Team Play

At the beginning of the season, when team coaches start teaching team concepts, they don't have enough time to teach beginner skills. There are just too many drills to cover. However, we can't ignore or forget fundamental skills. When the coach is given the responsibility of competing in a league with games right at the start of the season, then in order to play those committed games, the coach must teach team skills immediately. Since there is only so much time for coaching, something has to give, either basic skills or team skills. Coaches don't have time to teach both. Most of the time is consumed on team play. When coaches are forced to play scheduled games so soon, kids must learn the rules of the game. Consequently, basic skills are sacrificed for team skills.

Team coaches need to make a decision—spend the time they have on teaching beginner basics or spend it on team skills. Coaches have been trying to do both for years, but it is impossible to teach both because there are just too many skills involved. There simply is not enough time in team practices to cover both. Teaching team play is a full-time task for a coach. What we forget is that teaching basic skills is also a full-time task for someone as well, whether a coach or parent or group of parents.

Consequently, we expect too much from team coaches, who are obligated to immediately produce a product of team play for scheduled games and of course win. Therefore, due to this lack of time, team coaches in a sense are actually forced to skip the basics. As a result, beginner skills are left out and some are totally missed forever. It is not just a coaching problem. The minor hockey associations must address this issue and provide leadership.

When is a beginner ready for team play?

Not only do players require basic skills for team play, but they also need a certain amount of maturity. Beginners do not have the basic skills at first, nor do they have maturity. All kids do not have the same maturity, and they do not develop maturity at the same rate. All seven-year-olds don't have the same maturity; therefore, they are not all ready for team play at the same time. All eight-year-olds don't have the same maturity, and so on. Parents and hockey program organizations should not rush putting beginners on a team. They must have basic skills plus have some maturity before they are comfortable enough to succeed in team play.

Once a player has completed the basic skills, in most cases, they have developed enough maturity to stop chasing the puck all over the ice. However, this is not true for all kids. Some still play as individuals and continue to chase the puck regardless of the team situation on the ice. If this is the case, then they are not ready and should not be on teams, especially in the higher tiers. On the other hand, some kids do have the maturity to play the team game before all the basic skills are covered. They will be ready to start team play sooner.

After completing all the basic skills, kids are ready for team play only when they have the maturity to stop continually chasing the puck with their head down all over the ice. During the course of the game, they need to have the ability to stay in their zone on the ice and wait for the puck to come to them. In fact that is what team play is. They should not go after the puck blindly into an area where a teammate already has control of the puck. This is the discipline aspect of any team sport. Kids are not ready for team play in the higher tiers until they can purposely go to a spot or a position on the ice, away from the puck, as planned and directed by the coach. In other words they must have their heads up and have vision to see the whole rink. Again, remember hockey is a team sport, not an individual sport. If kids continue to chase the puck on the ice all the time under all circumstances, then they are just not ready for team play. Remember, these kids are young. In order to know where their teammates are on the ice, they must be able to skate with the proper skating stance and with their head up all the time. They will learn this following the concepts in this book.

Once kids have the basic skills and when kids are able to follow directions from the coach and are capable of being at a specific location on the ice, away from the puck, then they are ready to play on a team in tiers 1 and 2. It comes down to maturity. The degree of a kid's maturity is indicative of the tier the kid should be playing in. The higher the tier, the more maturity needed. The lower the tier, the less maturity needed.

Some kids can play team play at five years old; others can't do it at ten years old. I must admit that some in old-timer's hockey can't do it at fifty years of age. This is the mental part of the game and is very difficult to assess and teach. When body contact is not allowed, it is easy to try to chase the puck and then carry the puck around opponents who can't hit you. Successful competitive teams require good team play, rather than simply relying on one-on-one capability. A player who keeps the puck all the time, disregarding his or her teammates on the ice, is not ready for team play or needs better coaching. However, chasing the puck playing keep-away (Lone Ranger—type hockey) can be good and is even recommended for nonteam type of hockey for the youngest kids. More about that later in this book. There is nothing wrong with kids playing a full season of shinny without rules while learning the basic skills.

Can we Learn both Beginner Basics and Team Play at the Same Time?

What do you do when you are assigned to a team of beginners and there are games scheduled within the first few weeks? You know the kids do not have the basics yet, however you can't just disregard the basic skills. Kids need to learn as many basic skills as possible before team play is introduced. So although not ideal, as is in most cases, we must find a way to cover both of these different training modes, basic skills and team skills at the same time. *The Hockey Method* provides a means of doing both at the same time by categorizing drills into separate levels or concepts. These concepts are singled out as different entities, and therefore, they can be taught separately. In fact each concept can be considered a different skill level and can be graded and taught completely independent from each other. Parents or instructors can teach basics to kids completely independent and separate from team practices. The goal of this book is to prepare beginners for team play by teaching basics first; however, it also can accommodate teaching both at the same time.

The Hockey Method rates all the drills so they can be taught, then practiced separately from team play. Not only are the drills rated in four different levels of difficulty (E, M, A, U), but they are numbered sequentially and can be graded and easily implemented at any time and at any pace. When the skills are documented and grades recorded, you can come back to them and teach and practice them any time during the season. You can start anytime, at exactly where you left off the last time. Therefore, beginner drills can be instructed completely separate to the team practice. More important, anyone can teach them at any time. For example, you could reserve one ice session each week to do nothing but basic drills, such as those listed in *The Hockey Method*. It may take all season at once a week to cover and grade all E (Elementary) drills or all M (Medium) drills. You can practice these basics completely independent from team practices anytime, i.e. when the team has spare ice time available during the season, or perhaps just more additional ice.

If managed smartly, this could free up more time for team coaching when needed. As basic skills are successfully completed, one drill at a time, record it then move on to the next drill at a pace depending on the time available for each individual. It doesn't matter whether E and M drills are spread out over a long period of time or compressed into a short hockey-school-type session during the winter season or in the spring or summer. Doesn't that sound similar to taking swimming lessons? Summer hockey schools should be run this way as well. When a player starts the season with a new team, he/she should be able to show the new coach the grading record from the hockey summer school. Once a player's grade is recorded on a checklist, you will be able to come back at any time and resume the drills exactly where you left off. Once a skill has been mastered, it is only a matter of reviewing it periodically to maintain that skill level.

Instructing Beginner Skaters

Beginner Skaters

Learning how to skate well requires a lot of work. Like in most sports, a great deal of practice is required to reach a high skill level. How do you get kids to work hard? Young kids will give an extra effort only if they are having fun while doing it. In his book *Outliers*, Malcolm Gladwell refers to ten thousand hours of work or practice in a lifetime as the requirement to reach a level of excellence in any endeavor. This includes sports, the arts, etc. No matter how gifted an athlete is, he or she must practice a great deal. It will take years of practice to learn how to become an elite hockey player at a junior A level. They have to like doing it because they must practice, practice, practice. Whether being a violin player or a hockey player, he states that it takes ten thousand hours of good training over a lifetime to master all the skills. I assume in hockey, it is ten thousand hours of practicing skills correctly and not practicing mistakes. Start eliminating some of these mistakes by insisting that the knees are bent all the time while on the ice. This is one of the more difficult concepts to drive home. Kids will tend to keep the knees straight even after you directed them not to. As the instructor, you must continually monitor and keep reminding them.

Kids will never make ten thousand hours if they are not having fun. They don't have fun falling on the ice all the time. This book makes skating as easy as possible for beginners by keeping drills simple and short. Simple, achievable drills make success easy; therefore, they make it fun. For coaches or instructors, it is important to keep this fun in the practice. Kids like to compete with each other. No one is more competitive than a kid, even at the earliest age. Use numerous races or relays during practice. Most drills can be made into simple races end to end or across the rink. Especially try to use races that can incorporate some of the basics you are trying to teach them at that time. The promise of a fun game can be a carrot for good success, and continuing with a boring drill can be the stick. Reward them during the practice; don't wait until the end of practice to do it. If they do drills well, let them play a fun game of shinny for ten minutes at any time. When they don't give a good effort, use the threat to continue the drill longer. Kids also like to show off what they can do. Let each kid be the demonstrator for at least one drill. This will give them each a chance to show what they can do and be the leader.

Beginners should never be lined up in a row or single file for a drill. This is called SIL, or standing-in-line drills. With this type of drill, most beginners spend the majority of their time waiting for their turn to do a drill. SIL drills cause several problems. Ice time is not utilized efficiently. Players get bored waiting. When their turn comes up, they either forget to concentrate on the drill or sometimes they completely forget how to do the drill. Keep SIL drills to a minimum for beginners.

The beginner should use a hockey stick as an aid for balance for most drills in this book (unless they are carrying a puck at the same time). When possible, keep the stick blade flat on the ice or on a hard surface at all times. For balance, they should hold the stick at the upper end (butt end) of the stick with one hand only.

Beginners should have a warm-up at the beginning of a practice and a warm-down at the end of practice by doing numerous simple slow-speed balance drills. Kids should not skate as hard as they can, then immediately and go off the ice at the end of a practice. This could create a health problem especially going into a warm dressing room immediately after skating hard in a cold rink.

Age Considerations

At what age should a youngster start skating? Most drills in this book are very simple and can be attempted at a very early stage. I said early *stage*, not early *age*. Age does not matter. A beginner could be four years old or thirty years old or sixty years old—it doesn't matter. The fact is they can learn to skate at any age. Fundamentals are fundamentals for all human bodies, regardless of age. The difference is that a four-year-old is much more flexible physically and mentally possesses less fear of failing. They are not embarrassed when they fall flat on their face. Also, it is easier for the body to adjust to new skills at a younger age. However, anyone can learn to skate by following the sequence and practicing all of these drills.

You don't need to be a gifted athlete to learn how to skate. Any person, at any age, with average athletic ability can learn the fundamentals of hockey. Everyone has the ability to learn how to skate, and certainly all kids have the ability. Old-timer's hockey includes players who are in their eighties, and many of them never played minor hockey when they were young. Others did not start skating until in their thirties. Any individual can learn sufficient skating skills to enjoy playing the game of hockey as a recreational sport for the rest of their life. The key for even recreational hockey is skating.

Let's face it—we can't teach a kid to skate at two years old, and we can't really coach a kid of four or five years old for that matter. What we can do initially is try to point them in the right direction toward making skating easier for them. Beginners can start learning at two years old with these drills, but only as a fun exercise like walking and jumping on their skates at home. They can start at home on the basement floor with their skates on, or on any hard surface, or an old piece of carpet. This is one reason parents are in a good position to instruct beginners, because they can start right at home.

Parents can help kids familiarize themselves with the new sensation of wearing skates. If there is an ideal age, I would say five years old, when old enough to follow some directions and also at an age when they are very competitive with their friends (peers) on the ice. They want to compete immediately and start racing each other. The beauty of this age is they have no bad habits. It is surprising what a keen four—or five-year-old can do. First of all, they are usually willing to try; this, in itself, is all you need to start the skill development process. The best age to start depends on the individual. The right age to start varies for different individuals and depends on when the boy or girl is interested enough to be willing to try. When a kid is not interested in doing drills, wait until he or she is more interested. If they are not interested at five or six years old, it does not mean they will never make the NHL. When they are on the ice and uninterested, leave them alone and let them walk around the ice by themselves if they want to. Eventually, they will surprise you and decide to follow the others, but at their own pace when they are ready. I watched this happen many times with the youngest players on the ice. Using another kid as a drill demonstrator will help to encourage a beginner to follow, and using a friend as a demonstrator will create a major challenge for competition.

Adult Beginners

Skating and playing hockey games can be enjoyed at any age. As stated above, you can learn how to skate at any age. You don't have to be a kid at the novice or at the atom age. Anyone can learn how to skate no matter how old you are by simply following the structured plan of concepts and drills in this book. I have taught adults how to skate, even some who have just recently moved to Canada from Asia. In fact, one adult was from Australia and had never seen an ice rink before.

Recreational hockey such as old-timer's hockey is very popular across Canada with divisions in age groups of 35+, 50+, 60+, and 70+. The Canadian Adult Recreational Hockey Association (CARHA) (www.carhahockey.ca) helps organize teams in every province. In Victoria there is the annual Playmakers Old Timers international hockey tournament for every age group starting at 55+ and includes a 75+ and 80+ division as well. In fact, I attend that tournament each year as a player on the Edmonton Vintage 70+ team.

There are numerous recreational adult hockey programs out there. Canlan Ice Sports (www.icesports.com), headed out of Toronto, organizes what they call Adult Safe Hockey Leagues (ASHL) in several provinces across Canada. In Edmonton there is the North of 50 Hockey League comprising of twenty-one teams of players fifty years of age and older. These leagues are meant for adults who know how to play hockey. Every kid eventually becomes an adult, so there is no shortage of adult hockey players. There are adult leagues in every city in Canada. No-contact hockey for adults is becoming very popular, and it can be started at any age.

Yes, there are adult beginner hockey programs as well. An adult hockey league just for beginners in Western Canada is organized out of Calgary as part of their NCHL or Non-Contact Hockey League program. They have a beginner division running in Calgary and Edmonton for adults who have never skated. They learn how to skate, then learn hockey basics by starting their beginner league with two classroom sessions followed by eight on-ice sessions. After that, they begin their fun hockey career in the NCHL beginner division of the league (www.nchl.com).

Communicating with the Beginner

To communicate with kids at an early age, you need to talk to them at eye level and make eye contact while being very close to him or her, especially when beginning a new drill. This will allow you to get into their comfort zone. Sit down on the ice or kneel down. Never spend more than thirty seconds talking at any one time; actually ten seconds of explanation would be better (you can always come back and talk again later). Of course, only teach one thing at one time.

The younger the player, the shorter the attention span. After about twenty or thirty seconds, a young player will lose interest. Some kids can't focus longer than two seconds. For beginners, no drill should last more than thirty or forty seconds in duration. This is another reason to be working several drills at the same time. Later in team play, they can practice drills in duration of four or five minutes, but not at this stage. Usually, one minute is too long for any drill at this age, except fun games like racing or shinny, which they can play all day long.

Praise good performance and encourage improvement. Express awareness of their failures before instruction so they know you have some understanding for their feelings and difficulty. Sometimes kids just can't understand that they are not doing a drill properly. No matter how often you explain that they are doing it wrong, they still think they are doing it correctly. Some basic skills, like bending too far forward during the forward stride or not lifting the knees high enough, kids will say, "I am doing it." In cases like this, you will need to find a way for them to actually see themselves doing it. Either watch a video recording or look at a giant mirror while they are actually doing the drill. For some skills, kids need to see it through their own eyes, not yours.

Exaggeration Technique

Most hockey programs use exaggeration to reinforce drills. This book is no different. Skills are broken down into small easily achievable parts, then exaggeration is used to reinforce those skills. Exaggeration of the mechanical movement of the human body during skating is important for most drills. Exaggerating some of the basic skills beyond what is normally done is needed because it makes normal execution of skills much easier. Then with practice, skills can be done automatically without having to think about it. Exaggeration makes the otherwise "proper" position feel normal or comfortable.

Many of these drills greatly exaggerate the actual skating motion, so they may not seem to be needed, but in fact they are very important. Teaching kids to turn their toes out ninety degrees for the stride would be an exaggeration because you actually turn the toes out only about forty-five degrees during the stride. The reason for exaggeration is, the normal forty-five-degree skating motion becomes much easier and tends to become more automatic during the heat of the game. However, you do need to turn the toes out ninety degrees for other agility skating techniques like starting and pivots.

Beginner Confidence

Young players just want to get their stick on the puck and play the game without thinking about how to skate or how to get to that puck. This is how it should be for beginners. Of course, the better developed the player's balance and skating skill is, the better chance of them getting to the puck in the first place. Anyone who wishes to master a specific skill in hockey, psychologically will feel more relaxed and at ease when he or she is introduced to the skill with easy, simple incremental steps. Once drills are introduced, allow kids time to experiment on their own so they can improve at their own pace. More important, practicing easy, simple drills will allow skills to be done automatically, without kids having to think about them. Easy, achievable small parts of a skill will boost early confidence. The easier the drill, the more confidence kids get. The sooner kids are able to complete numerous simple drills, and given passing grades, the more confidence they will gain. Then the sooner they will have fun and the sooner they will start to enjoy skating and playing hockey.

Beginners feel more satisfied with themselves as they gain more confidence. Confidence will result in much more success. Let kids gain confidence by being successful with as many easy, simple drills as possible. Grade them with a rating such as "needs improvement," "good," or "excellent" to show their successes on paper, a grading sheet just like they get at school. The confidence kids gain in this process is unbelievable. They gain self-satisfaction and will want to get out back on the rink and practice harder to get to the next grade, just like getting to the next swimming level. They say "I can do it next time" or "I think I can get an 'excellent' on that one." The reaction of kids looking at their grading reports is beyond belief. Remember, these enthused beginners may be naive, but they are also honest, very smart, and can adapt quickly. If they can't do something, they will figure out a way to do it. Kids are amazing!

Kids like to be the leader and demonstrate drills. This is a big confidence builder. Let each kid demonstrate by leading at least one drill across or along the ice in front of the other kids. Each kid can be the best at something, even if it is only walking short steps across the rink. The designated demonstrator can lead the others across the ice with everyone else following simultaneously and immediately behind. Once a kid becomes the designated leader for a specific drill, he/she will take ownership of that drill and want to demonstrate the drill every time. They will try to specialize in that drill and want to do it even better than before. Not only will this build individual leadership, but it will also create a challenge for the other kids to do it as well. Remember, kids like to compete and enjoy a good challenge. Giving each beginner an opportunity to show off his or her success or achievement to the rest of the group is a form of mentorship. Assign the better or older kids to demonstrate difficult drills, then let them mentor weaker and younger kids. This works especially well when you have first-year and second-year kids on the same team.

It's great if parents and instructors can demonstrate drills, but it is not essential. In fact, as stated earlier, you don't need to know how to skate to teach beginner skating. Remember, it is easier for kids to demonstrate drills because they are more flexible, learn more quickly, and are better at balancing. Have you ever seen what the average fourteen-year-old can do on a skateboard? They can do far more than any forty-year-old. Kids can usually do basic drills like balances better than any adult. Adults normally demonstrate only the more difficult and complex drills they learned years earlier. Kids can learn to demonstrate any skill and will do it better.

Parents

Parents as First Instructors

Beginners need the most help because every drill is new, and this is when instructing and teaching have the most impact. Beginners start from scratch; therefore, they need to improve the most. Everything is new. They must go from walking on skates all the way to carrying the puck on their stick with their head up. These are big leaps in expectation. It turns out that first-time skaters can easily be taught or instructed by parents or older kids when skating is being introduced and when hockey knowledge is not as important. You should teach beginners only what they can handle. Parents are the ones who know their child's interest level and learning limits the best.

After being away from coaching minor hockey for years, to my surprise, I find coaching in minor hockey has changed very little. Good coaches tend to move on to teams with older kids who possess higher skill levels than beginners. Consequently, from a coaching perspective, beginners often are overlooked by minor hockey programs. As it turns out, most coaches of novice and prenovice teams are parents anyway, and they probably took the job as a last resort. They are default coaches. Therefore, I think it is time to present hockey skills in a format parents can use to teach their own kids.

This sounds like an oxymoron in that you want the best coaches at the earliest age, but you need parents to do it. It turns out that what is really needed the most for first timers is one-on-one direction and instruction. Coaches or parents can do it, but parents are a better choice to instruct beginners because they have the time and interest to dedicate one-on-one instruction to the beginner at this early age. After all, kids at this age must have at least one parent or some other adult in attendance at the practice in order to tie on skates. So parents are usually there anyway.

Beginners need instructors, not coaches, to teach basic skills. Team discipline, system play, and the mental part of the game should be taught by coaches later. Basics skills should be taught one-on-one by instructors. Parents as instructors turn out to be the best choice.

However, when kids are ready for team play, coaching becomes critical, and this is where the best-trained coach should be. Up to this point, parents can do a better one-on-one job. As soon as beginners are no longer beginners, after they have completed the drills in this book, they should be ready to start playing on a hockey team. This is the point where good coaching becomes imperative. The best coaches are needed by kids immediately after the transitional phase for beginners has been completed. In other words, the best coaches are needed on the kid's first team. The best coaches should not move up to the older-age groups where all the talent is. They should teach beginner teams who need them the most.

As stated earlier, beginners need super simple drills at first, and those drills are so simple you don't need to be a coach to teach them. Instructors don't even need to know how to skate to teach beginners. Believe it or not, parents who can't skate can successfully teach beginners how to skate. This book will enable any parent to teach beginner-level skating and puck control to any kid. All the parent needs is a simple guide that is easy to understand and follow, with simple easy drills for beginners to practice. Parents need to know which drills to practice and when to practice them. This book does all of this; it breaks skills down into minute elementary skills and provides an easy, sequential path for anyone to follow. Learning to skate takes a great deal of time and effort, so it makes sense for parents to get involved. When the coach has a team that did not complete their basic skills yet and the coach does not have sufficient time to teach fundamentals, then the coach can delegate parents to lead and instruct specific basic drills described in this book. This can be done separately from the normal team drills. Separate practices can be set up to cover only basic drills. In fact, various parents can take turns leading a set of drills and document the grades at these separate practices for the team coach to refer to. On the other hand, parents can simply do it on their own, at their pace with their own kid. They just have to follow the drill list in this book and read the drill descriptions.

As John Mighton stated his book, "A simple program [i.e., beginner skating] gives people who are not experts [i.e., parents], the opportunity to relearn or learn by explaining it to children." Beginner skaters need customized learning at their own pace. This is difficult to make happen in today's world, where everyone is busy and everyone seems to want to win as soon as possible. Although difficult in today's minor hockey paradigm, at this early stage, one-on-one teaching is the key. This is one reason why parents should teach kids to skate.

One-on-one support by parents can become an enjoyable experience for both the beginner and for the parent. The parent has more time for one-on-one teaching with kids than coaches do. With practice, drills become easier for the beginner to complete. With more practice, simple skills will become automatic like they do in swimming. Parents and kids will become proud and enjoy their achievements together.

Lone Ranger Hockey for Kids (Keep-Away)

Once kids learn a few skills, then they want to play hockey right away. At this early age they should do what they do best—that is, have fun. And for them that means hockey with no rules—we call that shinny. Kids need to learn the basic skills while having fun early by playing informal shinny. When games are scheduled for kids in their first year, they should be played across the width of the rink instead of the full length of the rink. They don't need rules to get the puck and score.

Kids at this stage don't need team instruction. They don't need coaches. What they need is adult supervision on the ice. Some coaches may hate me for saying this, but from my coaching perspective, at this beginner stage, kids should actually be coached opposite to what we as team coaches will want to teach them later. Beginners at first should only chase the puck, then keep it until they score. Basically, play keep-away and score if you can. Remember, at this stage these beginners have not gained good balance yet and are falling down all over the ice during the course of a game. Maybe six or more out of the ten skaters on the ice fall down at the same time. In this type of novice or prenovice hockey, a player has to try to get the puck, then carry it while avoiding five players from the opposition team plus the other four players on his or her own team. In other words, players need to carry the puck and keep the puck away from nine other players. These other players actually make up nine obstacles on the ice, with most of them lying down on the ice like pylons. We used to call this keep-away or Lone Ranger hockey (after the cowboy hero on radio and movies in the old days). There is nothing wrong with this Lone

Ranger type of hockey before they have learned the basics. With nine obstacles on the ice, it is nearly impossible to pass, so why waste your effort trying? This would be like an NHL'er trying to pass through six or seven pros lying on the ice at the same time. If professionals can't do it, does it make sense for beginners to try to do it?

Beginners can learn a lot from playing keep-away hockey. They are not ready for passing, so I recommend they play Lone Ranger hockey until all nine obstacles (players) are able to stay on their feet and skate without falling down. Beginners should play simple keep the puck away from everyone else until they can score. By "everyone," I mean kids, not adult coaches. Adults should never participate in shinny with beginners. Not only is it unfair, but more important, it deflates the kids' confidence. For at least the first year or until kids complete the drills in book 1 and book 2, there should be no rules, such as off-sides in organized hockey games. Shinny should only be played across the rink, not the length of the rink. Let's face it, youths want to hog the puck anyway. So let them have fun with the puck until they have completed fundamental skills. This is ideal for the transition from a first-time skater to being ready to join an organized team.

My six-year-old grandson played in a prenovice tournament the past couple of years. The tournament was well set up for this age group. They had an excellent arrangement for these five—and six-year-olds' games. First, they played across the width of the rink; two games could go on at the same time. However, the most important rule was, only the first three goals by any individual player counted for their team. After a kid scored three goals, if he or she wanted their team to score any more, they had to pass the puck to someone else to score for their team. This worked out well. It solved several problems. Any kid could play Lone Ranger for the first three goals. If they were good enough to score three goals, they were probably ready to pass the puck to a teammate. This prevented bigger and better players from dominating the game and taught them to pass.

Beginner Hockey Equipment Considerations for Parents

General

All hockey equipment must be checked for proper fit before these drills are tried. Equipment manufacturers are doing an excellent job providing safety-approved hockey equipment for all ages in any size. If a sports shop does not have it, they are able to get it in a few days. Today there is no reason for boys and girls to not be properly fitted with equipment, other than money of course. Manufacturers do a good job, considering all the protection and safety provided to young players. This was not the case twenty years ago. The competition between manufactures has kept prices, while not cheap, at least relatively low. Now parents can rely on most good sports shops for their input and advice for hockey equipment.

Although it is not essential, the full set of hockey equipment should be worn from the start so beginners can get used to it. Playing shinny is what hockey is all about, and wearing all the hockey equipment will prevent many bruises and injuries. Most red-blooded Canadians who played shinny when they were young will attest to the fact that the best hockey games and the most fun were those played with hardly any hockey equipment on.

Skates

The skate is the most important item for consideration at an early age. There are many different skates on the market today. Parents may have his or her preference. The most important thing to remember is that a skate is not made for comfort. It is made for protection and skating efficiency. The skate manufacturer has to cope with the problem of supporting the whole body on two thin blades each with two thinner edges while providing maximum protection. If you consider the area of the skate that actually touches the ice surface to the size of the surface area of the shoe, which children walk around on all day, the ratio would be about 1,000 to 1 or greater. Now, how in the world are you supposed to be comfortable with all your weight on an area hundreds of times smaller than what you are used to all your life? Also, it will take six to eight practices before a skate is even partially broken in. It will take that long before kids get confidence it their new skates. So don't wear new skates for the first time in important game or tournaments. Break them in first.

The skate must fit snugly and have good support. At one time the ankle support was not there in skates. All skates have excellent ankle support now. To obtain a proper fit, put the skate on without laces or at least with very loose laces, then lift the heel of the blade off the floor about three inches, slide the foot forward until the toe touches the front end of the skate. When you are able to force your index finger behind the heel, then it should be a very close fit. In order to allow for a little foot growth, you should be able to put the index finger behind the heel. If there is any more space than the width of the index finger, the skate is too big. Normally, to maintain correct fit, skates need to be replaced each year. In case the youngster has had a spurt in growth during the hockey season, parents should check the size during the course of the season as well. Kids will let you know when the skate is too small because the skate will hurt their feet and they soon will complain. Usually the skate size is one size smaller than their shoe size.

Tip: Cold skates—when skates are left out of doors for a long period of time, they get cold. One quick way to warm them up is to put your feet in them for a few minutes before tying them up. Then walk around in loose skates for thirty seconds. Before you tie them up, take them off again for a minute or two, then put them back on then tie them up. By taking the skates off, the cold air is released from the skate boot, and the warm foot warms the boot.

Walking around the dressing room or at home with loose skates is a good practice for balance anyway. If you can walk with loose skates, you will have better balance.

Skate sharpening for beginners should be standard sharpening of one-half-inch cut; three-eighths of an inch is too sharp until they start playing competitive hockey. One-fourth-inch cut is even deeper and will last longer but is too sharp for kids. Sharp skates make it more difficult to turn and stop. When skates are first sharpened, youths find it difficult to stop, but the skates become dull enough for them very quickly. Do not try to learn to stop for the first time with sharp skates. It is too difficult. Wait until the skates are duller, then try stopping.

Waxed laces can be a problem. They are hard to tighten and even harder to loosen. However, a minimal amount of wax on laces will help keep laces tight and will not be as hard to unlace. Nine-year-olds can start to tighten their own skates when laces are lightly waxed. Ask the sports shop for lightly waxed laces.

Helmet

Again, manufacturers do a good job in developing excellent helmets and masks. The helmet, mask, and chin strap should be snug and meet all national sports safety standards. If a chin strap and mask is not worn, a beginner may fall and injure their chin or face on the ice. A mouthpiece should be worn when playing shinny and games.

Hockey Stick

In book 1 the hockey stick is used mainly for balance, and therefore, the lie of the stick is unimportant at this point. Expensive composite sticks are not required for beginners. Stick blades should be taped from the heel to the toe.

The length of the stick may be a little longer than normal for balancing purposes. However, for puck control, it is important to have the correct length of stick for puck manipulation. The recommended length of the stick is from the ice surface up to your chin while standing on skates (or up to your nose with skates off). Some say it should be even shorter. The player eventually will decide what works best for him or her. Some hockey players use two different stick lengths. A longer stick for defensive play in a tight checking game and a shorter stick for offense play with better puck control.

The Four Major Skating Problems for Beginner Skaters

When introducing beginners to skating for the first time, you will encounter four major problems.

1. Skate Feel
2. Toe-Heel Movement
3. Knee Movement
4. Balance

I try to analyze these difficult problems through a beginner's eyes and try to observe the thinking process a youngster must go through. In order to accomplish this, as stated earlier, I break down the mechanics of what the human body needs to go through during the process of skating. The beginner's skating motion consists of four fundamental mechanical movements of the human body. After analyzing the problems, I present solutions for these problems in the form of drills. I refer to these four problem areas as groups of concept. These concept groups are broken down into specific concepts, and again further down into specific drills.

Why is skating so difficult for beginners? What is the difference between walking on the floor every day and skating on ice? Most people don't stop to realize the difficulty involved when asking a youngster to skate for the first time. Empathy is needed to instruct beginners to learn how to skate at any age. Asking four—or five-year-olds to skate for the first time is asking something completely foreign to them. It is even more difficult when they are older. If you have ever attempted to show someone how to skate for the first time, you know it seems nearly impossible for them. As I said, you need to try to look through the eyes of first-time skater. To see it through kid's eyes requires a very different approach.

When you think about it and then analyze a young skater's predicament, it becomes understandable as to why this is so difficult the first time. Youngsters have spent all their life (three or four years) learning how to walk normally; they run, play, and have fun every day. They spent most of their young lives learning to walk on a floor, which is close to and right next to the bottom of the soles of their feet. They learned to walk with the full profile of the bottom of their feet in contact with a floor. They learned to walk with their toes pointing normally toward the front. They learned to walk on floors with friction with a lot of traction, with shoes that possess soles with much traction to prevent them from slipping. It took their brain ten or eleven months to learn enough balance to begin to stand up and start walking on a floor for the first time. Then to prevent themselves from falling forward, they started walking fast going forward, with their hands reaching out in front. Some kids started by running before they could walk so they would not fall forward. In fact, those kids who run before they can walk probably will be good athletes. What an amazing human brain to teach the body how to do all of this. Logically, would it not take longer than ten or eleven months to learn to do the same thing on a slippery sheet of ice, especially if it was done on two-inch stilts?

Once beginners have finally gained the confidence to learn how to walk on the ground or floor every day of their life, gain balance by running, jumping, and hopping on one foot while playing every day, then all of a sudden, they are instantly expected to be able to do all of this on skates on ice. What we are asking them to do seems impossible for them at first—that is, we are really asking them to do the following:

1. Walk on stilts two inches above a floor (blade height).
2. Walk on a small, thin blade that touches a very small part of the floor. The full foot profile of the foot will no longer be in contact with a surface.
3. Use only one small part of an edge of that small thin blade.
4. Be able to point their toes ninety degrees away from the normal walking position.
5. And do all of this on a very slippery surface called ice.

One consolation is that when a youngster puts on a pair of skates for the first time, he or she doesn't necessarily need to try to walk on skates on the actual ice. It is easier, in fact probably better, for a beginner to start at home on any hard surface, rather than starting on the ice. Once they are able to stand up and perform some basic balances on a solid surface like a floor, then they can try it on the ice rink. However, they should go on the ice before they become too reliant on a non-slippery surface.

From the beginning, skaters should be taught to lean forward just enough to prevent themselves from falling backward, and they should use a hockey stick for balance. The hockey stick blade should be on the ice or floor in front of them, with one hand on the upper end of the stick. They should learn immediately that the blade of a stick should be flat on the ice or floor when possible, because at this point the stick is mainly used to help with balance. It is better to practice without a stick, but it would be much more difficult. If a beginner is not using a stick for balance, then they should use their arms for balance. Simply reach both arms as far forward as they can for balance.

Remember, all hockey players were beginners at one time. A great deal of work has been done by Hockey Canada in breaking the game down into smaller skill parts for kids to learn how to skate forward and backward, pass, and shoot. *The Hockey Method* breaks skating down even further, then organizes and examines all the basic concepts involved in the movement of the human body while skating and controlling the puck. Drills are simple and meant to be practiced for short durations of time over many practices.

1—Skate-Feel Concepts

Problem

When first-time skaters attempt to skate or walk on the ice, he or she will attempt to do it the same way they have been walking every day of their lives. That is, they will try as if they are walking in comfortable shoes on a solid floor with traction soles on their shoes. They try to walk flat-footed or rocking with their weight transferred from their heels on to the toes while running. The problem with a beginner skater is he or she has no idea of the feel of the skate, which for the first time suddenly is now two inches above the floor/ice, on a very small skate blade edge and on a very slippery surface. They somehow need to get used to that vacant feeling between their actual feet and the elevated and narrow blade edge on a slippery ice surface. It is not simple.

Analysis

The Hockey Method, first of all, will introduce a youngster to the feel of the skate by breaking down the area where the skate makes contact with the ice into the following actual distances between the foot and the ice surface: the various distances between the actual point of contact of the skate blade to the ice, the actual location of the nearest part of the foot to the ice surface, and the distance from the outside of the skate boot to the actual surface of the ice. These are the five separate distances to consider:

    A—Foot Distance—between balls of the feet and the ice surface
    B—Toe Distance—between toes of foot and point where toe of blade touches ice
    C—Heel Distance—between heel of foot and point where heel of blade touches ice
    D—Side Distance—between side of the blade and outside of the skate boot
    E—Edge Distance—between bottom of skate boot and the ice surface

Solution

I refer to obtaining the feel of the skate as skate-feel concepts. This group of concepts consists of five simple concepts: walk, run, glide, jump, and rock. These concepts again are broken down further into solutions of elementary drills, which are simple and easy to learn. The idea is to direct beginners progressively through these simple drills, starting with drill 1. Learn how to walk on skates first, then run, then glide, then jump, and finally learn to rock on skate blades on the ice. Below are the skate-feel concepts and drills followed by a description and a picture for each drill. A DVD showing the drills will be available on this book's website soon.

Skate-Feel Drill Description

Skate-Feel Concepts

Walk—Concept 1

Drill 1E: Short steps forward OI P (baby steps)

The simplest and first concept is to walk. Starting off with drill 1, which is as simple as possible, just take small steps. This is the first drill in the book and is also the first drill designated with the property OI for off-ice. This means you don't even need an ice rink to start. Kids or anyone else can practice this drill off-ice at home or in an arena dressing room or anywhere else on any hard surface with their skates on.

Skates, like ski boots, are designed differently than shoes. Bend the knees slightly and stand on the ice (any surface for that matter) with a minimal upper-body lean forward, the hockey stick blade on the ice (one hand on the end of the stick). Walk forward slowly, taking small steps across the ice. When there is no stick available, extend the hands and arms as far forward as he or she can for balance. Who can take the smallest baby steps? Can they walk fast? This is only the beginning of developing the balance needed for skating. When teaching a group, have all of them walk across the rink at the same time. One kid may go first as a demonstrator or leader.

This drill also is the first drill designated with the property P (Puck). P means the drill can be done with a puck on the stick. So right off the bat you can start using pucks if your plan is to instruct hockey as well as skating. The earlier puck control is taught, the better it is for hockey. Carrying the puck can be introduced now or later on. Depending on the interest and capability of the beginner, you can start anytime by putting a puck on their stick when you feel it is appropriate. However, beginners must learn how to hold the stick and roll the wrists before they start using pucks. So before introducing pucks, whether at this point now or later, you must jump ahead to book 2 ("Beginner Puck Control") and cover drills 200-202 and 206. Beginners must know the proper way to hold the stick, what length the stick should be, and how to move the wrist for simple puck control. After completing drills 200-202, then as stated in drill 206, you come back and practice puck control as early as drill 1. This can be applied at any time to all drills in book 1 designated with a P (Puck).

Drill 2E: Giant steps forward OI P

Take long steps on the ice or on any hard surface (dressing room, floor, hallway, etc.). At first it does not need to be real long, just longer than the previous small baby steps. Then make them longer and longer. Who can take the longest giant step? Give the kid who does the shortest and longest steps praise. Let the kids take turns leading by being the drill demonstrator for the group. Give them each a chance to succeed and build their confidence. With a group of kids, line them up all along the boards or a wall and ask all of them to do the drill at the same time going across the ice (or any other hard surface). Any kid can be the designated demonstrator and can go first as leader.

Drill 3E: Down and up (get up off the ice) OI P HC

At this early point, if beginners haven't fallen, they soon will. So this is a good time to show them how to get up off the ice and on to their skates. Beginners have little balance and it takes a lot of strength in the arms to get up off the ice. It will take time to accomplish getting up, especially for the smaller, very young beginner. A good method is to start from a position lying on the ice:

1. Get on to the knees.
2. Lift one knee until the skate blade (of the same leg) is on the ice.
3. Put both hands on that knee.
4. Push down hard on that knee with both hands and at the same time try to get up on the other leg.

This will take practice and a good deal of effort. The stronger players, who are able to push down hard on their knee, will be able to get up quickly. Don't attempt this too many consecutive times in a row because it quickly becomes very tiring for kids. Try a few times and keep coming back during the other drills until they can get up on their own. With practice, you should eventually be able to get up by using either knee. Kids love it when they can get a grade of "excellent" with this drill. Encourage them by praising them and give them a good grade as soon as you can for these first few drills. Be lenient on grading these early drills to build their confidence.

Drill 4E: Beginner's stance OI HC

It is important to develop a good stance for beginners early. When in the skating stance, beginners must bend the knees until they can't see their toes. The knees should block the view of the toes. The upper body should have a slight lean forward with weight on the middle of the skate blades. The actual correct stance for the skating stride will be discussed in more detail later (drill 58) and will require much more knee bend than the beginner stance.

At this point, there are two main concerns. Firstly, try to develop forward lean with the upper part of the body. If the stick or arms are extended forward as they should be for these drills, it will soon become automatic. Secondly, it is imperative for beginners to learn how to continually keep the knees bent. This is not easy, and it takes time to get used to it. Even when you are standing around doing nothing in a stationary position, you should be standing with knees bent. The view from the eyes to the toes of the skate should always be obstructed by the knees. In fact, as you will see later, the knees should be bent even beyond the point of where you lose sight of the toes of the skates. From this point on, keep the knees bent as much as possible at all times when wearing skates on the ice and when off the ice as well. Sometimes I jokingly tell kids in hockey schools that you will not see the toes of your skates again for the next five days until the hockey school is over.

Drill 5E: Walk sideways OI P L&R

Walk sideways (side steps). Step laterally along the blue line (sideways) with toes pointed in front, ninety degrees out from the blue line. Use the blue line only as a guide. This may be done any place on the ice or on any hard surface. Do not cross the feet over at this point, make simple side steps. We will introduce crossovers later. This will help provide balance for crossovers later. Practice equally to both to the left and the right.

Drill 6E: Walk forward on toes OI P

Walk forward on toes across the ice (or any surface.) This is similar to drill 1, short steps forward, except now you put the weight on the toes, not on the middle or back of the skate blades. Use the hockey stick for balance by holding the stick with one hand at the top end of the stick while keeping the blade on the ice. With no stick, reach the hands and arms forward.

Drill 7M: Walk forward on heels OI P

This is the first drill rated as *M* for medium in difficulty. This is more difficult because the beginner must be able to balance himself and walk in a very awkward position on the heels, thus it requires more balance. Lift the toes up off the ice and put all the weight on the heels of the skates then walk forward on the heels. This is especially difficult with knees bent. So practice with knees straight at first. Later bend the knees and lift one skate up off the ice with each step and straighten the leg out as it lands on the heel.

This will feel very awkward at first and seem impossible to some. If you can't do it at first, keep coming back to this drill until you can do it well, and you eventually will. With practice, you will be able to walk on their heels easily. Most beginners are not taught how to put their weight on the back of their skate blades. However, this is very important for most skating skills. Beginners need to be able to put their weight on the back of their skates to be good skaters. Not putting enough weight on the back of the skate blade and not using the heels while skating is one of the most overlooked aspects of skating skills in hockey. This is very important because weight on heels provides power for the forward stride and provides balance for agility skating like crossovers and turning.

Drill 8M: Walk backward on toes OI P

Walk backward on toes across the ice (or any surface). This is difficult at first, and it will take practice to be able to do it. Remember, these beginner drills should last no longer than thirty seconds. So at first go across the ice rink once or twice only. Come back to this drill later and keep coming back to this drill until it is mastered. This is the beginning of balance for backward skating.

Drill 9M: Walk skates loose OI

You need to be very careful not to injure kids with this drill because they could easily twist an ankle. Therefore, if this doesn't seem appropriate, use your own discretion and ignore this drill completely if you think it inappropriate. However, I do know that to walk with loose skates will require a good deal of balance. This does enforce the idea of balance for the beginner without depending on the skate boot. Trying to walk with loose skates in the dressing room or at home will give the beginner a better sense of balance without having to depend on the support given by the skate boot. Walking around the dressing room with loose skates, you will gain balance on the balls of the feet.

Tip: Repeating a previous tip in this book (Hockey Equipment—Skates), this is a good place to walk with skates loose. When the skates are very cold (especially when skating outdoors), it can be a good idea to put your skates on and walk around with loose skates for a moment to let the skates warm up before skating. Then take the skates off and let them warm up for another few moments. Then put your skates back on again and then tie them up. The warm feet in cold boots will tend to warm up the skate boot, and warm feet in the cold boot forces the cold air out of the boot.

Drill 10M: Lateral one side step, then stop on whistle OI P L&R

Walk sideways (side steps, not crossovers). Step laterally along the blue line (sideways) with toes pointed in front ninety degrees perpendicular to the blue line. This may be practiced anyplace on the ice or on any hard surface. Do not cross the feet over at this point. On the first whistle, the beginner must lift one skate up and remain in a balanced position with one skate up off the ice or floor. Use the stick blade on the ice for balance. On the second whistle, bring the skate down but over one step to the side. That is, knee up on one whistle and knee down with one side step on the second whistle. Again, do not cross over at this point. Continue up and down on the whistle, across the ice. This is the first drill to use the property L&R. This is a reminder to go to the left and to the right an equal number of times. A good place to start when on the ice is across the blue line. All beginners on the blue line, lift one skate on the whistle at the same time, then at the same time, drop the skate down on the next whistle, making one step sideways.

Drill 11M: Lateral side steps fast on whistle across blue line OI P F L&R

Walk sideways (side steps). Step laterally along the blue line (sideways) with toes pointed in front ninety degrees perpendicular to the blue line. Go to the left and right an equal amount of time. This may be practiced anyplace on the ice or on any hard surface. Do not cross the feet over at this point. This is the first drill to use the F (Fast) drill property. Make side steps slow then fast on the whistle. Continue going lateral one step at a time, step slowly sideways on the whistle, then step fast on the next whistle, then again slow on the next whistle, and continue to go slow, then fast and so on, in one direction then the other.

Drill 12A: Walk backward on heels OI P

This is the first drill rated with an *A* for "advanced." It is very difficult because the beginner must be able to balance himself on the heels and walk backward in a very awkward position with the toes up off the ice and weight on the heels. Lift the toes up and put all the weight on the heels of the skates and walk backward on the heels. At first, trying to walk backward on the heels seems impossible. In fact, they won't be able to do it. Start with knees straight, then later practice with a slight knee bend. Once you understand what you are attempting to do and after several attempts, you will get the idea and eventually will be able to accomplish it.

You will find kids will practice this on their own between other drills. So you don't need to spend much time on this drill. This is the case, with most beginner drills, where thirty seconds is a long time. The key is to not spend too much time on any one drill but come back to the drill often. Most beginner drills should be practiced many times for short durations of time; for example, they could be done early in the practice, then during the middle of the practice, and then again at the end of the practice for very short durations of time. Kids will now start to become familiar with that space between their heels and the ice.

If this drill is too difficult, like all A-rated drills in this book, it can be done later when the beginner is more able to handle it.

Drill 13U: Short steps forward fast on whistle P F S (Combo 5)

Walk forward with very short steps slow, then on the whistle move the feet fast. Slow, then fast on the whistle.

Run—Concept 2

Drill 14E: Run on the spot slow OI P

Running is normal for kids, but the concept of running on ice is certainly not. This is very difficult. Start by standing on one spot (anyplace on the ice or on any surface) and run slowly by lifting the knees up high. The knees should be lifted as high as you can. We will determine how high the knees should go later. At this point, it doesn't matter where the weight is distributed on the skate blade. The weight anywhere on the blade is fine at this point.

Drill 15E: Run on the spot fast on whistle OI P F

This is the first drill to practice at three different speeds or three different gears. The first gear is to go slow to allow you to concentrate on balance. The second gear is to go faster and concentrates on lifting the knees higher. The third gear or high gear is to move your feet as fast as possible. I refer to this high gear as superfast and it will be used in many drills throughout this book and means move the feet as fast as you can. This is the method used to create acceleration for many skills.

For this drill, run slow on the spot, then when you blow the whistle, run fast on the spot. On the next whistle, run slow again. Continue this fast-and-slow action for no more than thirty seconds, then move to another drill. Repeat several times during the practice. When the beginners become good at this, try going superfast on the whistle—that is, first whistle, slow; second whistle, fast; third whistle, superfast (as fast as you can move your feet); then slow again on the next whistle.

Drill 16E: Run then spin on the spot OI P L&R

Run on the spot (any location on the ice or other surface), then on the whistle, spin 360 degrees on the spot while continuing to run on the spot. Don't forget to practice it to the left and the right.

Drill 17M: Run on toes forward across the ice OI P F

This is the same as walking forward across the ice, but now run instead. Run on the toes forward across the ice. For some drills kids will want to look down at their skates to see if they are doing it right. Who can run the fastest across the rink? Have a race. At this point, you are beginning to get the feel of distance between your feet and the ice surface. Practice it slow then fast on the whistle.

Drill 18M: Run lateral side steps knees high fast across blue line OI P F L&R

Run laterally doing side steps across the blue and/or red line, lifting the knees high similar to drill 11, but this time lift the knees higher (until the thigh is parallel to ice) without crossing the feet over. Go equally to the left and right. This is important for agility skating in book 3.

Drill 19U: Run on toes backward across the ice OI P

Same as running on the toes forward, except now run backward. This is difficult at first, so don't expect them to accomplish it the first time.

Glide—Concept 3

Drill 20E: Glide two feet P HC F&B

Now that kids can run on the ice, beginners are able to gain some momentum and move on to the concept of gliding. Take a running start and glide forward on both skates. This works the best going across the rink from one side of the rink to the other. Remember, these are short-duration drills, and it is a good idea to use one beginner as a demonstrator to lead. Give all the kids a turn to lead. The leader can go across the ice first, then all the others follow behind together across the ice all at the same time.

Once kids can glide forwards they can practice it going backwards. This is the first drill to use the property F&B (forwards and backwards) which indicates that the drill must be practiced going forwards then backwards.

Notice I have not used one SIL (stand-in-line) drill. Skaters don't need to line up behind each other. They all line up on the boards in parallel, and they all practice the drill going across the ice at the same time, except for the leader who can go several feet in front of the other beginners to lead.

Drill 21E: Glide two feet sitting F&B

Take a running start, then bend knees until you are in a sitting position and glide, then continue gliding as far as you can go. This requires extra good balance and strong legs. This will start to build up leg strength.

Once this drill can be done forwards it should be practiced backwards.

Drill 22E: Glide fast arm pump F HC (Combo 5)

While gliding with both skates across the ice, swing each arm back and forth, front to back. On the whistle, pump both arms faster and faster as if you are running at a track on a field.

Drill 23E: Glide two feet and swerve P F&B

Take a running start, put both feet on the ice and glide on both feet forward. Then glide and swerve in and out forward, to the left then to the right.

1. Take a running start.
2. Slide with both skates on the ice at the same time.
3. Swerve to the left, then right.

Once you accomplish this, then swerve through pylons. To make it fun, utilize partners in tandem; one player bends forward at the waist forty-five degrees and glides forward while another player pushes from behind. Take turns pushing. Try a tandem race with groups of partners of two for each group. One kid can push one direction and the other push the other direction coming back. Try setting up a relay race with one group against another. Once this drill can be done forwards it should be practiced backwards.

Drill 24E: Glide two feet, sit, and swerve P F&B

Take a running start, then get into a sitting position and glide forward on both skates. Bend both knees into a sitting position and then swerve in and out to the left and right. The thighs should be parallel to the ice. Once this drill can be done forwards it should be practiced backwards.

Drill 25M: Glide one foot forward P HC

Take a running start and glide forward on one skate with the other skate off the ice and in front. Go in a straight line. Practice one foot, then the other an equal amount of time.

Drill 26M: Glide one foot forward with supporting knee bend P HC

- Take a running start and glide forward on one skate with the other skate off the ice and behind. Then while gliding, bend the knee of the gliding or supporting leg up and down so that the body goes up and down. Do not perform this drill too long because this is hard on the knee. Over time this drill will provide strength in the knee. Practice one foot, then the other an equal number of times.

Drill 27M: Glide toe on puck P HC

Take a running start and glide forward on one skate. With the toe of the other skate held on top of a puck, slide the puck along by putting enough pressure on the puck with your skate to drag it along under the skate blade. Control the puck with the skate by moving the puck in front, then drag behind, then across the other side of the skating foot. Practice one foot, then the other an equal number of times.

Drill 28U: Glide one foot and swerve pylons P

Take a running start and glide forward on one skate with the other skate off the ice and in front. Then try to make a slight swerve to the left, then to the right between a row of pylons. Practice one foot, then the other an equal amount of time. This is an introduction to the edges drills later. With practice, you will eventually be able to do it while carrying a puck on their stick.

Jump—Concept 4

Drill 29E: Jump stationary OI P F

Jumping is normal for kids, but jumping on the slippery ice with skates on is a new concept. There is a different feel between two feet adjacent and touching each other on a hard surface compared to two feet side by side standing two inches off the hard surface. To get used to the two-inch feeling in height (two-inch stilt feeling), jump with both feet. Simply jump on a hard surface or on the ice. On the whistle, jump and land on their feet any way you can. At first, most will fall down. Then jump with both feet together. How high can you jump? You will need practice at this.

Now after trial and error, you should begin to get some knee bend. Jumping can't be done without bending the knees. Do not jump over sticks because if one should step on a stick, it will cause the stick to turn, causing others to trip and fall, and injuries could result. At this point kids are not ready to jump over pylons or other high objects. However, they can jump on the spot as high as they can and with both feet together, bending their knees as much as possible.

Drill 30E: Jump lines P F

Start at the goal line and skate to the other end of the rink while jumping over each line with both feet held together. Then disregarding the lines, practice jumping while skating along the ice and make fast consecutive jumps when you blow the whistle (fast on the whistle), then slow consecutive jumps on the next whistle.

Drill 31E: Jump high on boards OI

Doing a drill while using the boards or a wall as support is an introductory process used for many drills. This is the first drill that is introduced by holding on to the boards (or a wall) for support. In this case it introduces the idea of bending the knees more and more to jump higher and higher. Start from a low profile or sitting position. At first, hold on to the boards for support with both hands while facing the boards or a wall, then jump as high as you can with both skates together by bending the knees as much as possible. Then try jumping while holding the boards with only one hand. Who can jump the highest? The higher the jump, the more balance and knee bend is needed.

Drill 32E: Jump high over blue line/floor OI P

Skate around the rink or end to end on the rink and jump as high as you can over the blue line and red lines. The more the knee is bent, the higher you can jump. If off-ice, then make a high jump while stationary on the floor.

Drill 33E: Balance one foot stationary OI P HC

Stand on one spot with stick blade on the ice and with one hand on the upper end of the stick for balance (if no stick, then reach forward with both arms). Then on the whistle, lift up one skate off the ice in front and bend the knee in front ninety degrees (thighs horizontal to the ice). Stay stationary in that position as long as possible, using only the sick on the ice for balance. Try the other leg. Who can balance themselves the longest? Again, these drills are "thirty seconds or less" types of drills. So you need to come back to them often.

Drill 34M: Hop one foot stationary OI P F HC

Hop on one skate. While standing on one spot, lift one skate off the ice and in front. Then hop up and down on the other skate. Of course, it can't do it without a good knee bend by the supporting leg. The other skate should never touch the ice. Practice hopping on one skate then the other. The first time this is attempted, beginners may not be able to do it. You will notice kids will be able to jump or hop on one skate a little longer each time. This is a very important balance drill and should be used during warm-ups and warm-downs from now on.

Drill 35M: Jump one foot OI P HC F&B

Similar to the previous drill, hop on one foot, but now jump high and then higher and higher. Try by jumping on one skate over blue lines and red line. Always jump and land with the same foot. Practice it going backwards as well.

Drill 36A: Jump legs crossed OI P L&R

At first, beginners will probably find this very difficult and probably will not be able to achieve it at this early stage. However, this is a good time to introduce it. Cross the legs (or skates) and jump. In order to accomplish this, beginners will certainly require that feeling of the side-by-side distance between their skates. Beginners will also need to be able to bend their knees to a great extent to accomplish this. You will find some may not be ready to do it at this point. We will cover this further under knee movement later, but keep coming back to this drill until they can accomplish it because this takes much practice; it will become very important later. Some kids will surprise you, and others won't. Alternate L&R by jumping with the left leg over the right leg, then the right leg over the left leg.

Drill 37U: High jumps moving P S F&B

Continue to jump higher and higher on the whistle while skating around the rink. Who can jump the highest? Once this drill can be done forwards it should be practiced backwards.

Rock—Concept 5

The idea of the rock concept is to learn to rock on your skate blades while skating which can be very controversial. In fact, many coaches would disagree. The concept is that not only can you skate in a straight line with the forward stride, but you also can skate forward in a straight line with a different stride, a type of rocking-on-your-skate stride. I refer to this as the sprint stride. This is very similar to the way you normally run when wearing running shoes on a track and field. In theory it is accomplished by moving the knees up and down and then when the skate touches the ice, the weight is put on the heels first, then the middle, and then toes of each skate blade as you stride forward. Although this rocking on the skate blade concept seems impossible to do on skates on an ice rink, it is actually done by some very gifted athletes. A very small percentage of professional players, do this automatically without ever thinking about it. Even though it is hard to detect, many of the great skaters like Bobby Orr and Paul Coffey, accelerate with a rocking motion on their skate blades as they come out of a circle. Players who have advanced or exceedingly great coordination, accelerate fast out of a circle doing crossovers, and sometimes they continue to skate in a straight line while seemingly still doing crossovers. They are actually sprinting ahead in a straight line still with a crossover motions but actually they are rocking on their skate blades. That is what I refer to as the sprint stride.

Some of the great players in the NHL today do it several times during a game without any notice. Although only a few kids can accomplish this, we should attempt to give every kid the opportunity to learn it. As stated earlier in this book by John Mighton, "Kids are not given credit for the great potential of their ability" Many more kids have the capability to learn this rocking type or sprint stride, than the number of those who can do it now. If we practice this as a formal part of the forward stride, many more kids should be able to achieve this new challenge. All kids should have the same opportunity to at least attempt this new concept. This is discussed more in book 3 within the section Agility Skating. The rock drills are an introduction to this concept.

Drill 38E: Rock on boards on skates OI

This "rocking on skates" concept is very difficult, and few kids will be able to do it properly because it is very difficult to achieve. Most kids may never be able to achieve a good rocking motion on their skate blades on the ice. However, it should be attempted, and after many hours of attempts, some kids will learn how to do it. Those who can accomplish this will become very advanced skaters.

As an introduction to rocking on skates, start by holding on to the wall or boards with both hands and rock on both skates then one skate, then the other. Continue rocking from heel to toe back and forth. Then rock on both skates at the same time. Continue rocking from heel to toe back and forth.

Drill 39E: Rock on boards running OI F

This drill is also very important for agility skating. Hold on to the boards with one hand (or start with both hands), then rock back and forth on each skate blade in a running motion as if sprinting. Start stationary the slowly try to run on the spot. This should be like running in a race on a race track wearing running shoes. The weight should be transferred from heel to the middle of the blade, then to the toes of the blade, one foot then the other, like running on the ground. Once you are comfortable doing this rocking, then go faster on the whistle.

Drill 40M: Rock stationary on skate blade one foot OI P

Similar to rocking on boards, but now rock back and forth on one skate on the ice without help from the boards for support. While stationary, rock on one foot, then rock on the other skate (back and forth heel-middle-toes).

Drill 41M: Rock stationary on skate blades, two feet OI P F

While stationary on the ice or floor, rock with both skates on the ice at the same time. Rock back and forth, transferring the weight from heel to middle to toes of the blade, back and forth. Then slide each skate back and forth while remaining in a stationary position as if you are walking. This is more difficult than it sounds. If off-ice, rock on the floor.

Drill 42A: Touch toes with horizontal stick, then rock OI

Hold the stick with both hands at waist height and horizontal to the ice. Without bending the knees, touch the toes with the stick, while keeping the stick horizontal to the ice. Then while the stick is on the toes, rock on the skates. If off-ice, rock on the floor.

Drill 43U: Rock on skate blades while running OI P

This is an introduction to a new and very agile type of forward stride. Run across a rink and try to implement a sprinting motion by rocking from the heels to the toes on each skate blade, one foot at a time, as if you are running on a track or field with running shoes. While rocking with skate blades on the ice may seem to be unnatural, in fact, it actually is more natural for the human body than the traditional forward stride. You normally don't walk or run pushing your feet out 45 degrees like you do in the skating stride. This is actually an extension of doing crossovers and it will make more sense and be much easier after learning forward crossovers later. So we will come back to it again later. Most NA players do not have the extra athletic ability and balance needed to accomplish this difficult type of stride. Few skaters are gifted with the natural ability required to do this type of forward skating without advanced balance training. However, it is worth introducing it at this point.

In book 3 I refer to this as the forward sprint stride. It is a major plus for speed and acceleration. If this is introduced now, it will have a major impact later in advanced skating. The few who can do this will become excellent skaters with great speed, acceleration, and agility. Therefore, perhaps only 1 in 20 kids will be able to do it, but it is important to try it at this stage. Rocking on skates will provide a better chance of implementation later during forward crossovers. If kids are off the ice, try it on any hard surface.

2—Toe-Heel Concepts
Problem

Toe-heel movement involves turning the toes of one skate out and in ninety degrees from the other skate. This was originally described by Howie Meeker in his book *Howie Meeker's Hockey Basics* (see the bibliography at the back of this book). This was the method Howie used to try to unlock the hips. Turning the toes out and in ninety degrees is needed for many skating skills. Five—and six-year-olds normally can't stretch their ankle muscles and ligaments out ninety degrees, probably because they never had a reason to do it before and, therefore, never tried it. In the normal walking motion, of course, they never walk with their toes pointing ninety degrees out to the side, not to mention turning them in ninety degrees.

Toe-heel concepts also involve the use of both edges of the skate blade. It is very difficult for kids to turn and balance on only one of the two edges of the skate blade. They certainly cannot skate forward on one edge without help. The heel concept means lifting up the toes and then putting all the weight on the heels. This concept is an under coached skill today. Skills involving toe-heel movement is difficult for all skaters, especially beginners.

Analysis

Moving the toes out ninety degrees is a concept to aid forward motion while thrusting forward during skating. In order to obtain forward movement and to increase power into this motion, a youngster must be able to turn the toes out ninety degrees with each skate, one at a time. Although toes ninety degrees out is not needed for the stride, it does provide the exaggeration needed to be able to turn the toes out at least forty-five degrees for the forward stride. If you cannot turn the toes out ninety degrees, you cannot push back at the start to obtain the power needed for the forward start. Turning the skates out ninety degrees will facilitate pivoting and starting later as well.

Unlocking the hips is important for long strides. The concept of moving the toes in ninety degrees and then out ninety degrees is needed to unlock the hips. You want to unlock the hips for long stride extension. All good skaters develop a way to unlock the hips. Kids also need to turn the toes in ninety degrees for agility skating such as backward skating.

Most beginners don't realize that there are two edges on each skate blade. As kids turn the toes out then in ninety degrees, they will start feeling the difference between both edges of the skate blades. Not only are you asking beginner skaters to skate on a slippery ice surface and on a thin skate blade, but you expect them to do it on one sharp edge of one skate and only on a very small part of that sharp edge. This skate-blade-edge concept takes a great deal of balance to achieve; beginners certainly cannot do it at first, especially on one foot.

Solution

The concepts of turning toes out ninety degrees, then in ninety degrees, using both edges of a skate blade one at a time and putting weight on the back of the skate, are unnatural and foreign to the muscles in the human body, especially for beginners. This is foreign to the whole body—the feet, ankles, knees, thighs, hips, and back. These drills will introduce the beginner's skeletal body to all of these new foreign concepts.

Toe-Heel Drill Description

Toes Out—Concept 6

Drill 44E: Toes out 90 degrees sitting on ice OI

Pointing the toes out ninety degrees is an important concept for the forward stride. This is so foreign to beginners that they need special help at first. Kids normally do not turn their toes out very far when walking or running at school every day. This is a major obstacle to skating.

Start by sitting on the ice or the floor with the heels of their skates touching the surface and the toes pointing in the normal position, up and perpendicular to the ice or floor. Do not force the beginners' toes to turn out. You must help them turn the toes of the skate out, but you must be careful not to stretch the ankle muscles too much to soon. At first, the instructor should provide some resistance in the opposite direction of the outward motion. In order to stretch the ankles and toes outward, instructors should provide inward pressure in the opposite direction. The instructor can use his hands or some object like a puck, glove, or water bottle and let the beginner press in the opposite direction. That means use pressure inward against some resistance between the toes of both feet.

Kids may be able to turn the toes out only ten or twenty degrees at first. Repeat putting more inward pressure against the ankles by turning the toes in the opposite direction, inward. Keep trying by using this inward pressure until the beginner can turn the toes outward ninety degrees. This will take time and practice to reach the goal of turning the toes out ninety degrees. Practice both skates equally.

Drill 45E: Toes out 90 degrees standing on ice OI

Once kids can turn their toes out 90 degrees while sitting on the ice, practice it standing. Perhaps start with one hand on the boards for support. While standing stationary on the ice, lift one skate up one or two inches off the ice and move it forward until the heel is adjacent to the toe of the each foot.

Drill 46E: Toes out 90 degrees moving on ice

Take a running start and lift the right skate off the ice one or two inches. While gliding, turn the toes of the right foot out ninety degrees with the heel adjacent (one or two inches off the ice) to the toes of the supporting left foot. The right skate is then perpendicular to the left skate a few inches off the ice. Then move the toes back in line pointing in front but with the skate still off the ice. Practice turning the toes out and back. Practice equally with both skates.

Drill 47E: Toes out against the boards OI

Lean on the rink boards or against a wall with both hands for support and turn the toes out ninety degrees while the skate blade remains on the ice. Keeping the skate blade on the ice, push all the way back as you turn the toes out ninety degrees. Practice one skate, then the other. This is the beginning of C-cuts. Keep putting more pressure on the skate on the ice. This is the beginning of the forward stride, which is covered in book 3.

Drill 48E: Push boards (C-cuts forward) on whistle OI S

Put both hands on the boards and, while leaning against the boards, stretch the right foot back as far as you can go at a right angle to the boards while turning toes out. Put some weight on the toes of the pushing skate blade and push as far back as possible, like in a forward stride. Keep the left skate perpendicular to the boards; try to exaggerate and push the boards over with the hands on the boards and hard pressure into the ice from the right foot. Put weight on the right foot and push hard; let the skate blade slide on the ice as you push. In other words, push hard with the skate toe turned out and extended as far as you can. Then alternate pushing back with one skate, then the other. Alternate putting weight on the toes, then on the heels while pushing back. Practice pushing hard with one foot, then the other. Again for exaggeration, ask them to try to push the boards over.

With a group of kids and a whistle, with both feet together and knees bent, on the whistle all of the kids push out hard with the left skate. On the next whistle, return the left skate to the original position. On the next whistle, push out with the right skate. On the next whistle, return the right skate to the starting position. Continue alternating one skate, then the other on the whistle. Make a C-cut into the ice with the toes of the skates. This is the beginning of C-cuts and also the beginning of the forward stride, which is covered in book 3.

Drill 49E: Carry puck in skates OI P HC

Now that the beginners can turn their toes out while putting some pressure on the ice, let's try something new. Carry the puck with the skates by turning the toes out. As soon as you throw the pucks on the ice, the beginners all go wild with excitement; they all want to play hockey. *Stop.* Don't throw the pucks on the ice. First, put their hockey sticks in the player's box or somewhere safe off the ice. Rather than throwing the pucks on the ice, hand each child one puck. Place the puck in their hand and let them know that at the end of the drill, they each are to return one puck. Line everyone up at the goal line or along the boards. Drop their puck to the ice. Skate across the ice or to the other end of the rink, carrying their puck with the inside of their skate blades by turning their skate out ninety degrees.

Show them how you can turn their toe out and kick the puck forward with the inside of the skate blade, not with the front of the toe of the skate, as a lot of them will try to do. Amazingly, some actually will be able to kick the puck with their toes pointed straight ahead at zero degrees, but this is not the objective of this exercise. To ensure both skates are used, get them to use the right skate first, then the left, and then continue alternating each skate. This can be practiced off the ice as well, except the puck doesn't slide as easily. If you don't skate, then demonstrate by turning your shoe out ninety degrees. Beginners will pick this up very quickly.

Drill 50E: Knee drag with toes out HC P (Combo 5)

Skate around or across the rink slowly, bend one knee, and drag the other foot out behind as far as you can with toes out ninety degrees. Stretch the leg as far as you can with the dragging knee nearly touching the ice. Drag the toes as far as you can at ninety degrees out, letting the ice pull the skate back. Alternate dragging the left, then the right skate with toes out. This will stretch the leg in the toes-out position and is a common and very good stretch for warm-ups and warm-downs.

Drill 51M: Power one leg (C-cuts forward) toes out multipush P

Start at the goal line or along the boards in what is called the starting position. The starting position is as follows: One hand is on the upper end of the stick. Stick blade is on the ice. Knees are bent and upper body leaning forward in the beginner stance (drill 4). Left toe is pointing forward. Right toe is out ninety degrees.

When the whistle blows, push back with the right skate with toes out. Lift the right skate off the ice; bring it adjacent to the left gliding skate with the right toes still out while still gliding on the left skate. Drop the right skate to the ice and push again while continuing to glide on the left skate. Keep the left skate gliding on the ice all the time. Continue pushing with the right skate back and forth until you reach the other end of the rink. When you get to the other end of the rink, stop any way you can. Now repeat the same thing going the other way, but this time push with the left skate only, letting the right skate do the gliding all the way on the ice, and continually push with the left skate, toes out. Try a race. Who is the fastest pushing with the left leg? Who is the fastest pushing with the right leg? This is the part of the forward stride, which is covered in book 3.

> **Instructor tip:** Observe "fun" races carefully. Even at a very early age, some youngsters can be overly eager to compete and may start to take shortcuts. Ensure all skaters are attempting to complete the drills correctly so that bad habits don't prevail.

Drill 52M: Power one leg (C-cuts forward) toes out single push P

From the starting position (previous drill), push once with right skate, then keep the right skate off the ice. How far can you glide on the left foot without pushing again or stopping or falling? Now, who can push the hardest with one push and go the farthest on the left skate? Who can push the hardest and go the farthest on the right skate? Whoever pushes the hardest with one skate and keeps his or her balance on the other skate should go the farthest. We discuss knees later but for now, you may realize that the more you bend the supporting knee on gliding leg, the farther you can extend back with the other skate. The farther you can extend that pushing skate back the more power can be gained, and more weight you put on the pushing skate (push as hard as you can into the ice surface), the farther you go. Keep the pushing foot off the ice while gliding on the other foot. Remember, only push once. Practice until you develop a good powerful push. Alternate practicing both the left and right skates. This is the beginning of power skating.

A fun variation of this drill is to keep moving farther down the ice on one skate with momentum by propelling yourself more by kicking in mid air with the pushing skate when it is still off the ice. While gliding along the ice on one skate kick with the other skate in mid air behind. Youngsters find this difficult at first, but it can be fun once they get the knack of it. Start by taking a running start, lift one skate up off the ice, and keep your momentum going by kicking backward behind and into mid air. Bend that knee a great deal and create momentum by pumping the bent knee from front to back very actively back and forth maintaining the forward motion. Continue swinging the same leg back and forth and you continue to glide; with good balance, you will be able to propel forward all the way across or down the ice. This takes many fast knee pumps or skate kicks to go faster. Good balance and weight transfer back and forth on the one skate is needed. Try a race. Practice on one leg, then the other an equal number of times.

Drill 53M: Push heavy objects OI HC

A good way to develop power with the toe-out movement is to push objects. For example, tip a hockey net over and ask several beginners to sit on the front of the net, while several other beginners push the net from behind with toes out, thus giving each other rides. Or have the instructor sit or lean on the net giving the required resistance with their skates. Push a chair with someone sitting on it. If this is too easy to push, drag the skates for resistance. Use any heavy object you can think of such as a large heavy pail full of pucks and pylons. How about pushing another player?

Drill 54M: Pull heavy objects OI HC P

Pull a heavy object or pull another player by concentrating on turning the toes out and pushing back as far as you can. Use a belt and cord to pull a player on the ice. While pulling a player, the player being pulled should drop to one knee or both knees to provide resistance. Pull a partner by each facing the same direction while holding on to two sticks. The partner being pulled can drag his skate in order to put pressure on the pulling. Try having a tandem race.

Drill 55A: Penguin walk forward heel to heel OI

Walk forward with toes of both feet out ninety degrees. In other words, the heels point in, and the toes point out, then slowly walk straight forward in this position. This can't be done without maximum knee bend. Although this is not a normal skating position, it is an exaggeration for other skating skills. Most kids will not be able to do this at first; if they completed the previous drills they should be able to do it, if they can't do it now, try it again later.

Drill 56A: Heel-to-heel on the boards OI

This is an introduction to the difficult heel-to-heel movement. It is especially important if a beginner has difficulty doing the previous drill, the penguin walk. This seems impossible at first, so start by using the boards or a wall for support. With both hands on the boards, move the toes of both feet out ninety degrees. Move the body up and down by bending the knees up and down while both toes point out. At first, to make it easier, lift one skate slightly off the ice but still in the heel-to-heel position, then drop that skate down on the ice into the proper heel-to-heel position while still holding on to the boards for support.

Drill 57A: Heel-to-heel one skate straight line HC

With one skate off the ice, practice the heel-to-heel motion in a straight line (i.e. start by following along the blue line or red line as a guide). Glide with the toes of both skates pointing out ninety degrees and both heels pointing in. This is a very difficult drill at first. So to make it easier this drill will be done on one skate only for now. That is, glide in a straight line with only one skate on the ice and the other just off the ice, but both skates are in the heel-to-heel position. Practice going both directions on the left skate only on the ice, then with the right skate only on the ice.

We will try dropping the other skate down later. More on this later in drill 99, when we put both skates on the ice at the same time to complete this heel-to-heel movement.

Drill 58A: Full skating stance and hold OI

This is one of the most important drills. Once beginners can walk, run, glide, jump, rock, and turn their toes out, they are ready to learn the correct skating stance. This is a critical procedure for beginners because if they don't get this right, they will never skate with the full capability of their body. Young boys and girls of approximately eight to nine years of age do not possess the strength we as parents and coaches think they have. They are much weaker in the knees and legs than we realize. This is especially evident when you compare a December-born beginner to a January-born beginner. The weakness of the muscles of beginner knees and legs is completely underestimated by us adults, and this is probably the most significant reason why kids cannot skate fast compared to other kids born several months earlier. More kids born in January make tier 1 than kids born in December. One major factor is due to eight to twelve months of less muscle growth and subsequent strength.

Most people do not realize that skating speed is not determined only by how fast you move your feet. Speed on skates is primarily determined by two factors:

1. The full bending of the knees (the skating stance with knees bent ninety degrees)

2. Strong weight transfer and heavy push into the ice surface (with toes out forty-five degrees)

If a player can perform these two factors better, he or she can skate faster than a player with faster feet. Faster feet movement is genetic and nice to have, but believe it or not, knee bend with full stride extension and a strong hard push into the ice surface is much more important and is the major requirement for fast skating. This is one reason I insist on the knees being bent all the time, even when kids are standing around and listening to the instructor.

The strong or hard push into the ice is the beginning of power skating. When you watch replays of the great skaters like Sidney Crosby and Alex Ovechkin, you will notice that their feet are not necessarily moving any faster than other players on the ice. What they do is bend their knees more, thus creating a very long stride especially during crossovers. They also possess very strong legs and push harder into the ice with their skates than anyone else on the ice. Foot speed is nice, but it is not what makes a skater faster.

Most drills in volume 1 will emphasize both of these skating requirements. The "full skating stance and hold" drill is the first drill to practice it.

Full Skating Stance

The full skating stance involves hips, knees, ankles, and toes out forty-five degrees. Each stance will be somewhat different for the different individual body makeups. It involves the upper body leaning forward a little less than twenty degrees, pushing toes out approximately at forty-five degrees with weight on middle of the skate blade. The upper body leaning forward and the fully extended back leg make one continuous straight line. The gliding leg (supporting the weight) has a ninety-degree knee bend. In other words, a ninety-degree knee bend. This may seem extreme, but this is required to maximize the length of the stride. If the stride is longer, kids will skate faster. Do not sacrifice the length of the stride for foot speed. In Book 3 when the sprint stride is taught, the back will be kept straighter instead of the forward body lean in the traditional forward stride.

"Full Skating Stance and Hold" Drill Description

While standing stationary, go into the skating or full stance with a near twenty-degree body lean and knees bent to ninety degrees with both skates together, then hold that position for twenty seconds. Then straighten up for a rest. The first few times, kids will feel burning in the leg muscles. This means these muscles are weak and have been used very little up to this point. Repeat again after a twenty-second rest. Continue practicing this to develop knee and leg strength. Keep increasing the number or seconds as the player gets stronger. Kids can practice this at home on their own using an iPod for a stopwatch.

Remember, as we get into skating, all the skating is done from the hips down. The player should be about eighteen inches shorter with the knees fully bent at ninety degrees. This is not easy to achieve and must be continually practiced. It is so difficult that beginners will soon forget and go back to easier short strides. The instructor must continually monitor this by observation and continue to enforce it for all future drills.

Tip: To determine whether the knee is bent enough while in the skating stance or skating position (when the thigh is parallel to the ice surface), place a hockey stick on the thigh, then you will be able to see when the hockey stick is parallel to the ice or not.

Drill 59A: Full stance push alternating long strides P S

Although we don't cover the forward stride until book 3, this is just the beginning of the forward stride. Take long strides by alternately pushing with one leg, then push with the other leg and as far out as your skate can reach with toes out about forty-five degrees, wherever it feels comfortable. To start, skates are hip width apart, knees bent, hips and ankles flexed, making a V with the toes of both skates, keep low forward-profile with a full skating stance, then push back with a full extension with entire the skate blade. Learn to develop low quick skate recovery time back to the midline by keeping the skater blade close to the ice as you return to the middle underneath the body. Alternate one skate, then the other, with long extension pushes, hard into the ice. Try races for competition.

Drill 60U: Full stance push alternating long strides and tap P S (Combo 5)

This is the same as the previous drill, except now tap each skate together under the middle of the body to enforce a complete midline return. Alternate pushing back with one leg, then the other leg as far as you can. Make the return of the pushing skate low and as close to the ice as possible while gliding on the other skate. Make sure the pushing skate returns back adjacent to the gliding skate or the midline. This is called midline return. Tap the gliding skate with the returning skate to reinforce a midline return at the middle of the stride—that is, when the skates are adjacent to each other right under the middle of the body. In other words, make continuous long strides, toes out and with complete midline return, alternating one leg, then the other, tapping the skates together at the midline of the stride.

Hips, knees, and ankles are all involved. Try the toes out fifty-five, then forty-five, then less than forty-five degrees. The actual number of degrees will vary depending on individual body makeup. Upper body should be leaning at a little less than twenty-five degrees depending on the individual. Swing arms back then forward, not to the side. At the start, skates are hip width apart, bent knees, hips, and ankles, V skate start position. Keep a low forward profile, then push with a full extension with entire skate blade. Practice developing low skate recovery. Again, this is part of the forward stride, which is covered in detail in book 3.

Toes In—Concept 7

Drill 61E: Toes in sitting and against the boards OI

The toes in concept will help unlock the hips and enable even longer strides by incorporating the hips into the stride. Start by sitting on the ice, and assist the beginner by using resistance to put pressure on the toes in the opposite direction you want to go (out). The idea is to be able to turn the toes in as far as you can. Start by doing it a little at a time. Similar to learning toes out, aid them by stretching the ankle with pressure in the opposite direction. The instructor can provide resistance in the opposite outward direction with his hands or any other object for that matter. Keep increasing the number of degrees the toes can turn inward, a little at a time, until they can turn ninety degrees in. This will take a great deal of time and much practice.

Once you are comfortable doing it sitting down, then do it with one hand or two hands on the boards or a wall for support. Lift one skate up slightly off the ice and try to turn the toes in ninety degrees. This is very difficult, and kids can only accomplish ten or twenty degrees inward at first unless they spent a lot of time practicing sitting on the ice. This becomes major for backward skating later. With a lot of practice, beginners should eventually be able to turn their toes in ninety degrees on one skate, then the other. Remember to practice left and right skates equally.

Drill 62E: Toes in stationary (on ice) OI

While standing stationary on the ice and not touching the boards, lift one skate off the ice and turn the toes in ninety degrees. Then practice the other skate.

Drill 63E: Toes in, toes out, stationary and moving on ice OI P

Start in a stationary position and move the toes of one skate (off the ice) in ninety degrees, then out ninety degrees. Rotate the hip at the same time. Point out that this is called unlocking the hip and it is what the hip should feel like at the end of long stride extensions. Work one leg, then the other.

Once they can do it stationary, then skate around the rink and between the blue line and red line or, on the whistle, lift one skate off the ice and move the heel just off the ice and beside the toe of the gliding skate, then turn the toe out ninety degrees. Then turn the toes in ninety degrees. Try to rotate the hips as much as possible. Practice one skate then the other. This "toe in, toe out" movement to unlock the hips is very important for long forward strides and backward strides later in book 3.

Drill 64E: Toes out, toes in, semicircle on ice HC

While keeping both feet on the ice, with some pressure on the toes, move the right toe out ninety degrees and push mainly with the toes as you turn them out, then lift the toes only, off the ice and bring the right toe back while keeping the heel on the ice all the time, thus leaving a semicircle mark on the ice with the front of the skate blade. Repeat making these semicircles on the ice with the front of the skate blade as you move down the rink. Try to gain speed as you go forward using one foot to continually create momentum by turning the toes out while making a series of semicircle markings on the ice. The heel becomes sort of a swivel.

After kids can do this with one skate, practice with the other skate. Examine the markings on the ice. They should be significant, showing that the beginner is pushing hard on the ice with the front of each skate while keeping the heel on the ice.

Drill 65E: Backward C-cuts on the boards (toes in, then out)

Similar to drill 48 (push boards C-cuts forward), but this time make c-cuts with the toes in front of the middle of the body or torso and push back with the toes as if skating backward stride. Lean on boards and make a deep C-cut into the ice with one skate by turning toe in then out, marking a C on the ice. Make short and long C-cuts. Keep the supporting leg on the ice while making C-cuts with the other skate. This is the beginning of the backward stride, which is covered in book 3. Work on one skate then the other.

Drill 66A: Walk toes in OI

This is an exaggeration and not really needed for skating. However, some kids have extra flexibility and can do it. It was taught to me by a six-year-old, my grandson Lucas. If kids can do this, it will be a plus and will assist flexibility in skating for them. Remember, most kids can't do this, but it is only worth a try. Turn toes of both feet in ninety degrees so the toes on each skate are pointing in at each other, and try to walk this way. This will take a great deal of practice on their own. If you can't do it, don't worry about it because it is not necessary. This is opposite to the toes out penguin walk, drill 55.

Drill 67U: Power backward slow long C-cuts alternating skates P HC

Push backward with C-cuts alternating with both skates. Slowly make a long C-cut with one skate by turning toe in, then form a C on the ice by pushing and turning the toes out. Stretch the leg out farther and farther to make longer and wider C-cuts on the ice. Continue alternating with one skate then the other using C-cuts to propel backward along the ice. Keep the gliding skate on the ice until the end of the C-cut. Return the skate of the midpoint of the stride for a good midline return. This is the beginning of the backward stride, which is covered in detail in book 3.

Edges—Concept 8

Drill 68E: Edges forward (foot in front) P (Magic 6)

The edges concept is generally not well understood by skaters. Most don't realize there are two edges to each skate blade. Kids will try to skate mainly with the inside edge of the skate blade because it is easier. The difficult part is to be able to use the outside edge of the blades by learning to put the weight on the outside edge. Kids must be eased into using that difficult outside edge. After much practice, beginners will be able to use the outside edge automatically, again without realizing there are two edges on each skate blade. If they understand the concept, they will be able to use both edges sooner and more effectively. This first edge drill, edges forward, is also called inside-outside edges. This is only the beginning of using both edges of the skate blade.

Glide in and out (to the left and right) on one skate and balance yourself while swerving in and out, making a path on the ice like a snake. Beginners will be forced to transfer the weight from the inside then to the outside edge of the skate as they swerve in and out to the left and right. Use the other skate for balance by keeping it off the ice and in front of the gliding skate. Keep the hockey stick blade on the ice for more balance.

This is a very important drill and should be used often during all warm-ups and warm-downs from now on. As you get better at it, you will go faster and be able to swerve in and out wider and wider with a slight body tilt from side to side and with some weight on the heel. When you think you are ready then practice going through a row of pylons. As you continue practicing, keep weaving wider and wider. Practice on both skates, one then the other.

Drill 69E: Edges forward (foot behind) P HC

Skate on the edges forward the same as the previous drill (swerving to the left, then right on one skate) but now with one skate behind for balance instead of in front. Practice one skate, then the other.

Drill 70E: Slalom forward parallel P HC F

Skate with both skates on the ice at the same time, keeping both skates parallel to each other. Turn to the right with both skates turning in parallel to each other, then to the left as both skates turn in parallel to each other gliding along forward on the ice. This is similar to parallel skiing. You will find if you put some weight on the heels you will get more propulsion. Keep trying to parallel wider and wider, then fast on the whistle. Put weight on the heels to go faster and faster.

Drill 71E: Push and slide S

While going sideways across the rink, slide or drag one skate blade out to the side laterally on the ice, then drag the other skate blade along sideways with it as you move lateral across the ice. In other words, go across the ice sideways, sliding both skates laterally without taking either skate off the ice. Go across the ice equally to the left then to the right.

You need to develop a knack to do this with just the right pressure on the ice with the skate blades. At first practice by standing in a stationary position on one spot and slide the skate blades sideways back and forth on the ice. When skates are too sharp, some kids try to make the blades duller by doing this, although this is not the purpose here.

Drill 72M: Edges backward (foot beside, then behind) P HC

This drill uses both edges of a skate similar to drill 68 (edges forward) except it is done going backward on one skate while holding the other skate (off the ice) beside then behind for balance. In other words, you use both the inside and outside edges of the gliding skate, swerving backward in and out as you balance yourself with the other foot. Swerve in and out like a snake on that one skate.

This is a very important drill and should be used often during all warm-ups and warm-downs. As you get better, go in and out faster with sharper angles and with a slight body tilt to the side. Bend the knee of the leg that is off the ice, lift it by bending it up and down, and move it from side to side and back and forth to create momentum. With more practice, weave wider and wider.

Drill 73M: Slalom forward leading one skate P HC F

Skate the slalom keeping both skates on the ice at the same time in parallel. Then when turning left, let the left skate lead out in front, then when turning right, lead with the right skate in front to the right. Continue doing the slalom along the ice until you turn then let one skate lead in the turns.

Drill 74M: Slalom forward leading skate double pylons
P HC F

Skate the slalom with both skates on the ice, but instead of paralleling both skates all the way lead with one skate as you turn to left and then right. Similar to the previous drill letting the left skate lead in front to the left, then let the right skate lead to the right, turning right. Instead now use two rows of pylons (double pylons) to force a wider slalom. Also, you could use a series of hockey sticks lying parallel on the ice instead of pylons. Exaggerate by putting weight on the heels, trying to go faster.

Drill 75M: Short C-cuts two skates alternating backward
P HC F

Skate backward by pushing one skate backward with short C-cuts, then alternate the other skate, then keep alternating both skates one after the other. Practice fast on the whistle.

Drill 76M: Long fast C-cuts two skates alternating backward
P HC F

Similar to drill 67 but faster. Skate backward fast on the whistle, with long alternating C-cuts and good midline return. This is part of the backward stride, which is covered in book 3.

Drill 77M: Pull partner short C-cuts backward HC

Pull partner with hard short C-cuts backward while skating slalom backward. Use two sticks held by two skaters or use a belt and pull with a cord.

Drill 78M: Pull partner long C-cuts backward HC

Pull partner with hard long C-cuts backward while skating slalom backward. Use two sticks held by the both skaters or use a belt and pull with a cord.

Drill 79M: Pull heavy objects backward P HC

Kids pull each other skating backward any way they can, using a belt and cord. Create resistance by dropping to one knee, then two knees. Pull any heavy object.

Drill 80M: Dribble puck between skates P HC

Skate across the width or length of the rink by carrying the puck in the skates, moving (dribbling) the puck back and forth between the skates (from one skate blade to the other skate blade). Carry the puck between the inside of one skate blade to the inside of the other skate blade. This is different from toes-out drill 49 (carry puck in skates), which simply carries the puck straight forward with the inside or the skate blades.

Drill 81M: Figure 8 inside edges P HC

Make a complete figure 8 on the ice with the weight on the inside edges of both skates. Start with one skate going one direction, making a half circle, then the other skate in the same direction making a second other half circle for the second half of the figure 8. This makes up two halves of the figure 8. Then continue to complete the full figure 8 by turning and coming back in the other direction completing the full figure 8 with the inside edge of each skate (making the final two half circles of the figure 8). While the gliding knee is bent, the other knee should be bent and behind. Keep the stick on the ice.

Drill 82A: Figure 8 outside edges P HC

Similar to drill 81(figure 8 inside edges) but the weight is on the outside edges. This is much more difficult. Make a complete figure 8 with the weight on the outside edges of the skate blades. With one skate making one half circle and the other skate making another half circle going the other direction followed by going in the other direction to complete the figure 8 with two more half circles. Make a complete figure 8 on the ice with the outside edges of both skates only. The gliding knee is bent, and the other skate should be swing out to the side to force the weight on to the outside edge of the gliding skate.

Drill 83A: Ankles L&R

Skate forward in a near-squat position, then while squatting on one skate, reach out to the side with the other skate, as far out as you can reach. Stretch your ankle and skate out as far to the side as possible, then continue the same thing on the other skate to the other side. Bend the supporting knee as much as possible, go as low as you can eventually into a squat, then stretch the other ankle and skate as far out to the side as possible while swerving. Kids really need to stretch their ankles to do this. This will require much practice to get all the way down into a near-squat position. Alternate left and right skates.

Drill 84A: Slalom backward parallel P

Gain as much speed as you can by skating slalom backward. Keep both skates in parallel on the ice and put weight on the heels, then toes of the skates. Both skates go in parallel together to the left, then to the right.

Drill 85A: Half moon (half figure 8s) inside edges wide multi P HC

Skate end to end in the rink making multiple extra wide half figure 8s. Use the inside edge of the skate and make half figure 8s, wide across the ice as far as you can while you skate end to end down the rink. Similar to drill 81 (figure 8 inside edges) but making only half figure 8s to the left then right while skating down the ice. The weight is on the inside edge of one skate, then on the inside edge of the other skate, thus making half moons or half figure 8s. Keep the stick on the ice. The gliding knee is bent, and the other knee is also bent but behind with that skate off the ice.

Drill 86U: Half moon (half figure 8s) outside edges wide multi P HC

Similar to drill 85 (half moon inside edges) but the weight is on the outside edges of the skate blades. Skate end to end on the rink making multiple extra wide half figure 8s. Use the outside edge of the skate and make half figure 8s, wide as far as you can across the ice while you skate end to end down the rink. Similar also to drill 82 (figure 8 outside edges) but making only half figure 8s while skating down the ice. The weight is on the outside edge of one skate, then on the outside edge of the other skate, thus making half moons or half figure 8s. The gliding knee is bent, and the other skate should be swing out to the side to force the weight on to the outside edge of the gliding skate. Keep the stick on the ice.

Heel—Concept 9

Drill 87M: Walk on heels, then jump on heels OI

The heel concept is not what you would expect as a requirement for skating, but it is, and it is a concept that is usually overlooked in hockey. The concept is that you must put weight on the heels of the skate blade for many skating skills. It is difficult at first and requires much practice. Start by walking on the heels similar to drill 7, (walk forward on heels) then jump on the heels. Jumping on the heels is an exaggeration and is normally not done. However, it will enhance capability with other drills, thus enhancing the skating skill level.

Drill 88M: C-cuts forward with heels only P HC F

As stated earlier, the concept of having the weight on the heels is an overlooked skill. This is a real exaggeration with the heels. Make C-cuts forward with the heel instead of the toe by making a C-cut on the ice with the heel and with toes off the ice. Then try to make the C-cuts wider with the feet going wider with weight on the heels. Go fast on the whistle. This is very difficult at first and as I said it is an exaggeration but worth spending some time practicing. It will really help the forward stride in book 3.

Drill 89M: Sharp turns on dots or gloves P F (Magic 6)

Take a running start and make a sharp turn around a pylon or the face-off dot on the ice. When turning left, the left skate goes first and the right skate follows right behind. When turning right, the right skate goes first. The key is to be able to walk on your heels first. You need to emphasize lifting the toes up. That means all the weight is on the heels when turning. This is an exaggeration, so at this point the beginner must make sure the toes of both skates lift up off the ice while making the sharp turn. The faster you are moving, the easier it is to make a sharper turn, and the deeper the cut will be in the ice.

This is the basic sharp turn. More advanced turns are covered in book 3 where you learn how much weight to put on the back of the skate blades under different circumstances. For this basic turn, you need to put weight or pressure on the back of the skates. As most skills, this will take a lot of practice to accomplish. Try with each skate following in the same path, making a single cut on the ice as you turn. This is just an added challenge for beginners. Practice turning an equal number of times in both directions.

> **Instructor tip:** When attempting this sharp turn drill with the youngest of skaters, have them first try it without their hockey sticks. Tell the players that they are driving a school bus and they need to keep both hands out in front of them on the steering wheel. Steering the bus to turn a corner often causes a natural weight transfer to the inside foot as the player leans inward. This movement will also help shift weight to their heels. The more weight they put on their heels, the sharper the turn will be and the bigger the cut will be in the ice. Both feet may follow the same groove in the ice, making a deeper cut.

Drill 90M: Power turns stick horizontal or vertical S

Make sharp turns with the hockey stick held horizontal on the shoulders, then make sharp turns with the stick held horizontal waist high to the ice if front. After that make sharp turns with the stick held vertically in front.

Drill 91M: Quad turns 4 pylons P S F

Place four pylons in a square and make a sharp turn in front of each pylon while staying within the four-pylon square. Skate across and make a sharp turn in front of each pylon. Practice making sharp turns in both directions to the left and right.

Drill 92M: Stick (lying on ice) sharp turns S

Lay a stick on the ice and make sharp turns around each end of the stick. Practice both directions.

Drill 93M: Sculling P HC S F

Both skates snake out at the same time and then snake in at the same time. Opposite to slalom skating. Sometimes this is called the snake drill. Now that toes-in and toes-out drills have been completed, you should feel the hips rotating in and out. You should be able to do some weight transfer from skate to skate as you go in and out. This helps to unlock the hips, which is very important. Again try putting the weight on the heels.

In other words, make both skates crawl like a snake with both skates going out, then both skates go in at the same time, without lifting the skates off the ice. That is, from a dead stop (while keeping both feet on the ice), propel forward by moving both feet outward at the same time, then both feet inward at the same time. If necessary, let them take a running start to make it easier.

Drill 94M: Crossover sculls P S

Make one scull (drill 93) or snake stride (both skates go out, then both skates go in at the same time) followed by one crossover to the left, then one crossover to the right, then immediately continue the next scull (snake) move, repeating this across the ice.

Drill 95M: Flat-foot skating P S

Keep both skates on the ice all the time, similar to the slalom but skates shoulder width apart, skate forward while holding the stick horizontal on the shoulders. Start with the weight on the balls of the feet. Then for more power, put the weight on the heels of the skates. More power will also be gained with a lower-profiled skating stance by bending the knees more and making the stride longer.

Try flat-foot skating while shadow dribbling (imaginary puck) and then include carrying a puck on the stick.

Drill 96A: Scull jump P S F&B

Same as sculling (drill 93), jump from the insides of both skates when both skates are wide, then touch both skates at the top of the jump in midair and land on the ice with both skates on the ice. For this, kids need really good knee bend and strong legs.

Drill 97A: Euro shuffle both feet on ice weight on heels P S

Similar to the drill 70 (slalom forward parallel) but your weight is on the heels. Keep both feet on the ice, then shuffle fast to the left, then right with weight on the heels and the skates shoulder width apart.

156

Drill 98A: Heel-to-heel through single pylons P S

Skate through a single row of pylons and go around the pylons in a heel-to-heel motion.

Drill 99A: Heel-to-heel two feet straight line P HC

This is a difficult drill at first, but after the introduction to it by drills 56 (heel-to-heel on boards) and 57 (heel-to-heel one skate straight line), beginners should be ready to attempt it now. Figure skaters can do it—that is, glide forward with both heels touching each other while the toes on both skates are pointing out and in opposite directions. At first, without being able to fully turn both feet ninety degrees out at the same time, kids will tend to travel in a semicircle. So start by lifting one foot off the ice and don't drop it on the ice until in the proper heel-to-heel position. It is very difficult to go in a straight line so start by skating along the blue and red lines. Although difficult, kids with great flexibility will be able to do it. Skate in a straight line and glide with the toes of both skates pointing out in opposite directions and with heels in. The goal is to hold this position and glide in a straight line as far as you can.

Drill 100A: Heel-to-heel sit down OI

Skate in a straight line and glide with the toes of both skates pointing out and heels in. Then try to get lower by moving down into a sit-down position, then bend the knees to move the body up and down as you glide in a straight line. If you are off-ice, practice in a stationary position.

Drill 101U: Surfer heel-to-heel straight line stick horizontal waist high S

Skate heel to heel in a straight line with stick held with both hands horizontal in front waist high, bend knees, and keep a low position. This will help to open the hips for the forward stride. Practice in both directions.

3—Knee Concepts

Problem

In the skating motion, the knees should never be in a straight position except for the final thrust of the stride. The knees should always be bent and in front of the skates. But this is not normal for kids so it doesn't happen without practice, and beginners cannot do it at first. So far we have been touching on knee bending with many of these drills. Now beginners need to bend the knees farther, they must bend the knees until they can't see the toes of the skates, and then continue bending the knees even beyond that point. Bend the knees another two inches.

Most people don't realize that kids physically can't flex their knees enough. As stated, when kids are on the ice, they should never be able to see their toes when they look down. Proper skating techniques require a ninety-degree knee bend. Beginners simply can't bend their knees that much without practice.

Analysis

Proper knee bend is another under coached area in North America. Europeans have more knee bend with better balance while the knee is bent, resulting in better agility thus allowing them to create more acceleration. Canadian coaches teach the knee bend skill but it is not enforced all the time. They do not make it compulsory throughout all skills. Coaches seem to instruct the knee bend at the beginning or as an introduction to skills only. Then it appears to be forgotten after that. Maximum knee bend is imperative for all skills and it must be enforced all the time not just at the beginning of a drill.

Proper knee bend is a ninety degree bend, but that is only part of it. Hockey players must learn to also use all of their body weight with the knee bend to gain acceleration in all skills and in as many drills as possible. They must learn to get all their weight behind each stride (including crossovers and sharp turns) all the time, especially during games. This is not enforced enough in Canadian hockey development by coaches. Full knee bend is stressed in Hockey Canada development programs but it is just not being implemented. Canadian hockey players lack agility while the knee is bent, and do not put sufficient body weight behind their strides to gain as much acceleration as Europeans do.

The concept of bending a knee seems simple, but for beginners, bending the knee ninety degrees is not easy because this is not normally done during everyday walking or running as kids. Beginners always try to keep their knees straight as they learnt to do every day normally standing and walking. To make this even more difficult, the supporting knee, with all the weight on it, should also be bent at the same time. Bending of the supporting knee is much more difficult and will not be achieved without a great deal of practice. This is especially hard on the knees, so don't push it too hard at first. Small kids do not have the strength needed. These drills will help strengthen the knees.

Normally, kids don't have a reason to lift their knees high. It is amazing, as active as most kids are, running or playing all day, they don't make a complete knee movement with a ninety-degree bend. Considering they spend half of their time running around the house or yard, their feet are moving like little machines, but they simply don't lift their knees very high. As it turns out, in order to skate efficiently, maximum knee bend is essential. The knee movement should be bent until the thigh is parallel to the ice. This is needed to obtain speed in most running sports like sprinters. Kids don't do this very well in any sport, even when they reach their teens and start playing school sports like basketball. Probably the main reason for this is they just never stretched the muscles and ligaments to that extent.

Solution

These groups of knee concepts build up to where kids will have the strength and flexibility to bend the knees ninety degrees and to be able to have maximum leg extension. They include the concepts of knee bend, knee extension, lateral, drop, kicks, and advanced jumps. The drills with pictures and descriptions follow:

Knee Concepts Drill Description

Knee Bend—Concept 10

Drill 102E: Bend knees 90 degrees on the boards OI

The knee-bend concept is important because most kids can't bend their knees the required ninety degrees. This is probably because kids normally have no reason to bend their knees that much. You can see in this picture that the demonstrator has superior knee bend even beyond 90 degrees. Sorry hockey players, she is not a hockey player. She has great knee bend because she studies and practices Irish dancing. Most kids can't do this at first.

Start by holding on to the boards or a wall for support with one hand and bend the knee ninety degrees. Exaggerate a knee bend to even more than ninety degrees if possible. You may need to use your hand to assist moving their knee up and down. If they can't do it, use your hand to provide some resistance in the opposite direction as they try to lift their knee up. Make sure you can eventually bend both knees ninety degrees. If you can't do it now, keep practicing and come back to this drill until you can. You notice you can bend your knee a little more each time you try it.

Drill 103E: Balance one skate other knee high OI P

Stand on the ice or any surface with the stick blade on the ice for balance as usual, then while on one skate, lift the other skate as high as you can. When the knee is high enough, the thigh will be parallel to the ice surface or ground. Then balance by holding that position for ten seconds (with only one skate and the stick blade touching the ice). If no stick use the hands and arms for balance. Practice both left and right knees.

> **Instructor tip:** In order to fully achieve the proper knee bend, it's important to develop the required flexibility and strength. To enforce the exaggeration of this movement, a simple prop can be used, such as a puck. By placing a puck on the player's thigh while the knee is brought up, you can challenge the youngster to see how long they can keep the puck from falling.

Drill 104E: Run on spot knees high OI P F

One method of getting beginners to bend their knees is to run on the spot with knees high. While they are all running on the spot, go around and hold your hand above their knees to the correct height, asking them to lift their knees until it touches your hand. Move your hand higher until the beginner's thigh reaches the point where it is parallel to the ice. Line the players up across the blue line and ask the beginners to hit your hand with their knee as you go by holding your hand above their knee. Raise your hand until they can run on the spot and reach or touch your hand with their knees bent ninety degrees. On one whistle, get them to run slowly; on the next whistle, run on the spot faster. Then slow, and then fast, and then superfast as in a third gear. Always lift the knees as high as possible.

Drill 105E: Run backward and spin backward OI P

While running backward, on the whistle, make a 360-degree spin while continuing to run going backward. Of course, kids need to practice spinning in both directions to the left and right.

Drill 106E: Mini crossover circles P F F&B

Run on the spot and spin while running on a spot, then try to make a mini circle around the outside of the dot by crossing the skates over each other a little at a time making a small circle. Then while still running on the skates in a small circle, make the circle a little larger. As you make the crossovers a little bigger, it will automatically make the circle larger and larger. Make the circle larger and larger until eventually you can make crossovers around the full face-off circle. Then start over and do this backwards with short crossovers. This is the beginning of forward and backward crossovers for agility skating in book 3. Don't forget to do it both directions.

Drill 107E: Crossover stability—circles stick horizontal on shoulders with crossunders HC F&B

This is the beginning or using your body weight to provide power in crossovers and eventually into the stride. Skate crossovers around a circle with stick horizontal in front then after that on the shoulders. Cross over with one skate, then cross under with the other skate. In other words, when crossing over to the left, lift the right skate over, doing a crossover, and then push left skate across but underneath the other skate. Always put your body weight into the pushing skate. Go in both directions to the left and right and also do it backward.

Drill 108E: Crossovers circles forward on whistle P F (Magic 6)

Skate around a circle doing forward crossovers in one direction then later in the other direction later. Start slow, then on the whistle go fast, then on the next whistle go superfast (as fast as your feet can move) for only a few seconds. Always transfer all the weight into the pushing skate. This drill is a key part of the Magic 6 special group of drills used later in the book.

Drill 109E: Run across rink on toes, then balls of the feet knees high OI P F

Run across the rink on the toes while lifting the knees high. Try a race. Then run across the rink lifting the knees high and concentrate on putting the weight on the balls of the feet (middle of the skate blade). Practice fast on the whistle.

Drill 110M: Rocking crossovers in circle on whistle P F

Similar to drill 43 (rock on skate blades while running), but now rock while doing crossovers. Skate doing forward crossovers around a circle, and rock on the skate blades as you crossover. Rock on the skate blade by transferring the weight from heels to middle of the skate blade, then to the toes of each skate as you cross over. This is using the skate similar to sprinting on a track or field wearing running shoes. Both directions, of course.

Drill 111M: Jump and turn toes 90 degrees out in parallel stationary OI P

The reason we are doing this parallel jump drill here rather than earlier is because kids need good knee bend and knee movement first. While standing stationary, with both skates together (or parallel), jump and turn and land with both skates parallel and ninety degrees out without falling. Alternate turning to the left and right. Later in drill 161 (jump 90 degrees while skating) we will practice this while moving instead of stationary.

Drill 112M: Squat (OI stationary) F&B

At an early age, most kids have not developed strength in their knees and legs yet. They also do not possess a full range of knee movement. As stated several times, strengthening the knees and legs is very important for beginners. For the first time trying this drill, start in a stationary position while holding on to the boards with one hand for support. Bend both knees until you are sitting down real low and basically sitting on the heels of their skates. Once you can do it on the boards, try it without support from the boards. Then do it while moving, as you skate across the ice, slowly bend both knees until you are sitting down very low and basically sitting on the heels of your skates. Most beginners cannot get down low enough. This drill is called the squat and can be done in a stationary position off the ice as well.

In other words, while on the ice, take a running start and slowly bend the knees and sit down as low as possible, all the way down to the skate heels, then glide as far as you can. If the other knee movement drills have not been completed yet, you will not be able to do this drill. You will just not be able to get low enough. You need to bend their knees to maximum. Basically sit on the heels and keep the skates shoulder width apart to glide. For balance, as usual, the stick should be held out as far as possible out in front (stick on the ice). Kids can try this without hockey sticks with arms extended out in front, but this is more difficult. Once you can do it forward, practice it backward as well.

Drill 113A: Sit-down balance F&B OI HC (Magic 6)

As you skate forward across the ice slowly, bend both knees until you are sitting down real low and basically sitting on the heels of the skates. In other words, the squat position. Then as you are moving across the ice slowly, lift one skate off the ice and glide on the other skate. Practice doing it with each skate. This is also known as the flatiron drill or shoot the duck. It requires the player to squat all the way down on both skates, shoulder width apart, then lift one leg off the ice and glide. It is very difficult at first as it requires exceptional balance and knee bend and knee strength. Hence, this is a very good drill to practice. If beginners can't do the squat, they will not be able to do this drill. This drill is difficult will take a long time to learn. Over time, skaters should be able to master it. Once you can do it on each skate, practice it going backward. To be rated as "excellent," you should be able to do it going backward.

Drill 114A: Elbow balance OI

While gliding slowly on the left skate, bend the left knee as much as you can, then stretch the right leg and skate out to the back as far as you can and to the right. Then the idea is to bend the left knee even more until you can touch the ice with the left elbow. This is very difficult and requires strong knees. Practice with one leg and elbow, then the other leg and elbow. This drill requires much knee strength, so beginners must strengthen their knees first with the other knees drills. If they can't do it now, come back later and practice it when their knees are stronger. For off-ice, try it in a stationary position. Off-ice makes it even more difficult. Someone may need to hold on to the player to provide some balance.

Drill 115A: Step over and under stick (over and under twirl) OI S F&B

As you skate, step over the stick with one skate then the other skate while you pass the stick underneath the legs. In other words, twirl the stick continually under the body and all the way around as you step over the stick as it twirled underneath the skates. Try in a stationary position when off the ice. Twirl the stick it in both directions.

Drill 116A: Step over and under stick jump (over and under twirl) OI S F&B

As you skate, twirl the stick under the skates as in drill 115 (step over and under stick), but now jump over the stick with both skates together instead of stepping over. So twirl the stick under you, jump over the stick with both feet together. Try in a stationary position when off the ice. Beginners need good knee bend to do this.

Drill 117U: Crossovers circles backward on whistle P F (Magic 6)

Skate around a circle doing crossovers backward in one direction, then the other. Start slow, then fast on the whistle, then superfast on the next whistle for only a few seconds.

Knee Extension—Concept 11

Once kids are able to bend their knees ninety degrees, they must learn to be able to stretch their knee and skate as far as they can reach. Knee extension is a concept that is unusual because in most sports, you don't need to stretch the knee and leg out as far as in hockey. Not only do you need to extend or stretch the knee as far as you can, but you also need to be able to flex and turn the knee while it is still in an extended position. Receiving a hit or running into another player while the knee is bent or extending and is the cause of many knee injuries in hockey. This is why kids must learn to do all of these drills with their heads up at all times, and is the reason I include pucks into as many beginner drills as possible.

Drill 118E: Knee drag P

Start by taking a running start, then slowly drag one leg behind with the knee close to the ice and toes out. Beginners must bend the supporting knee a great deal in order for the dragging knee to be close to and if possible touch the ice. This a good stretch during a warm ups. Practice with each knee.

Drill 119E: Three knee motion glide (25-45-90), then horizontal side to side HC F&B

Take a running start and, while gliding on both skates, on the whistle bend both knees twenty-five degrees and continue gliding. On the next whistle, bend both knees forty-five degrees and continue to glide. On the next whistle, try to bend them more, up to ninety degrees, and then glide. You should be in a sitting position at this point. On the next whistle straighten up and start over again. Practice it backward as well.

Then take a running start and lift one knee until the thigh is horizontal to the ice. Hold the stick horizontal to the ice and pull it against the knee. Then pull the horizontal stick in against the knee toward the body to stretch the knee muscles inward toward the body. Then practice it without the aid of the horizontal stick. After that, take a running start and lift one knee until the thigh is horizontal and move the knee back and forth from left to right. After mastering this, try bending the knee even higher. Practice both knees. Do it forward and backward.

Drill 120E: Single stick stepovers forward and backward S F&B

Stationary—Start by lying a stick flat on the ice and then cross over the top of the stick from one side to other side of the stick. Practice crossing over the stick to the left and to the right, going back and forth from side to side across the top of the stick.

Moving—Skate from one end of the stick (lying on the ice) to the other end of the stick and cross over the top of the stick as you skate from one end to the stick to the other. Stop at the end of the stick and turn and go forward again in the opposite direction and repeat, always keep going forward.

Backward—Do the same thing backward.

Drill 121M: Forward scissors wide on outside edges P HC

Most kids can't do this drill because they don't know how to use the outside edge of their skate blade. The previous edge drills should have helped solve this problem for them. Start by slowly making a wide crossover (called a scissors motion), with one skate crossing over the front of the supporting leg. Start with a long push with one skate, then cross it over the leg in a scissorlike motion, going wide laterally to the side, then repeat with another crossover with the other leg going to the other side. Try to stretch wider and wider from side to side each time. When you can stretch far enough, the weight will be on the outside edge of the skate blade, which is the objective. Skate end to end or across the rink slowly while making crossovers as wide as you can with the weight on the outside edges of the skate blade. This is a very good warm-up drill.

**Drill 122M: Forward scissors narrow on outside edges fast
P HC F**

Make narrow crossovers by moving one skate over and across the other. Start with a short fast push, then cross the legs in a short scissorlike motion from side to side. Weight is on the outside edge of the skates. Slow then fast on the whistle, then superfast on the next whistle, then slow again on the next whistle.

Drill 123A: Forward scissors wide outside edge jump lateral P HC

Similar to drill 121 (forward scissors wide outside edges), stretch a wide crossover across and over one skate, but jump laterally with a long lateral push with the outside edge of the pushing skate blade and cross over in a scissors motion to the outside edge of the other skate. Jump from side to side as wide as you can. You need good use of the outside edges to accomplish this drill. Good, strong knee bend is required. Weight is on the outside edge of the skate all the time.

Drill 124A: Backward scissors wide on outside edges P

Similar to drill 121 (forward scissors wide) but now do it backward. Going backward, slowly stretch a long crossover wide across over each leg. Start with a long push with one skate and cross the legs in a scissorlike motion going wide from side to side. Weight is on the outside edges of the skate. Make the crossovers wider and wider.

Drill 125A: Backward scissors narrow on outside edges fast P S F

Similar to drill 122 (forward scissors narrow on outside edges) but now it backward. Stretch to get the weight on the outside edges of the skate and make short crossover backward scissors. Start with a short, fast push, then cross over in a scissorlike motion from side to side. Weight is on the outside edge of the skate. Slow then fast on the whistle, then superfast on the next whistle, then slow again on the next whistle.

Drill 126A: Backward crossovers with tight 360 turn S

Make backward crossovers with tight 360-degree turn by using a backward sharp turn and crossovers in a 360-degree turn. Do it to the left, then to the right.

Drill 127U: Outside, inside, and under scull (snake) P S F&B

Similar to drill 93 (sculling), while weaving both skates out, then in at the same time, with both skates on the ice (sometimes referred to as a forward scull or snaking motion), with both skates on the ice, drag one skate behind the other skate, then across and behind to the outer side of the supporting skate (need good knee bend). In other words, snake both skates out, then both skates in at the same time and then move one skate behind (under) and across to the other side and continue on to the next snake move. This is called crossunders. Skate with one skate going under, and the next time, alternate the other skate going under as you snake forward on both skates.

Lateral—Concept 12

Drill 128M: Lateral crossovers on blue line, stop then fast on the whistle OI P HC F L&R

Crossing the feet over each other while running is not normally done except when playing or perhaps in some sports. Beginners normally don't do it very much. Therefore, they do not have the strength in the knees and they need a great deal of practice to strengthen the knees. Not only does it need leg strength but much balance is required. You must bend the supporting knee as well, however, you do not want to overwork the supporting knee because it is very hard on the knee ligaments. Bending the supporting knee while crossing the other knee over is very difficult because all the weight is on that supporting knee.

Start by spreading the beginners along the blue lines and center line. Make certain each kid is at least one and a half stick length apart from each other and not too close to the boards. With the stick blade on the ice, lift the right knee up high until the thigh is horizontal to the ice and try to bend the left knee (other supporting leg) at the same time, then cross the right skate over in front and across the left skate, then down. Then move the left skate back to the normal side of the right skate. Do the same the other direction, crossing the left skate and knee over. After going back and forth in this manner several times, on the whistle everyone stop with one knee suspended and thigh in the horizontal position. After ten seconds, blow the whistle again and continue, thus continuing with the crossover drill. Remember, always have the toes of the skates point forward, thus at right angle to the lines (in other words, pointing to the instructor). When the players understand the drill, they can do this drill anywhere on the ice, forgetting about the blue or red lines. Go in both directions equally.

The lateral concept is difficult, especially if the previous drills have not been completed. Often this is a skill that is undercoached. Ensure there is a ninety-degree knee bend and, more important, make certain the supporting knee is bent as well. If the knee is not lifted up until the thigh is parallel to the ice and with little bend in the other supporting knee, making crossovers will be very difficult, if not impossible.

Once beginners are comfortable doing these lateral crossovers, start slow, then go fast on the whistle, then superfast on the next whistle, then slow again on the next whistle. Go in both directions equally.

Drill 129M: Double stick stepovers forward and backward (over sticks lying on ice) HC F F&B

Lay two sticks flat on ice end to end, butt ends touching. Skate forward and step over the sticks twice as you skate to the other end of the sticks. Then make a sharp turn at the end of the sticks and go forward in the opposite direction and again step over the sticks twice. A second player can repeat the same thing while the first player rests, thus taking turns in tandem. Then do it by jumping over the sticks with both feet together twice instead of stepovers.

Do the same thing skating backward, doing two stepovers with pivots instead of sharp turns at each end of the sticks.

Drill 130M: Double stick stepover pivots forward backward S

Lay two sticks flat on ice end to end, butt ends touching. Skate forward but instead of stepping over, now pivot (from forward to backward) over the sticks, twice as you go to the other end or the sticks. Pivot instead, from forward to backward, then backward to forward. Then make a sharp turn and start over. This can be done in tandem, where a second player repeats the same thing while the first player rests, thus taking turns.

Drill 131A: Forward crossovers 3-2-1 P (Magic 6)

While skating end to end in the rink, make three crossovers each way to the left then to the right, keeping the stick blade on the ice. Then practice making two crossovers each way and then one crossover each way. Once you are used to it, do all three, two, then one crossover while shadow stickhandling (dribbling a virtual or imaginary puck). Once you can do that, carry the puck with normal dribbling while skating.

Drill 132A: Forward crossovers three speeds P F

Similar to drill 131 (forward crossovers 3-2-1), while skating end to end down the rink doing three or two then one crossover to the left and right, we now will incorporate three various speeds. Start slowly, then on the whistle go fast, then on the next whistle go superfast. On the next whistle go slow again and continue repeating this. Practice with three crossovers each way, then two crossovers each way, then one crossover each way. These speed crossovers are the beginning of generating acceleration and quick feet.

Once you are used to it, do all three, then two, and then one crossover while shadow stickhandling (dribbling a virtual or imaginary puck). Once you can do that, carry the puck with normal dribbling while skating these 3-2-1 crossovers end to end in the rink.

Drill 133A: Backward wave with crossovers P F

Spread the beginners out across the ice, then the instructor waves his stick left, and the kids follow doing backward crossovers left. Then wave them right and they do crossovers to the right. Go backward to the left and right until the instructor drops his stick blade on the ice, then the beginners break for the corner by pivoting and skating forward hard to the corner that the instructor's stick is pointing to. Try while carrying the puck. Then fast on the whistle.

Drill 134U: Backward crossovers 3-2-1 P F (Magic 6)

Skate backward doing three crossovers each way to the left and right. Once this is accomplished, try to do two crossovers, then one crossover to the left, then to the right backward. Then go fast on the whistle.

Once you are used to it, practice three, two, and then one crossover while shadow stickhandling (dribbling a virtual or imaginary puck). Once you can do that, carry the puck with normal dribbling while skating.

Drop—Concept 13

Drill 135E: Drop to one knee while stationary and moving OI P F&B

The dropping concept is where beginners need to bend the knees a great deal in order to drop to the ice and get up again quickly. Start while standing stationary on the ice or any floor surface, then on the whistle, drop to the knees and get up as fast as you can. Then try dropping on one knee then the other.

After that, do it while skating forward. Continually drop to one knee then the other as you skate forward. Once you can do that then do it backward.

If you can get a full bend in your knee, it is easier to get up off the ice after you fall during a hockey game, and you will be able to get up much quicker. This drill will improve on the recovery time needed to get up off the ice. Kids can have a race to see who can go the fastest. Try fast on the whistle and also with a puck on the stick.

Drill 136E: Drop to both knees while moving, then continue P F&B

Drop to both knees while skating and then get up quickly. While skating, on the whistle, drop to the knees and get up as fast as possible and keep skating. At first you will tend to lose control. Practice until you can drop to the knees without losing control and continue to remain in a straight line as you get up, that is, without turning or swerving while on your knees. Continue dropping to the knees on the whistle and getting up as quickly as possible while continuing to skate in a straight line.

If your intension is to teach hockey as well as skating, try to dribble the puck on one knee then the other. Try this in a stationary position first. Drop to one knee and keep skating. Dribble the puck any way you want (side to side, diagonal, back and forth), then drop to their knees and continue dribbling. Then get back up on the feet. Continue going up and down on one knee then the other on the whistle while skating and carrying the puck.

While we are into puck control, try to dribble on two knees. Try this in a stationary position first. Drop to both knees and keep dribbling the puck.

What happens? The stick is too long, and a kid can't dribble the puck. So what should a beginner do to solve this problem? The answer is simple—choke up on the stick by dropping both hands on the stick shaft until the stick blade is flat on the ice. It happens many times during a hockey game when you end up on your knees in front of the net after being knocked down and you get a chance with the puck. Learn to shoot and pass from this position on the knees and also while moving or sliding on the knees.

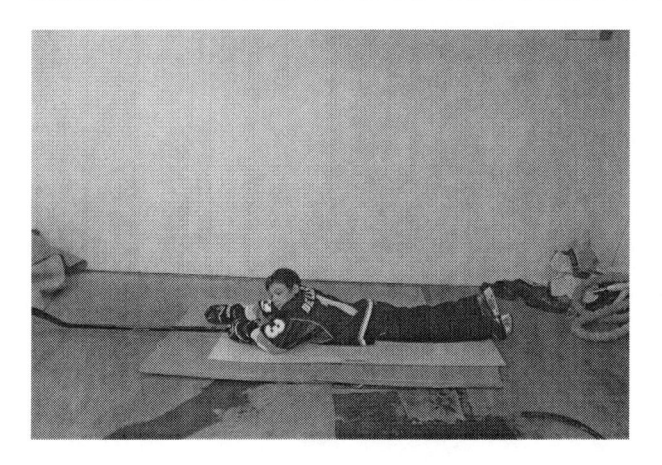

Drill 137E: Drop to stomach while stationary OI P

While standing stationary, drop to the stomach on the whistle and get up as fast as you can.

Drill 138M: Drop to stomach while moving P

While skating, drop to the stomach on the whistle and get up as fast as you can and continue skating.

> **Instructor tip:** The quickest way to get up from lying on your stomach is to pull your elbows in toward your knees. Attempting to bring elbows and knees together while sliding forward results in minimal lift being required to pop yourself back up into a forward stride position.

Drill 139M: Drop to stomach and roll OI P S

While skating, on the whistle drop to the stomach and roll 360 degrees on the ice and get up as fast as you can, then continue skating.

Drill 140A: Drop to knees and do 360 spin on knees P S

While skating, on the whistle drop to the knees and spin 360 degrees while on the knees while moving, then get up as fast as you can after the spin and continue skating in a straight line.

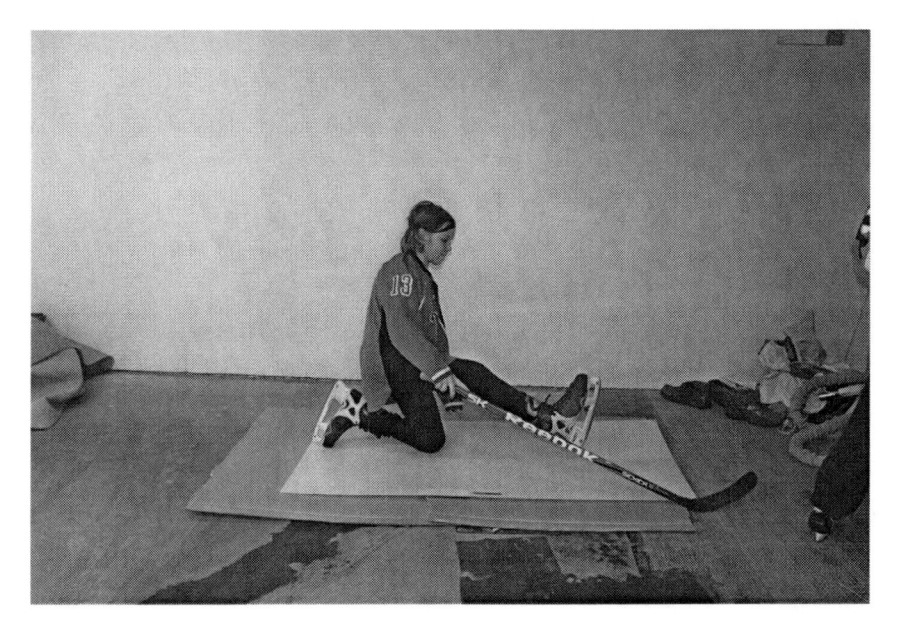

Drill 141U: Russian knee drop OI P S F

Alternate dropping to one knee, then to the other knee as fast as possible while skating forward. This will appear as if you are walking on their knees. Move knees up and down fast. One knee is always on the ice until the other knee drops to the ice (lift one skate, then the other as you move forward along the ice). Try stationary off the ice but it is easier on the ice.

Kick—Concept 14

Another concept within the knee movement concept group is what is commonly referred to as kicks. This develops more balance while the knee is in various positions. There are a variety of different kick drills.

Drill 142E: Rotate skate in circle in air OI P F

Start by gliding on one skate and lift the other skate up off the ice in front and rotate it in a circle in mid air. Rotate that skate in one direction and then the other, clockwise and counter clockwise. Practice the same with the other skate. Practice fast on the whistle and with a puck. If you are off the ice, practice it in a stationary position.

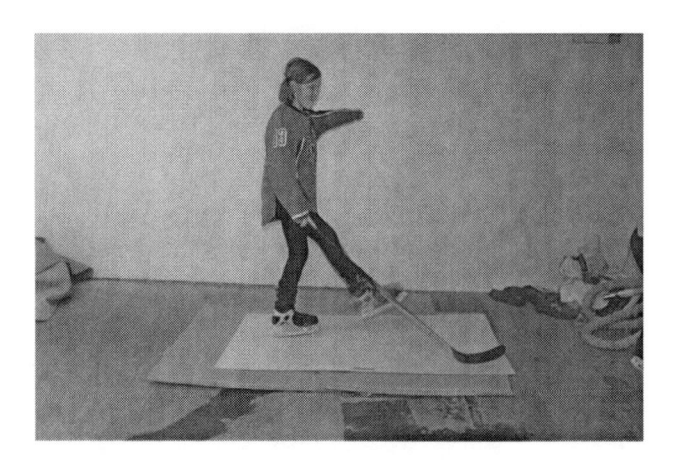

Drill 143E: Side kicks OI P F

While skating, balance on one skate and, with the other foot, make a short kick out to the side and then toward the front at about forty-five degrees. Do the same with the other skate. Practice fast on the whistle and with a puck on the stick. If off the ice, practice it in a stationary position.

Drill 144E: Front kicks OI P F

While skating, balance on one skate and make a kick straight to the front as high as you can with the other foot. Alternate with both skates. Practice fast on the whistle and with a puck. If off the ice, practice it in a stationary position.

Drill 145M: Back kicks OI P F

While skating forward, balance on one skate and, with the other skate, make a short kick behind. Practice with both skates. Practice fast on the whistle and with the puck. If off the ice, do it in a stationary position.

Drill 146A: Balance (stick horizontal) trio kicks OI F

Repeat the kick drills (trio kicks—side, front, back) while holding the stick with both hands horizontal to the ice out in front of you about shoulder height. Then put your weight on one skate and try to kick three times with the other skate. Try to kick the front kick high enough to touch your stick (which is held horizontally in front). Repeat this while skating, first the left leg, then the right leg. You want a minimal bend in the supporting knee. This is hard on the supporting knees, so don't overdo it. If you can't bend the knee with all the weight on it, then attempt it with the leg straight at first. Practice fast on the whistle. If off the ice, practice it in a stationary position.

Drill 147U: Kicks skating backward P F

Make trio kicks while skating backward (front, back, side). Start with the stick held horizontal in front and waist height. Then make trio kicks going backward while carrying a puck on the stick. Then practice fast on the whistle. Practice it equally with both skates.

Advanced Jump—Concept 15

Drill 148M: Crossover tripod jump S

The advanced jump concept is to be able to jump high and maintain balance as you land. All high jumps need maximum knee bend. By now the beginner should be able to do simple high jumps on the ice. Now with two tripods lined up touching each other making a vertical row, forming a low vertical fence, jump lateral over the middle of the tripods by making a crossover as you skate across and over them. Practice crossing over to the left and right.

Drill 149A: Forward 2-foot tripod jump P S

Jump high over two tripods (held in horizontal position) that are set up like a high fence. Jump with both feet close together. Try with the tripods in a low position at first.

Drill 150A: Forward 1-foot tripod jump P S

Jump over two tripods (held in horizontal position) that are set up like a low fence. Using one foot, jump and land on the same foot. Try with the tripods in a low position at first.

Drill 151A: Hurdler high jump with one skate and land with the other P S

Similar to drill 149 (forward 2—foot tripod jump), jump over two tripods (held in horizontal position) that are set up like a fence. Jump with one skate and land on the other skate. Try with the tripods in a low position at first. Practice jumping with the left foot first and then with the right foot first.

Drill 152A: Forward to backward transition jump P S

Jump over two tripods (held in horizontal position) that are set up like a fence. While skating forward, jump forward and land backward. Also skating backward, jump backward and land forward. Start with the tripods in a low position first.

Drill 153U: Jump 360 from forward to forward P S

Jump over two tripods (held in horizontal position) that are set up like a fence. While skating forward, jump over the tripods and spin 360 degrees over the fence and land forward. Few kids have enough strength in their legs to accomplish this drill. At first start by jumping and spinning 360 degrees over blue and red lines then with the tripods in a low position.

4—Balance Concepts

Problem

Kids have a lot of balance but not enough for skating and hockey. They need to develop balance specific to the body movements used in hockey. Balance is the key to hockey, and it takes much practice to develop. Good balance results in good skating. Good skating means good hockey. Before youngsters can start to develop good balance, they should have completed the previous concepts. By this time they should be comfortable with the concepts of the feel of their skates and turning their toes in and out ninety degrees, and they should have attained good knee movement. After going through these first drills and with a good deal of practice, skaters will begin to feel the two-inch distance between their feet and the ice, toes out with good knee movement. Remember the knees should always be bent, even when the kids are just standing around waiting or listening to the instructor. They should never be able to see the toes of their skates.

> **Instructor tip:** Remember, what you do on one skate, you will always have to practice on the other skate an equal amount of time. Don't let your young skaters favor one foot or direction over the other. Something to watch for is the tendency for beginners to only attempt a drill with their "good" leg or in their preferred direction.

Analysis

The key to learning good balance is to continue breaking the skating motion down into small, simple, easy balances to start with. Now we want to do balances by putting more weight on the supporting skate. These small parts of the skating motion may not seem to be a part of skating, but in fact, they are very important. Most balance drills on the ice should be done while moving slowly. It is sometimes more difficult to do it slowly. A good way to do balance drills is, while skating around the rink, doing the balances between the blue lines or between the blue lines and goal lines. Another good method is doing balances across the rink (side boards to side boards). All players should be doing the drill at the same time, not standing in line (SIL) and having to wait.

As you probably realize by now, we have been getting into balances throughout this book, right from the first drill. It is easier for a beginner to do a balance drill holding a hockey stick for balance. As stated earlier, hold the upper end of the stick with one hand while keeping the stick blade as flat as possible on the ice. All good skaters have good agility with extensive flexibility, are able to pivot with ease, and will possess power in their skating stride.

Solution

Balance concepts include agility, flexibility, pivot, and power concepts. Although power drills are starting to go beyond beginner skating, it is a good time for an introduction to the power skating concept. The power concept involves pushing extra hard into the ice surface during the forward and backward stride.

Balance Drill Description

Agility—Concept 16

Drill 154E: Touch ups and touch backs OI S F

The main objective of agility is quick movement. These drills will start force all the weight on the supporting foot with bent knees. The first drill for the agility concept is to lift one skate up high in front and touch it with opposite glove, then lift the other skate high in front and touch it with the opposite glove (i.e., touch left skate with right glove). This is called touch ups. Practice it while skating slow at first then fast on the whistle.

Then practice the same thing lifting the skate high to the back and touching the opposite skate with the glove. This is called touch backs—that is, lift one skate high behind and touch it with opposite glove behind, then lift the other skate high behind and touch it with the other glove behind. Practice it while skating slow at first then fast on the whistle.

Drill 155E: Touch combo OI S

This is doing touch ups immediately followed by touch backs. Do both previous drills consecutively, one after the other, making four touches per sequence. Touch the skates with the left glove then right glove in front, then immediately follow by touching with the left glove then right glove behind. Practice it slow then fast on the whistle. This gets complex for beginners. They have to start thinking.

Drill 156E: Single stepover forward tap S

Similar to drill 120 (single stopovers), with a stick flat on the ice, skate then tap the ice with each skate once or twice before you step over the stick as you skate back and forth forward doing stepovers over the stick.

Drill 157E: Multitap skate with other skate (while skating) (toe, side, heel) OI P

Skate around or across the ice with long strides and return each skate all the way back to the middle of the stance until it is adjacent to the gliding skate. This is called the midline return and this drill will force a midline return. Tap the supporting skate with the other skate when you reach the midline of the stride. This is also similar to drill 60 (full stance rap). While skating, as you return the pushing skate to the middle of the stride, tap the supporting skate with the other skate at the middle of the stance. As you reach the midline on the return, tap (not kick) lightly on the heel of gliding or supporting skate, then practice taping the toe of the gliding skate, then practice taping the middle of the gliding skate. Practice all three taps (toe, middle, heel of the supporting skate), with one skate then tap with the other skate on the alternating or next stride.

Drill 158E: Tap skate with stick (by instructor or another player) OI P

Skate forward around or across the ice with long strides while returning each skate all the way back until it is adjacent to the gliding skate in the middle of the stride (midline return). While skating, the instructor or another player taps one of the skates with their stick. Very light taps only. Do not tap hard enough to trip the skater. This happens often during the game, and good balance is required in order to stay on your skates and not fall down every time your skate is touched. You will find you will have better balance if the knees are bend.

Drill 159E: Walk and run with stick up OI F F&B

Hold the stick horizontally with both hands about shoulder width apart. Lift the stick above the head, keeping it horizontal to the ice or ground, and reach up as far up as you can. Then walk holding the stick horizontally up above the head. At first walk on the toes forward and backward. After that walk on the balls of the feet (middle of the skate blades). Then try it on the heels. The stick should not be resting on the helmet. When your arms get sore after a few seconds, take a rest and then continue. Once you can walk, practice the same thing running. Practice fast on the whistle and practice it backward.

Drill 160E: Horizontal stick touch toes, then roll shoulders OI F&B

Hold the stick with both hands shoulder width apart, horizontal to the ice and above the head. Without bending the knees, touch the toes with the stick while keeping the stick horizontal to the ice. Go up and down with the stick while skating. In order to accomplish this, you need to transfer their weight from the balls of their feet to their toes and back again. Then with the stick on the shoulders, do a shoulder roll from side to side.

Drill 161M: Jump 90 degrees while skating (beginning of the stop) OI P L&R

Now that you know how to jump and know how to bend the knees, you should be able to jump and land with both feet together and toes pointing ninety degrees to the left or right. Similar to drill 111 (jump and turn 90 degrees stationary), this is the beginning of the stop drill. While skating, jump and turn toes (both feet at the same time) out ninety degrees to the side without falling. That is, take a running start, then bend the knees, then jump up and land with both skates parallel but ninety degrees out to the left, then later practice the same thing to the right.

There are two keys to this drill, first-you need good knee bend, therefore bend the knees into a sitting position and, secondly—most kids try to do this when skating too slowly, so skate with some speed.

This is the beginning of the basic stopping process, which is covered in book 3. This is very important for learning how to stop properly. In fact this is the basic two-foot stop. A good number of kids should be able to make a stop at this point.

> **Instructor tip:** Stopping is a book 3 drill. However, as a hint, here are the steps required:
>
> 1. Take a running start.
> 2. Keep feet together.
> 3. Bend knees.
> 4. Jump and turn ninety degrees.

If you keep your balance and don't fall, you will have stopped.

Drill 162M: Stick mirror speed drill S

Start with two sticks lying flat on the ice end to end, making a vertical line with the butt ends of the sticks touching. Two players face each other across the sticks in a mirror image. Start with both gloves touching the ice, facing each other and ready to go. Then with one player leading and the other following, the leader starts with crossovers and quickly makes crossovers to the left or right, while still facing each other across the sticks, they reach the end of the sticks on the ice, they stop and touch the ice with both gloves and immediately start again going back the other way to the other end of the sticks. They are facing each other all the time with one player leading by going quickly back and forth, stopping and using crossovers, while the other player follows tying to be a mirror image. The leader is stopping and going back and forth, touching the ice with the gloves and stopping various spots. Each takes a turn leading while the other follows and tries to keep up in a mirror image.

Drill 163A: Partner stepover mirror (faster and faster) F S

This can be done individually or in tandem with two players taking turns. Arrange two sticks flat on ice end to end with the butt ends touching. Facing each other, but this time on the same side of the sticks (instead of across the sticks), while facing each other, do stepovers across the sticks, with one leading and the other following like a mirror image. The leader goes faster and faster. If done individually, the one player goes faster and faster on his or her own.

Drill 164A: Heel-to-heel turn through double pylons P

Similar to drill 98 (heel-to-heel through single pylons) but now arrange pylons in double rows instead. Skate and make a turn with the heel to heel motion around the double pylons. Using double pylons forces a longer turn while in the heel-to-heel position.

Drill 165U: Lateral crossover touches S

While skating forward, make two crossovers to the left, then touch the ice with the left glove, then make two crossovers to the right, then touch the ice with right glove. Continue as you skate end to end or around the rink.

Flexibility—Concept 17

Drill 166E: Automobile (OI stationary)

The main objective of flexibility is to bend the body. The first drill for the flexibility concept is to take a running start and glide on both skates. Bend the upper body and knees into a sitting position and swerve from left to right like driving a car by transferring the weight from side to side on both skates. Kids can hold the stick in a horizontal position in front and use it as a steering wheel to swerve left and right. You can also practice it off-ice on any surface by sitting in a stationary position and transferring their weight appropriately from side to side.

Drill 167E: Airplane (OI stationary)

Take a running start, glide on one skate while bending forward at the hips with arms stretched out to the side as far as you can reach. The other leg should be extended straight back parallel to the ice. Arms, upper body, and back leg should all be parallel and horizontal to the ice surface, all at the same time. No stick needed. Glide with torso and elevated leg horizontal to the ice with the arms making the wings of an airplane. Practice one skate then the other and swerve side to side gliding on one skate like an airplane flying in the sky.

Drill 168E: Ride on stick (OI stationary)

This is one of the simplest balances which intrigue most beginners. All kids try it on their own at some point anyways, but few know how to do it properly. First of all, use a long stick. At least make sure the stick is not too short. Put the stick between the legs and sit on the stick with the blade on the ice. This is more difficult than it sounds. Start trying it in a stationary position and make sure to put most of the weight on the stick. The stick blade should remain on the ice. Bend the knees ninety degrees. Take a running start then place the stick between the legs with both hands on the upper end of the stick and sit down on the stick. While sitting on the stick, balance the weight equally between the stick blade and the skate blades. See how far you can go without falling. Start with some speed and then turn left and right by twisting the handle of the stick in the direction you want to go. This works only if most of the weight is on the stick. Swerve between pylons or other objects for practice. When kids get good at it, select partners and have one push the other in a tandem race even through pylons.

Drill 169M: Push puck off the line (inside outside blade) P

Two players face each other in a stationary position and try to push the same puck off the blue line. First with the outside of the stick blades, then after that, with the inside of the stick blades. This is to develop strength in the hands and balance on the skates. Practice this drill for only a few seconds because the arms get tired quickly at this young age. You need to practice this many times to gain the strength need by beginners.

Drill 170M: Squat jump OI P S F F&B

While moving in a gliding low-squat position, with skates close together, jump as high as you can. Do not make high jumps, only short squat jump just enough to kick both feet out in front at the same time then off the ice and back under the body again. If kids are off the ice, do it in a stationary position. Practice doing it fast on the whistle and also practice it backward. Kids will find a way to do it with a puck on the stick.

Drill 171M: Shumpka jumps (high jumps touching skates behind) OI S

While skating, get in a sit-down position and make a high jump. While at the height of the jump, touch the skates behind with the gloves. Hold the stick beside you with one hand in the middle of the shaft. Continue making Shumpka jumps as you skate end to end or across the rink. Try to do it in a stationary position if you are off the ice.

Drill 172A: Russian jump OI P S

Similar to drills 93 (sculling) and 96 (scull jump), but this time while both skates are wide, jump lateral from the inside of one skate blade to the other. So while doing the sculls or snake drill (both skates go in, then out at the same time), you make a lateral jump. While the skates are wide, make a jump off the inside edge of one of the outside skates, lateral across to the other skate—that is, when the skates are wide apart, put all the weight on the right skate by bending the knees and jump to the left skate. While skates are still wide, repeat jumping from one skate to the other as you skate sculls down the ice. When off-ice, jump side to side from a stationary position.

Drill 173A: Edge extreme drill S

Skating through pylons, stretch to the extreme inside edges by leaning until you can reach the ice with your glove, then stretch the hand even farther to allow the glove to reach to the extreme until you are nearly falling, then do it on the other side (reach far out by bending the knee to maximum until the glove reaches ice). The left hand is down and the right skate up as you go left on inside edge of the left skate and vice versa, going the other way. Then practice around the rink without pylons.

Drill 174A: Stick behind horizontal down to skate heels OI S

Similar to drill 160 (horizontal stick tough toes), but now we will do it behind the back. Hold the stick horizontal to the ice with both hands shoulder width apart, move the stick from the front over the head, then letting the hands slide wider on the stick shaft, bring the stick down behind the back, keep the stick horizontal until the stick reaches all the way down to the heels of the skates then back up over the head and in front again. At first most adults can't do this, but most kids probably can. First start while in a stationary position. Then try while skating around the rink. If you can't do it while skating then practice it in the stationary position only.

Drill 175U: Serdachny shuffle OI P S F&B

This is similar to drill 113 (sit down balance). Get into the sit down balance while gliding then make small jumps from one skate to the other while remaining in the sit-down balance position. You don't need to extend the legs all the way out in front like the sit-down balance. While gliding in a squat position, extend one skate in front and jump from one skate to the other skate while kicking out in front with the other skate. Do this while going forward. As you move along, you do not get quite low enough into the sit-down balance position. Shuffle or alternate bouncing from one skate to the other by lifting one skate up a few inches off the ice, then in turn lift the other skate off the ice. Practice it backward as well. I first saw this drill at the Steve Serdachny Elite Power Skating Camp. See the bibliography at the back of this book, "Drill Sources and References".

Pivot—Concept 18

Drill 176E: Mohawk turn OI P HC

The pivot concept is basically changing direction from backward to forward, and forward to backward while skating. Start with a standard two-foot turn (180-degree turn or pivot), called the Mohawk turn. This turn allows you to easily change direction from forward to backward or from backward to forward on the ice by shifting weight from one foot to the other. Glide forward on the ice on both skates then turn about forty-five degrees to the right, then lift the right skate off the ice, leaving the weight on the inside edge of the left skate as you are turning clockwise to the right. Then bring the right skate (still off the ice) next to the left skate with toes pointing backward and perpendicular to your left supporting foot. The heel of the right foot should point to the middle or heel of the left skate. Place the right foot down on the ice and at the same time lift the left foot off the ice by transferring your weight from the left foot to the right foot. Turn your body straight in line with your right (now the supporting) foot. You should now have completed a 180-degree pivot. When pivoting to the left, do the same thing but to the other side. Everything is the same except you are going to pivot to the left instead of to the right.

Drill 177M: Partner pivots holding sticks OI HC S

While stationary, two players hold the end of both sticks with both hands while facing each other. Then both players, at the same time, spin (pivot) all the way around (360 degrees) while holding on to both sticks, moving the sticks up and over both of their heads as they spin all the way around. Practice both to the left and right.

Then do the same thing while skating but still facing each other. While one player skates backward and the other skates forward, again spin at the same time (pivot) all the way around (360 degrees) while holding on to both sticks. Practice in both directions, and each takes turns going backward.

Drill 178M: Straight line pivot on blue line stick horizontal HC

Skate sideways going across the blue line on one skate with toes out ninety degrees (the other skate off the ice and also toes out 90 degrees), hold the stick horizontal to the ice in front waist high. Then alternate transferring the weight from one skate to the other skate while the toes of both skates are pointing out ninety degrees, like in a heel-to-heel motion. Go across the blue line with left toes pointing left and the right toes pointing right, while you keep gliding along the blue line on one foot then the other. This is exaggerated pivoting and can be done anywhere on the ice.

Drill 179A: Slalom pivot S

Similar to drill 70 (slalom forward), skate the slalom forward then pivot backward (180 degree) while continuing the slalom. Both skates always remain on the ice and in parallel, including during the pivot. Then practice it from backward to forward as well.

Drill 180A: Stick chases (two sticks lying on ice) S

Lay two sticks on the ice in a vertical line with butt ends of the sticks touching. One player chases a second player around the sticks using heel-to-heel moves. Each player takes turns chasing. After that instead of using only the heel-to-heel move, continue using any means in a normal one-on-one chase around the sticks.

Drill 181A: Spin forward (360 degrees) P HC L&R

While skating forward, spin or turn 360 degrees on the whistle or at the blue and red lines. Keep the puck on the stick. Pivot with the mohawk turn or heel-to-heel motion and slalomto pivot. Practice it spinning in both directions, to the left and to the right and with a puck.

Drill 182A: Spin backward (360 degree) L&R

While skating backward, spin or turn 360 degrees on the whistle or at the blue and red lines. Try starting with a backward sharp turn then using short backward crossovers to complete the 360 turn. Practice spinning in both directions.

Drill 183A: Circle pivot P S

Two players face each other on the face-off circle. One player acts like a mirror image of the other. The leader skates around the face-off circle, pivoting back and forth to the left and right on the circle by transferring the weight from one skate to the other (toes out) in one direction then the other direction while going around the circle. The other player tries to follow as a mirror image. They take turns being the leader.

Drill 184A: Backward crossover pivot 90 degrees P S

Skate backward crossovers, then pivot ninety degrees to one side (pivot with a heel-to-heel move) and skate forward toward the boards, then pivot ninety degrees and do backward crossovers to the other side or end of the rink. Go equally to the left then to right. This is very important for one-on-ones. Do it with a puck to help make it occur automatically. You can also use a whistle to control the pivoting.

Drill 185A: Pivot drive S P

Stop, turn, and burn—Skate toward the net but toward and into the face-off circle. While always facing the same direction, stop and then reverse pivot backward (forming a small circle around the dot of the circle), away from the net, using backward crossovers. Then with a quick start, accelerate forward again toward the net while still facing the goalie, then shoot on net.

Drill 186A: Starbust 360 pivots around ice S

Similar to drill 172 (Russian jump), lateral jumps with inside edges. Make wide edge-to-edge jumps around the ice like ballroom dancing. Exaggerated inside edge jumps.

Drill 187A: Bart Simpson P S

With two rows of pylons wide apart, skate across the ice toward the boards and reverse pivot and skate backward through all the pylons, always facing the same direction. So skate forward, pivot, and skate backward always facing the same direction and continue through all the pylons making pivots while always facing the same boards or side of the rink.

Drill 188U: Skiing one foot P

Similar to drill 68 (edges forward), while skating forward edges in and out on one skate, with one skate high in front or beside for balance, pivot backward (reverse) and go in the opposite direction (the same direction you came from) while remaining on the same skate. This is an exaggerated edges drill with a reverse or pivot on one skate. Of course, practice it on the other skate as well.

Power—Concept 19

The power concept is an introduction to power skating, which requires even more balance. It also starts introducing opponent players into drills to provide resistance to the body, which is encountered during a game. Kids need agility, flexibility, and power to accelerate during a game. Most importantly they must incorporate all of their body weight into the stride to gain maximum thrust.

Drill 189E: Power outside 8s S

Make a figure 8 with a combination of drills 81 and 82 (figure 8 inside and outside edges), but now make a figure 8 while facing the same direction. That means go forward on the inside edges and make one half of the figure 8 then do not turn, instead skate backward on the outside edges to complete the figure 8 on the ice. Try to use more power by bending the knees and pushing hard into the ice while making the 180-degree C-cuts (or half moons).

Drill 190E: Gauntlet (skates, stick, shaft, shoulder, combo) OI P

With players lined up in two rows, the first player in the row skates through the gauntlet between the two rows of players. The players making the gauntlet lightly tap the skates of the skater on the toe, blade or heel of the skate, or stick even the shoulder as he or she skates through the gauntlet. The player goes to the end of the gauntlet line, and the next player goes through the gauntlet, and so on until all the players have had a chance to go through the gauntlet.

Drill 191E: Isolation push—stick horizontal behind, multi and alternating leg push S

Similar to drill 51 (power one leg multi push), skate forward with multi push with one leg but with the stick held horizontal to the ice behind and with hands shoulder length apart. In other words, continuously (multi) push with one skate with the stick is held horizontally behind, making long extension with the pushing skate and a quick skate recovery. Practice pushing back one skate then with the other.

Then continue the drill by alternating one skate the other skates, making long strides with stick still horizontal to the ice and behind.

Drill 192M: Acceleration circle drive S

Skate around the face-off circle in front of the goal net, turning in a direction away from the net. Pick up a puck on the way, near the goal line as you go by. Using crossovers, accelerate all the way around the circle, then take a shot from in front of the net. You can use a checker as well to make it interesting.

Drill 193M: Acceleration turn—sharp turn with two crossovers S

Similar to drill 192 (Acceleration circle drive), and skate around the face-off circle in front of the goal net, turning in a direction away from the net. The difference is that now when you pick up a puck near the goal line, start making a sharp turn, then convert the turn into crossovers to accelerate around the rest of the circle, then shoot on the net. Same as acceleration circle drive, except you use a sharp turn for the first part of the circle. In other words, start with a sharp turn followed by crossovers for acceleration. You can use a checker as well.

Drill 194M: Steeple—backward and forward with stick horizontal and glide S

With the stick held horizontally to the ice in front at shoulder height, in the sit down position, skate forward by pushing back with one skate, then with the other skate, going all the way down the ice. Practice backward as well.

Drill 195M: Power push OI S

Players face each other along the blue line. Two players hold on to the same stick, horizontal to the ice at shoulder height, and then try to push each other across or off the blue line. This can be done off-ice as well.

Drill 196M: Stick pull backward OI S

Players face each other along the blue line. Two players hold the same stick horizontally at shoulder height, and try to pull each other off or across the blue line, like in a tug of war. This can be done off-ice as well.

Drill 197A: Stick battle backward OI S

Players face each other along the blue line. Two players hold two sticks with one hand on each stick, then pull each other across the blue line backward, like in a tug of war. This can be done off-ice as well.

Drill 198A: Own the stick OI S

Two players hold the same stick horizontally to the ice at shoulder height, and push and pull and twist to get the stick out of the other player's hands and away from the other player. This can be done off-ice as well.

Drill 199U: Alternating long stride forward stick vertical and glide HC

Skate forward by pushing behind with one skate then the other skate, alternating down the ice, with the stick held vertically on the ice in front and with an upper body lean and in the sitting position.

Special Combination Drills without the Puck

Combo 5

This is a special combination of drills from book 1 to introduce forward stride fundamentals. This covers as many forward stride fundamentals as possible in the shortest period of time. These drills should be done consecutively in this sequence while skating end to end or across the rink. This is a good introduction to practicing the proper forward stride. The instructor should monitor and observe the fundamentals of each drill. The skaters must focus on doing each drill correctly. Once kids get to know this sequence of drills, they should be able to do all of them within only two or three minutes.

1. Toe drag toes out (50E)
2. Short steps fast on whistle (13U)
3. Gliding arm pump fast (22E)
4. Full stance long strides with tap (60U)
5. Put it all together doing all of these drills at the time into a good fast forward stride

This sequence of drills can be used periodically as review of the introduction to the forward stride.

Use a different kid to demonstrate and lead each drill. They can become the specialist for their specific drill.

Magic 6

This is another special combination of drills from book 1 to cover the greatest number of agility skating fundamentals within the shortest period of time. These drills should be done at one end of the rink, across the ice, and around the face-off circles, consecutively in this sequence. The instructor should monitor and observe the fundamentals of each drill. The skaters must focus on doing each drill correctly. Once kids get to know the sequence of drills, they should be able to do all of them within only two or three minutes. In order to reduce boredom, from time to time the first two balances may be replaced with different balances of your choosing.

1. Sit-down balance (113A)
2. Edges forward (68E)
3. Crossovers circles forward (108E)
4. Crossovers circles backward (117U)
5. Two crossovers forward and backward (131A&134U)
6. Sharp turns (88M) two each way (left and right)

This sequence of drills can be used periodically as a quick review of basic agility skating skills.

Use a different kid to demonstrate and lead each of the six drills. They can become the specialist for their specific drill.

Book 1:
Beginner Skating Drill List (Book 1)

Skate-Feel Concepts
Walk—Concept 1
1E Short steps forward OI P
2E Giant steps forward OI P
3E Down and up (get up off the ice) OI P HC
4E Beginners stance OI HC
5E Walk sideways OI P L&R
6E Walk forward on toes OI P
7M Walk forward on heels OI P
8M Walk backward on toes OI P
9M Walk skates loose OI
10M Lateral one side step then stop on whistle OI P L&R
11M Lateral side steps fast on whistle across blue line OI P F L&R
12A Walk backward on heels OI P
13U Short steps forward fast on whistle P F S

Run—Concept 2
14E Run on spot slow OI P
15E Run on the spot fast on whistle OI P F
16E Run then spin on the spot OI P L&R
17M Run on toes forward across the ice OI P F
18M Run lateral side steps knees high fast on whistle across blue line OI P F L&R
19U Run on toes backward across the ice OI P

Glide—Concept 3
20E Glide two feet P HC F&B
21E Glide two feet sitting F&B
22E Glide fast arm pump F HC
23E Glide two feet and swerve P F&B

24E Glide two feet sit and swerve P F&B
25M Glide one foot forward P HC
26M Glide one foot forward with supporting knee bend P HC
27M Glide toe on puck P HC
28U Glide one foot and swerve pylons P

Jump—Concept 4
29E Jump stationary OI P F
30E Jump lines P F
31E Jump high on boards OI
32E Jump high over blue line/floor OI P
33E Balance one foot stationary OI P HC
34M Hop one foot stationary OI P HC F
35M Jump One Foot OI P HC F&B
36A Jump legs crossed OI P L&R
37U High jumps moving P S F&B

Rock—Concept 5
38E Rock on boards on skates OI
39E Rock on boards running OI F
40M Rock stationary on skate blade one foot OI P
41M Rock on skate blades two feet OI P F
42A Touch toes with horizontal stick then rock OI
43U Rock on skate blades while running OI P

Toe-Heel Concepts
Toes Out—Concept 6
44E Toes out 90° sitting on ice OI
45E Toes out 90° standing on ice OI
46E Toes out 90° moving on ice
47E Toes out against the boards OI
48E Push boards (C-cuts forward) on whistle OI S
49E Carry puck in skates OI P HC
50E Knee drag with toes out HC P
51M Power one leg (C-cuts forward) toes out multi push P
52M Power one leg (C-cuts forward) toes out single push P
53M Push heavy objects OI HC
54M Pull heavy objects OI P HC

55A Penguin walk forward heel-to-heel OI
56A Heel-to-heel on the boards OI
57A Heel-to-heel one skate straight line HC
58A Full skating stance and hold OI
59A Full stance push alternating long strides P S
60U Full stance push alternating long strides tap P S

Toes In—Concept 7
61E Toes in sitting and against the boards OI
62E Toes in stationary (on ice) OI
63E Toes in toes out stationary and moving on the ice OI P
64E Toes out toes in semicircle on ice HC
65E Backward C-cuts on the boards (toes in then out)
66A Walk toes in OI
67U Power backward slow long C-cuts alternating skates P HC

Edges—Concept 8
68E Edges forward (foot in front) P
69E Edges forward (foot behind) P HC
70E Slalom forward parallel P HC F
71E Push and slide S
72M Edges backward (foot beside then behind) P HC
73M Slalom forward leading one skate P HC F
74M Slalom forward leading double pylons P HC F
75M Short C-cuts two skates alternating backward P HC F
76M Long fast C-cuts two skates alternating backward P HC F
77M Pull partner short C-cuts backward HC
78M Pull partner long C-cuts backward HC
79M Pull heavy objects backward P HC
80M Dribble puck between skates P HC
81M Figure 8 inside edges P HC
82A Figure 8 outside edges P HC
83A Ankles L&R
84A Slalom backward parallel P
85A Half moon (half figure 8s) inside edges wide multi P HC
86U Half moon (half figure 8s) outside edge wide multi P HC

Heel—Concept 9
87M Walk on heels then jump on heels OI
88M C-cuts forward with heels only P HC F
89M Sharp Turns on dots or gloves P F
90M Power turns stick horiz or vertical S
91M Quad turns 4 pylons P S F
92M Stick (lying on ice) sharp turns S
93M Sculling (snake) P HC S F
94M Crossover sculls P S
95M Flat-foot skating P S
96A Scull Jump P S F&B
97A Euro shuffle both feet on the ice weight on heels P S
98A Heel-to-heel through single pylons P S
99A Heel-to-heel two feet straight line P HC
100A Heel-to-heel sit down OI
101U Surfer—heel to heel straight line horizontal waist high S

Knee Concepts
Knee Bend—Concept 10
102E Bend knees 90 degrees on the boards OI
103E Balance one skate other knee high OI P
104E Run on spot knees high OI P F
105E Run backward and spin backward OI P
106E Mini crossovers circles P F F&B
107E Crossover stability—circles stick horiz on shoulders with crossunders HC F&B
108E Crossovers circles forward on whistle F P
109E Run across rink on toes then balls of feet knees high OI P F
110M Rocking crossovers in circle on whistle P F
111M Jump and turn toes 90 degrees out in parallel stationary OI P
112M Squat (OI Stationary on ice) F&B
113A Sit down balance F&B OI HC
114A Elbow balance OI
115A Step over and under stick (over and under twirl) F&B OI S
116A Step over and under stick jump (over and under twirl) F&B OI S
117U Crossovers circles backward on whistle F P

Knee Extension—Concept 11
118E Knee drag P
119E Three Knee Motion glide (25-45-90) then horizontal side to side P F&B
120E Single stick stepovers forward and backward S F&B
121M Forward scissors wide on outside edges P HC
122M Forward scissors narrow on outside edges fast P HC F
123A Forward scissors wide outside edge jump lateral P HC
124A Backward scissors wide on outside edges P
125A Backward scissors narrow on outside edges fast P S F
126A Backward crossovers with tight 360 turn S
127U Outside inside & under scull (snake) P S F&B

Lateral—Concept 12
128M Lateral crossovers on blue line, stop and fast on the whistle OI P HC F L&R
129M Double stick stepovers forward and backward (over sticks lying on ice) HC F F&B
130M Double stick stepover pivots forward and backward S
131A Forward crossovers 3-2-1 P
132A Forward crossovers three speeds P F
133A Backward wave with crossovers P F
134U Backward crossovers 3-2-1 P F

Drop—Concept 13
135E Drop to one knee while stationary & moving OI P F&B
136E Drop to both knees while moving and continue P F&B
137E Drop to stomach while stationary OI P
138M Drop to stomach while moving P
139M Drop to stomach and roll OI P S
140A Drop to knees and do 360 degree spin on knees P S
141U Russian knee drop OI P S F

Kick—Concept 14
142E Rotate skate in circle in air OI P F
143E Side kicks OI P F
144E Front kicks OI P F
145M Back kicks OI P F
146A Balance (stick horizontal) kicks OI F
147U Kicks skating backward P F

Advanced Jump—Concept 15
148M Crossover tripod jump S
149A Forward 2 foot tripod jump P S
150A Forward 1 foot tripod jump P S
151A Hurdler—high jump with one skate and land with the other P S
152A Forward to Backward Transition jump P S
153U Jump 360 from forward to forward P S

Balance Concepts
Agility—Concept 16
154E Touch ups & touch backs OI S F
155E Touch combo OI S
156E Step over forward tap S
157E Tap skate with other skate (while skating) (toe, side heel) OI P
158E Tap skate with stick (by instructor or another players) OI P
159E Walk and run with stick up OI F F&B
160E Horizontal stick touch toes then roll shoulders F&B OI
161M Jump 90º while skating (beginning of the stop) OI P L&R
162M Stick mirror speed drill S
163A Partner stepover mirror faster and faster F S
164A Heel-to-heel turn through double pylons P
165U Lateral crossover touches S

Flexibility—Concept 17
166E Automobile (OI stationary)
167E Airplane (OI stationary)
168E Ride on stick (OI stationary)
169M Push puck off the line (inside outside blade) P
170M Squat Jump OI F P S F&B
171M Shumpka jumps (high jumps touching skates behind) OI S
172A Russian jump—lateral jump off inside edge of outside skate laterally OI P S
173A Edge Extreme drill—thru pylons stretch to inside edges extreme S
174A Stick behind horiz down to skate heels OI S
175U Serdachny Shuffle—sit down jump F&B OI P S

Pivot—Concept 18
176E Mohawk turn (forward to backward and backward to forward) OI P HC

177M Partner pivots holding sticks OI P HC S
178M Straight line pivot on blue line stick horizontal HC
179A Slalom pivot—forward then pivot backward (feet together) S
180A Stick chases (two sticks lying on ice) S
181A Spin forward (360 degrees) P HC L&R P
182A Spin backward (360 degrees) L&R
183A Circle pivot P S
184A Backward crossover pivot 90 degree P S
185A Pivot drive—accelerate toward net then pivot backward shoot S P
186A Starbust—pivots around ice continuously doing 360s like dancing S
187A Bart Simpson—pylons in 2 rows and pivot thru them facing one direction P S
188U Skiing one foot edges and pivot and go other direction on same foot P

Power—Concept 19
189E Power Outside 8s—stationary power arc 180 around each skate S
190E Gauntlet (skate, stick, shaft, shoulder, combo) P OI
191E Isolation Push—stick horizontal behind, multi and alternating leg push S
192M Acceleration circle drive—circle in front of the net crossovers to accelerate then shoot S
193M Acceleration turn—sharp turn with two crossovers S
194M Steeple—backward and forward with stick horizontal & glide S
195M Power Push—2 players hold stick and try to push against each other OI S
196M Stick pull backward—2 players hold stick and pull OI S
197A Stick battle (backward) OI S
198A Own the stick—2 players one stick push and pull stick OI S
199U Alternating long stride forward stick vertical in front then glide

Special Combination Drills
Combo 5 (50E toe drag, 13U short fast steps, 22E fast arm pump, 60U long stride, all together stride) P
Magic 6—113A sit down balance, 68E edges, 108E circles forward, 117U circles backward, 134U 2 crossovers fwd & bkwd, 88M sharp turns

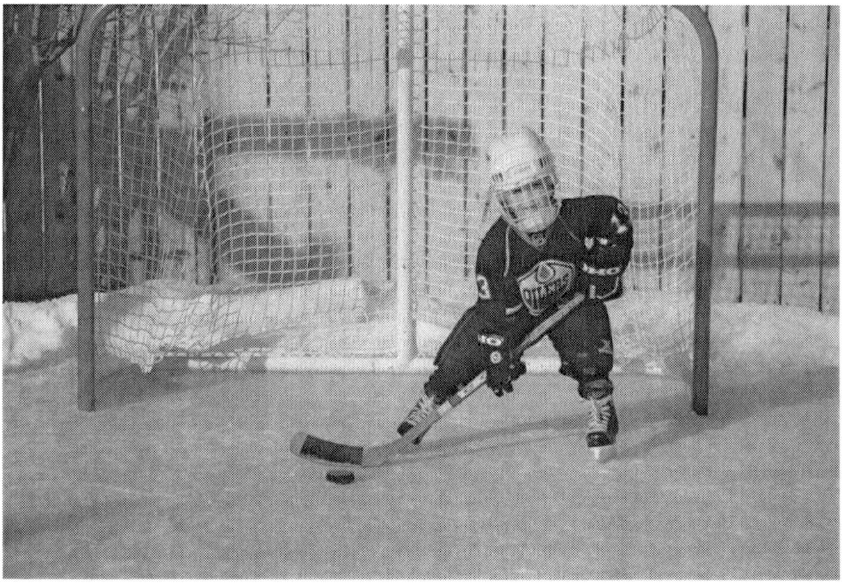

Book 2

Beginner Puck Control

Why Beginner Puck Control?

The most controversial issue in professional hockey today is the problem of concussions. The number of head injuries is on the increase and, therefore, critical to the future of the sport. Similarly in minor hockey, head injuries from body contact are a major concern. Even though hockey is a body contact sport, too many injuries are caused by unnecessary body contact. Ice hockey is such a fast-moving sport that injuries are inevitable. However, in order to decrease the number of injuries, we need to control body contact better. (More about body contact and kids at the end of this book in the epilogue.) There are many reasons, but two of the main causes for injuries are lack of vision and poor puck control. Many players skate with their head down, and most kids don't control the puck effectively. Unfortunately, if proper puck control is not taught early, kids must look down at the puck to control it. Hence, they can't see other players to avoid being hit. Without proper puck control, kids are very vulnerable to body contact. This is the reason for this Book 2. It teaches kids how to keep their head up while controlling the puck, right from the very beginning while they are learning how to skate. This book teaches beginners to control the puck and keep their head up even before they learn the forward stride.

Puck control is one of the most difficult skills to teach in hockey. This is part of the transition from being a first-time skater to being ready to play the team game. In order to control the puck properly, beginners need to handle the puck without having to look down at it. In practice, kids need to look around and recognize where their teammates are. They need to learn to manipulate the puck and keep control of the puck while their head is up. This is not easy or simple. When playing the game of hockey, kids must be able to look up and around the rest of the rink to see where the other eleven players (five teammates and six opponents) are and what they are doing. Kids must know where their teammates are in order to make a pass to them, but more important, they must see their opponents, whose objective is to check or hit them. If you are going to be an accurate shooter, you need to look at the target when you shoot, not down at the puck. The concept of puck control with head and eyes up is very difficult. It is critical that it becomes automatic and an inherent part of the skating process. Proper puck control takes a long time and will develop slowly. The drills in Book 2 will teach you how keep your head up and control the puck at the same time.

The sooner you introduce puck control into the skating process, the easier it is for kids to learn. You want puck control to become an automatic part of skating. That is the reason why I introduce puck control to beginners before teaching the actual forward stride. Kids have no preconceived ideas as to what they can or can't do. They are not afraid to try something new. They are not worried about making mistakes. As seen earlier in this book, kids have much greater ability than given credit for. Once they have been given proper direction, they will experiment on their own. I have always had the best success introducing puck control to the beginner before teaching the forward stride. Kids are able to learn a great deal of puck control before they have acquired enough balance for forward and backward skating. Self-protection from body contact becomes critical in any contact sport. Beginners must learn to either avoid or minimize the impact of a collision with another player. This is impossible if kids don't keep their head up.

The Five Major Problems for Beginner Puck Control

Teaching kids to play with their head up should start at the very beginning of their skating skill development. In this book you can start puck control as early as drill 1. Drills that can be done while manipulating a puck on the stick are identified with the property P (Puck).

Kids can start to learn how to keep their head up as soon as they learn how to walk on skates. They can be taught to protect themselves better from head injuries by learning to handle the puck early, when they have the capability of developing the vision needed to automatically handle the puck without having to look down at it. This volume introduces pucks to beginner drills as early as possible. You can start using pucks as early as drill 1 in book 1 if you choose. However, in order to use pucks early, kids must learn how to hold the stick and dribble the puck. You can do this while in book 1 at any time, but first you must jump ahead to drills 200-202 and 206 in book 2. These drills will teach kids how to hold the stick, the stick length, and wrist roll before doing drills with the puck on the stick. Depending on the individual beginner, parents can determine when to start using pucks. The sooner they start handling a puck, the easier it is for kids. Once beginners learn the simple hands concepts in drills 200-202, they can go back where they left off and repeat most drills in book 1 (marked with P [Puck]). Throughout book 1, a puck is implemented into as many drills as possible, including acceleration speed drills.

However, doing the same skating drills with a puck on the stick is much different, especially if you ask beginners to keep their head up and not look down at the puck. It is very important to learn to skate with pucks. It will help kids to eventually automatically keep their head up. Also, with practice, kids will be able to perform skills automatically and not need to think about any specific skill while playing the game. While carrying the puck during a drill, when they lose the puck, let them continue and finish the drill, then pick the puck up on the way back on the next try. With practice, you will be amazed at how kids figure out ways of keeping control of the puck while doing balances such as the squat. They are very creative and will learn how to do a lot of puck control by trial and error without coach input.

There are five puck-control (or stickhandling) problems encountered by beginners and, for that matter, by all hockey players. These problems may not seem important at first; nonetheless, a weakness with any one of these problem areas will be a major detriment to good puck control later.

Major problems are the following:

1. Hands
   Grip
   Stick size
   Wrist roll
2. Eyes (keeping eyes off the puck)
3. Puck
4. Stick
5. Puck-control balance

These five problems are solved with five solutions or basic concept groups. It starts with the hands and eyes, then it involves actual puck feel and stick manipulation, followed by puck-control balances. Once this is accomplished, it is important to learn to get used to the long stick. In order to control the puck in hockey, somehow you need to feel the puck on the stick blade at the end of the long stick shaft. These five problems make up the five basic skill concept groups involved in puck control. They are refined further by being broken down into more detailed concepts with various simple drills each. The use of pucks is assumed for all drills in book 2.

1—Hands Concepts

Problem

Handling and controlling the puck at the end of a long stick, with a short stick blade, is nearly as difficult as skating is for the first time. The problem is this is not natural to the human body, especially for a beginner who up to this point has manipulated everything directly by the fingers and hands, like in hand ball or in other games. The beginner must learn to be able to manipulate a puck at the end of a long stick instead of manipulating a ball that fits directly in the grasp of the fingers and hand.

Analysis

First of all, a hockey player must know how to hold the stick. Then he or she will need to practice manipulating the puck on the stick blade.

However, the biggest problem is learning to take the eyes off the puck and keep the eyes looking up around the hockey rink at the same time. You need to gain a feel for the puck in your fingers nearly as if the puck was directly in your hand. Once you get to that point, you can get into serious puck control.

Solution

The solution starts with simple drills and progress in difficulty as you go on. The hands concepts consist of three concepts: the grip, wrist, and puck repeat (repeating drills in book 1 with a puck) drill. Hands concepts and drills are as follows:

Hands Drill Description

Hands Concepts

Grip—Concept 20

In order to learn how to control the puck, the first thing to learn is how to hold the stick. The grip concept consists of two drills: the first one shows you how to hold the stick with both hands, and second shows you how long the stick should be.

Drill 200E: Stick grip OI

The grip concept is to learn how to properly hold the hockey stick with both hands. Up to this point we have been using only one hand on the stick for balance. For puck control we need to use two hands on the stick. The proper grip is to place the top hand one-half inch below the top of the stick shaft. Place the lower hand wherever it is comfortable on the stick for now. Later we move the lower hand up or down for different drills. It doesn't matter whether you hold the stick left or right; the theory is the same. Place the V between thumb and index finger of both hands in line with the middle of the top edge of the shaft (the narrow side of the stick shaft). You will get better wrist roll and be able to make harder shots and passes if both Vs are lined up with the middle of the narrow side of the stick. Kids usually forget and let the V of the lower hand slip off the center line. Beginners must be monitored to ensure they keep the V of the lower hand on the middle of the stick. They also tend to want to point the

V of the upper hand to the right shoulder for left shooters and to the left shoulder for right shooters, but this will also cause problems.

- First-time beginners need to see the V of their hands on the stick the first time they do it, so take the gloves off and show them the V between the index finger and the thumb and show them where it should go on the midline of the stick. All puck-control drills should have both hands on the stick unless stated otherwise. It is imperative that instructors continually check and correct the grip. If they are not corrected, it will result in weak shots and weak passes. When a player's shot or pass suddenly seems to become weaker, then suspect the V of the grip; it is probably slipping off the midline of the shaft.

Drill 201E: Stick length OI

This drill is simple. In order to control the puck, you must cut the hockey stick to the correct length.

Stick length—when you buy a hockey stick, the length is at the maximum length, so it will fit everyone. Therefore, you must cut the top end of it to make it shorter. What should the stick length be? This can be a controversial question. Generally, the stick should be no longer than up to your chin when your skates are on or no longer than up to your nose with skates off. However, this is a very general rule, and there are exceptions to the rule. It is important to remember that the idea is to put the stick blade flat on the ice when a player is moving in the skating motion and carrying or passing the puck. Unfortunately, to get the blade flat on the ice while skating at full speed is different for each individual. It depends on the makeup of the individual's body—height, width, thickness, and weight. The lower your skating profile, the shorter the stick could be. Some skate with maximum knee bend, and others do not. It also depends on the type of stride and how you skate. So in fact, stick length is a little different for everyone. For beginners, the general rule "to the chin with skates on" is good for most.

An alternative method to determine stick length for good puck control is stated by Howie Meeker in his book (see the bibliography at the back of this book, "Drill Sources and References"). That is, stand straight up, knees perfectly straight, hand straight down the side of the body; you should be able to hold the stick one-half inch from top end of the stick while the blade is flat on the ice. If the stick blade is not flat on the ice, slide the upper end of stick higher up or down through the handgrip until the blade is flat on the ice. Do not change their stance or move their hand at this point. There should be less than one-half inch above the hand to the end of the top of the stick. Cut off the rest of the stick. This is from Howie Meeker's book, and for some this is a good method for determining stick length for puck handling. Others may find this length too short as it is a couple of inches below the chin when skates are on. Howie Meeker's suggestion turns out to be 2-4 inches below the chin. This is good for stickhandling but not as good for checking. This is discussed in more detail in book 4, "Passing."

Stick size includes the length of the stick shaft and blade together as one unit, but you must also consider the actual length of the blade, thickness of the shaft, the weight, and the flexibility of the stick, as well as the angle between the shaft and the blade. This angle is called the lie. Usually it is not indicated in sports shops; unless they indicate otherwise, the standard lie sold in sports shops today is probably 5. Normally, sports shops don't offer different lies anymore. A lie of 7 would provide the blade at a narrower angle, and thus the puck would be closer to the feet. As far as stick size is concerned, for five—and six-year-olds, take advantage of a youth stick that is narrower, lighter, and has a smaller blade.

Wrist—Concept 21

The wrist concept consists of the following four drills:

Drill 202E: Wrist roll OI

The wrist concept is simply being able to roll the wrist to sufficiently control the puck. An incorrect grip on the stick (drill 200 above) makes a good wrist roll nearly impossible. In order to control the puck, beginners must roll the wrists to a great extent. While standing stationary on the ice (or any hard surface), put a puck on the ice (or any hard surface) in front of them. Then place the heel of the stick on top of the puck. Then lift the heel of the stick blade a little off the top of the puck. Leaving the heel of the stick above the puck and using it as a swivel, rotate the wrist until the tip of the blade touches the ice on one side. The heel of the stick should remain in the same place and swivel in the air. Then rotate the wrist in the opposite direction, all the way around until the tip of the stick touches the ice on the other side of the puck. Rotate back and forth, letting the heel of the stick swivel above the puck and the tip of the stick rotating back and forth, touching the ice with the toe of the stick on both sides of the puck. This requires an extreme wrist rotation.

Beginners will find this wrist roll can't be done properly unless the V between the thumb and index finger is directly on the middle of the narrow side of the stick. If you can't turn your wrists all the way around, then keep coming back to it until you can. If this is too difficult at first, ask them to go halfway around, then three quarters of the way and eventually all the way around until the toe of the blade touches the ice or hard surface. Later beginners will need to be able to cup the puck on both sides of the stick blade. Any exercise that will provide strength and flexibility to the wrist will help.

Drill 203E: Find the puck OI

Put the stick heel on top of the puck. Then raise the stick up and look up, then put the stick back down on top of the puck without looking down for it. Much practice will be needed. Dribble (moving the puck from side to side with the stick blade) the puck, then stop with your stick on the puck and without looking down, verbally state where the puck is. Is the puck on the toe, heel, or middle? Stop dribbling, lift the stick up and down to same spot without looking down, and then keep dribbling the puck back and forth.

Drill 204M: Balance puck on both sides of stick OI

This is an exaggeration of the requirement for hockey, but it gives the hands a feel for the puck. First, balance the puck on one side of the blade of the stick. How far can you skate without letting the puck fall off the stick blade? See who can go the farthest. Now practice the same thing with the puck on the other side of the stick blade.

Drill 205U: Bounce puck on stick blade OI HC

This is not something usually done during a hockey game; however, it definitely takes a special feel for the hands to accomplish, and it is a good challenge for the beginner. Few can do this well, and it takes much practice. Practice bouncing the puck on both sides of the blade. Do a Sidney Crosby and bat the puck into the net while the puck is in the air. This is a fun aspect of the drill.

Puck Repeat—Concept 22

Drill 206M: Repeat book 1 drills

The puck-repeat concept is to simply go back and repeat the skating drills in book 1, implementing a puck into those drills. Once you can roll your wrists, you should be able to do most drills in book 1 while keeping a puck on the stick. In other words, now with the proper grip and a good wrist roll, kids can go back and repeat most skating drills with a puck on the stick. The drills in book 1 that can be done with a puck on the stick are identified with P (for "puck") in the drill name.

The instructor will need to decide when a beginner is ready to include a puck into their skating drills. It will depend on the individual beginner, but it can start as early as drill 1. Start by trying it with drill 1. If this is too difficult for them, then you can try to implement it at any other time. Just go back later and do the drills that have been missed. Kids usually want to and they should start using pucks as soon as possible. From now on, keep a puck on the stick for as many drills as possible.

2—Eyes Concepts (Eyes Off the Puck)

Problem

The problem is, beginners look down at the puck when carrying it. While skating, a player should be looking up and around the ice instead. Players need to play hockey without looking down to see the puck. Some people call this puck feel or peripheral vision or split vision. Whatever you want to call it, players need to acquire the knack of handling and controlling the puck without bringing the eyes down to look at it. Although this is very difficult to teach and requires much practice, it is a skill that can be learned by all players, especially young beginners. The "eyes on the puck" problem will also slow down the skating speed by a great factor. When the head is down, kids can't see the rest of the play on the ice. The common result is, often even with pro hockey players, you get hit by another player when your head is down (with your eyes on the puck) instead of looking where you are going and who is coming toward them.

Analysis

The ability to keep the eyes off the puck while skating is indeed a skill that can be taught to all players. As difficult as it is, beginners can do it better than adults because they have no preconceived notions. Today puck control is not taught early enough. This is the main reason this book introduces puck control before actual regular skating. There is not enough emphasis placed on proper puck control at the beginner stage. More drills should be done with a puck on the stick. Too many players skate with their head down, especially when they are trying to skate at full speed. Kids will learn to keep their head up by keeping a puck on their stick during as many drills as possible.

Today players spend too much time practicing without the puck. They are taught to skate without the puck for too long a period of time before they are allowed to carrying the puck. Teaching kids to skate without a puck on their stick should be minimized. You should include pucks into as many beginner skating drills as soon as possible. Teach it in very small steps at first, starting with how to hold the stick and to roll the wrists for control of the puck. Then they can practice most skating drills with a puck while keeping the eyes off the puck and while looking around with the head up.

For most kids, you can start including pucks into drills right at the very beginning with drill 1. It is easier to make puck control an automatic part of the skating motion, before beginners start regular skating, because beginners are ready to accept new ideas without question. They will try anything as long as you make it easy enough. Kids are amazing and will adjust quicker to these new ideas and weird concepts before older players can.

The game is moving too fast to take the eyes off the surrounding ice activity. When a player learns to skate before learning to carry a puck, he or she will develop the bad habit of keeping the head down during the game. Unless they are taught differently, kids subconsciously always look down for the puck. If not taught early enough, then no matter how often they practice to correct the habit, it never really is completely overcome. Therefore kids must learn to carry the puck from day one, before the bad head-down habit sets in.

The longer you wait, the more difficult it is to learn. This is why puck control is so difficult to teach. Consequently, this is the main reason to introduce puck control before forward skating. Kids must learn to control the puck automatically without looking down for the puck. In other words, the head and eyes are up all the time, except when you initially receive the puck. Manipulating the puck on the stick blade without looking down at the puck is a very difficult task to learn at any time. The earlier, the easier it is for a beginner.

Solution

The best time to learn how to keep the head up is as soon as possible. The best way to learn how to keep the head up is by keeping a puck on the stick blade during as many drills as possible. These drills will not only give confidence to beginners to dribble the puck, but will force kids to take their eyes off the puck and look around the rink instead. i.e. practice simple balance drills with a puck on the stick during warm-ups at the beginning of a practice and warm-downs at the end of a practice. Eyes concepts include dribbling the puck and balance while dribbling a puck. Eyes concepts and drill descriptions follow below.

Eyes (Off the Puck) Drill Description

Dribble—Concept 23

Drill 207E: Puck feel (eyes off the puck) OI

The first concept within the eyes concept group is the dribble concept. That is to be able to dribble the puck from side to side with the stick blade. Standing in a stationary position, move the puck back and forth from side to side. Start by dribbling without wearing hockey gloves to get a better feel for the puck. Kids need to learn to dribble the puck with the head and eyes up. Put the gloves back on and dribble by not looking down at the puck. Simply move the puck back and forth with a wrist roll. After a lot of practice, kids will eventually be able to dribble a puck without looking down very much. Practice with the head up and eyes looking around the rink (and not looking at the puck). Ask the players to look up at the stands on the sidelines or at some other part of the rink while dribbling the puck back and forth. For all of these drills, practice keeping the eyes off the puck.

Drill 208E: Dribble narrow (short) stationary OI HC F

Standing in a stationary position, move the puck back and forth, from side to side, in a narrow or short dribble and concentrate on letting the wrists roll and do the work. Practice doing it fast on the whistle.

Drill 209E: Dribble wide (long) stationary OI HC F

Standing in a stationary position, move the puck back and forth, from side to side, in a wide or long dribble and concentrate on keeping the blade at right angle to the puck path. Roll the wrists to cup the puck on each side with the stick blade. For extra long dribbles, release the lower hand at the widest point for a longer reach. Practice doing it fast on the whistle.

Drill 210E: Dribble slow stationary arms extended OI

Standing in a stationary position, move both hands, arms, and elbows extended out in front (for exaggeration), then move the puck back and forth, from side to side, as you dribble the puck while keeping the shoulders square to the puck path.

Drill 211E: Dribble fast stationary OI F

Standing in a stationary position, dribble any way you want (narrow, wide, etc.), slow then fast on the whistle.

Drill 212M: Dribble narrow and wide combo moving HC F

Dribble narrow then wide on the whistle, then narrow again on the next whistle while skating.

Drill 213M: Dribble three zones stationary OI F

While standing stationary, dribble three zones—forehand side, backhand side, and in front. Go fast on the whistle.

Drill 214A: Dribble eyes closed stationary OI F

While standing stationary, dribble with eyes closed. Concentrate on letting the wrists do the work and try to let the fingers obtain a feel for the puck. Practice fast on the whistle.

Drill 215A: Dribble superfast stationary OI F

Dribble slow then fast on the whistle while keeping the blade at right angle to the puck path. Then on the next whistle, dribble superfast (as fast as you can). (Superfast is like a third or high gear.) Then slow again on the next whistle and continue repeating all three speeds on the whistle.

Drill 216A: Knob drill (narrow-wide-fast) OI S F

Holding the stick with the blade up and the knob end down on the ice, dribble the puck with the knob end of the stick instead of the stick blade. You would not use this in a game, but it gives a much better feel for the puck. Practice fast on the whistle.

Drill 217A: Dribble rotation HC

Start in a stationary position and slide the stick blade along one side of the puck, then slide it along the other side of the puck in the opposite direction, causing the puck to rotate or spin. Keep the puck spinning by continually sliding the stick back and forth along each side of the stick. Once you are successful, do it while skating. This will appear as though the puck never leaves the stick (some call this the puck on a string). Practice spinning the puck in both directions.

Drill 218A: Shadow dribbling no pucks HC F&B F

Skate around the ice without a puck but dribble as if you had a puck. This is called shadow dribbling, similar to shadow boxing. Practice shadow dribbling (or stickhandling) in the three zones (forehand, backhand, and in front) while at the same time skating with three crossovers to the left, then the right. You can include shadow dribbling in many other drills with pylons and without pylons. Practice while skating three crossovers forward and backward. Practice fast on the whistle.

Drill 219A: Long wide stride inside edges dribble narrow S F

Skate extra long wide strides on the inside edges of the skates while dribbling narrow. Practice dribbling fast on the whistle.

Drill 220U: Dribble wide through double rows of pylons while skating HC

With double rows of pylons, skate inside the double rows of pylons while dribbling the puck, side to side, outside the pylons. Double pylons will force a wide dribble. This will develop long puck handling moves.

Then skate outside the double rows of pylons with the natural move and the opposite move.

Natural Move-skate through the double row of pylons and dribble the puck wide from outside of the stick blade (forehand side of the blade) to the inside of the stick blade (backhand side of the blade). This is the most common move to get around a player. It provides the maximum reach to move the puck around another player. It is the most natural movement by the human body to get around a player and therefore called the natural move in hockey.

Opposite move-opposite to the natural move. Skate through the double row of pylons and dribble the puck wide from inside of the stick blade (backhand side of the blade) to the outside of the stick blade (forehand side of the blade).

Balance—Concept 24

Drill 221E: Dribble one skate (stationary and moving) OI HC F&B F

The balance concept teaches balance while dribbling the puck. The first puck-control balance concept is to stand on one skate. Dribble with only one skate on the ice or any hard surface. Stand on only one skate while dribbling. Practice while standing stationary then while skating. Practice both skates. Then fast on the whistle as well as backward.

Drill 222E: Dribble one hand (upper) (stationary and moving) OI HC F&B F

Dribble with only upper hand on the stick. Practicing this will provide hand, wrist, and forearm strength. Do while stationary then while skating. Practice fast on the whistle and backward.

Drill 223M: Dribble one hand (lower) (stationary and moving) OI HC F&B F

Dribble with only lower hand on the stick. Practicing this will provide hand, wrist, and forearm strength. Do while stationary then while skating. Practice fast on the whistle and backward.

Drill 224M: Dribble hands together (stationary and moving) OI HC F&B F

Dribble with both hands close together at the top of the stick. Do while stationary and while skating. Practice fast on the whistle and backward.

Drill 225M: Dribble hands wide (stationary and moving) OI HC F&B F

While dribbling, loosen the lower hand and slide it lower than normal on the stick shaft, making it wider between the upper hand and lower hand. Dribble moving the lower hand up and down in different positions on the shaft of the stick. Do while stationary and while moving. Practice fast on the whistle and backward.

Drill 226U: Dribble one leg three zones while moving
F&B HC F

Similar to drill 221 (dribble one leg), now while skating on one skate, dribble the puck in all three zones: the forehand zone, the backhand zone, and the front zone. Remember, practice on the left skate then the right skate as well. Practice it fast on the whistle and also backward.

3—Puck Concepts

Problem

Players don't know where the puck is on the blade of their stick. They can't tell whether the puck is on the heel, the toe, or the middle of the blade without looking down at the puck. You need to learn to be able to feel the puck in your hands even though the stick blade it is a long distance from the hands. Puck control is very difficult for everyone; it is especially difficult for kids. Fortunately, kids are more open to trying new concepts for the first time than adults.

Analysis

Instead of relying on the eyes to look down at the puck, beginners need to develop a sense of feel for the puck on the stick blade. They must keep their eyes on the play around the rest of rink, not on the puck on their stick. Puck control or stickhandling is manipulating the puck with the stick blade. In order to control the puck, you actually move the puck back and forth from side to side with the stick blade. This is like basketball where you bounce a ball up and down on the floor. In hockey you bounce the puck along the ice from side to side with the stick blade instead of dribbling a basketball up and down. Consequently, it is referred to as dribbling the puck. Beginners need to develop a light, smooth touch to dribble the puck efficiently and with control. After a great deal of practice and with these drills, kids will develop a feel for the puck.

Solution

Concepts to develop a feel for the puck include soft hands and puck control while moving the body with a good deal of agility. The drill descriptions and pictures follow:

Puck Concepts Drill Description

Soft Hands—Concept 25

Drill 227E: Switch hands OI HC

The concept of soft hands starts with exaggeration by dribbling (stickhandling) the puck while holding the hockey stick opposite to the normal way you hold the stick. Start in a stationary position. If you normally shoot left, then hold the stick right and vice versa; thus hold the stick the wrong way. This is difficult, but it is important in order to develop the full use of the hands. Practice dribbling the puck holding the stick the wrong way while stationary and then while skating. A few gifted players can play hockey effectively holding the stick either left or right, and some can even shoot effectively both ways.

Drill 228M: Dribble inside edge control one leg long OI

Similar to drill 219 (long wide stride dribble narrow on inside edges), dribble the puck while skating on the inside edge of one skate forward, but this time glide on the skate as far as you can go and as long as you can go. Continue dribbling as fast as you can while you are gliding. After practicing with one skate, then practice with the other skate.

Drill 229M: Dribble through legs stationary OI HC

Right-handed shooters—while standing stationary, move the puck around to the right outside of the skate and drop it behind and then put the stick blade between the skates and behind to retrieve the puck, then bring the puck back up to the front. Opposite for those who hold their stick left-handed.

Drill 230M: Dribble through the legs moving

Same as drill 229 (dribble through legs stationary) except you do it moving. Move the puck around to the right outside of the skate and drop it behind and then put the stick blade between the skates and behind to retrieve the puck, then bring the puck back up to the front. Opposite for those who hold their stick left-handed.

Drill 231A: Puck scoops stationary and moving HC

Scoop is to be able to pick a puck up off the ice with the stick blade. You don't need to use scoops in the game very much, but it is fun and will give beginners a better feel for the puck.

Forward scoop—With the stick in the forehand position, scoop with the heel of the stick on top of the puck while the stick blade is nearly flat or parallel to the ice, then scoop forward and flip the blade under the puck. This is not something you usually need to do during a hockey game; however, it definitely takes a special feel of the puck to accomplish it. Few can do it consistently. This is a good challenge and can be fun but takes a great deal of time to develop.

Backward scoop—In the front zone, start with the stick blade flat on top of the puck on the ice, then slide the stick upside down (backhand side of the stick blade on the puck) and on top of the puck back along the ice across to the other side, then scoop backward and up under the puck.

Scoop and catch—Pick up the puck with the stick blade. Scoop with the heel of the stick, with the stick blade nearly flat, parallel to the ice. Now flip the puck up in the air and catch it with the stick blade.

Scoop and carry—Scoop and carry the puck on the blade of the stick.

Drill 232A: Pick up puck and stick off the ice with glove OI

Practice picking the puck up off the ice or off a hard surface with the glove. Although this is not essential to playing hockey, it can be a very useful tool to have when playing hockey. If you can't do it, you may have some restriction with your gloves. Gloves could be too stiff, too big, etc. The glove should be flexible enough to pick a puck up off the ice with the glove. If not, then the glove should be modified without reducing any protection to the hand. If you can't pick a puck up off the ice with your glove, you probably do not have enough flexibility in the glove for advanced stickhandling moves.

Also, practice picking the stick up off the ice with their glove without taking the glove off, like many minor hockey players do. Most new gloves are not flexible enough to allow you to do this. Manipulate your glove to a state where you can do it. This is often required when you lose your stick during the game. You should be able to pick their stick up off the ice without taking your glove off.

Drill 233A: Control stick flat on ice OI

Put the stick flat on the ice without letting it go, and lift it up again without losing control of the stick. Most gloves do not allow you to do this. You should manipulate or modify the glove to accomplish this. Putting your stick flat on the ice and then picking it up without losing it can become a very useful checking technique to intercept flat passes along the ice. This is covered in more detail in volume 2.

Drill 234A: Dribble silent OI F

While standing stationary, start by dribbling the puck fast and hard, making a loud stickhandling noise. Then dribble without making any noise at all. In order to be as silent as possible, you need to slow the dribble down and feather the puck back and forth from side to side with a smooth, light touch. If you can accomplish this, you have a really good feel for the puck, and eventually, you should be able to increase the speed of the silent dribbling with no or little noise. When you can dribble silently, then practice silently and fast on the whistle.

Drill 235U: Dribble puck outside on backhand side, and back between the skates HC

Those who normally shoot left move the puck with the stick blade outside around the right skate and back up to the front between the legs. Opposite side if you hold the stick right-handed.

Agility—Concept 26

Drill 236E: Dribble through single pylons P HC F F&B

The second concept of the puck concepts group is agility which involves quick muscle movement. It is one of the most important drills in book 2 especially at a super speed. Start simply with narrow dribbling between a single row of pylons while doing crossovers. Start slowly, then on the whistle move both feet and puck fast, then on the next whistle go superfast (as fast as you can dribble and as fast as you can make short crossovers). Then slow again on the next whistle. Superfast requires much energy, so superfast should last for only a few seconds. This should be practiced backward at all three speeds as well.

Drill 237M: Dribble 2 pucks F&B HC

While standing stationary, dribble two pucks but one at a same time. After that, while skating carry both pucks and dribble both pucks at the same time. To dribble both pucks, dribble one then the other, as you skate along. Kids are very creative and will figure out a way to do it. Try it skating backward.

Drill 238M: One-on-one in the corner

This is really starting to get into the game of hockey and kids like it. Start at the blue line. The instructor dumps the puck into the corner. Two players go in and play one-on-one in the corner, each going after the puck and trying to score on the goal. In other words kids play one against one in one corner at one end of the rink. They can try to get the puck away and get a shot on the goal. Then the instructor blows the whistle and the next group of two will do the same.

Drill 239M: One-on-one in the corner teams

Start at the blue line and dump the puck in the corner, and two players go one-on-one into the corner after the puck and try to score on the goal. Make two teams of two players each (one on each team go in at one time, one-on-one in the corner). Count the number of goals to see which team wins. After one shot (or two or even three shots), replace the two players with the other two players who are waiting and resting, like during a line change in a game. The instructor or the kids can keep the score themselves.

Drill 240M: Two-on-one in the corner

Start at the blue line and dump the puck into the corner and go two-on-one in the corner after the puck and try to score on the goal. Take turns being the single defender.

Drill 241M: Two-on-one in corner and chase

Start at the blue line and dump the puck into the corner and go two-on-one in the corner after the puck and try to score on the goal. Take turns being the single defender. On the whistle, chase whoever has the puck all the way to the other end of the rink (with the other two back-checking) and take a shot on the net. Any player (whoever has it when the whistle is blown) will carry the puck and the others chase from behind. The player carrying the puck tries to get a shot on the net at the far end of the rink, while being back-checked by the two other players all the way to the other end of the rink. Then the next group starts while the first group rests.

Drill 242A: Dribble three pucks

This is very difficult but worth attempting. Skate slowly and try to carry three pucks by dribbling with the stick and skating at the same time. Do whatever you can do, including using your skate blade, to carry the three pucks with you. Kids will figure a way to do it. They may have to use their skates to carry a missed puck.

Drill 243A: Three-man keep-away in front of net

The player with the puck tries to keep the puck away from the other two and attempts to get a shot on the net. Whoever can get the puck becomes the offensive player, and the other two are defenders.

Drill 244A: Russian dribble

While skating, let the puck drop outside and behind the left skate, then bring it up to the front between the skates, using the inside toe of right skate blade. Then let the puck drop back between the skates and bring it back up again between the skates with the inside of the skate blade. Also practice the other side with the other skate. The Russian dribble is to skate continuously alternating bringing the puck up with the left inside skate blade then the right inside skate blade between the skates and outside the skates.

Drill 245A: Dribble two pucks feet HC

While skating, dribble one puck, skate past a second puck and pull it up with inside of the skate blade at the same time. Practice both left and right skates.

Drill 246A: Heel-to-heel half circle each side S

Skating from one end to the other end of the rink making very wide heel-to-heel half circles to the left then right as you skate carrying the puck.

Drill 247A: Heel-to-heel half circle one-on-one S

Start at the red line and go one-on-one against a defender where the offensive player with the puck uses heel-to-heel half circles to go around the defender and then tries a shot on the net. Kids can start this with a tripod at first.

Drill 248A: Puck catch S

Start at the blue line. Quickly start skating and catch a puck thrown up in the air ahead of you (by the instructor). You can start anyway you want. Starts are covered in book 3. You can use a quick V start or crossover start, which are covered in book 3, to accelerate as the instructor throws a puck up in front of the skater, and the skater catches the puck with a glove while acceleration straight ahead.

Drill 249U: dribble one puck with stick and feet while moving

Dribble the puck between the stick blade to the inside of the skate blade of each skate while skating forward. Go from stick blade to inside of one skate then back to stick blade, then to the inside skate blade of the other skate and so on.

4—Stick Concepts

Problem

Players continue to lose control of the puck while skating. You have no sense of where the puck is without looking down at it. Consequently, you need to slow down the skating speed in order to look down. You have no control when you reach out for the puck with the stick. Most players cannot move the stick square to the target and do not draw the stick back far enough to generate enough passing or shooting power, resulting in weak passes and poor shots.

Analysis

Manipulating a round ball in your hand takes practice. Using a long hockey stick to manipulate a small disc certainly makes this much more difficult. It is similar to what a beginner skater had to go through when he or she puts skates on for the first time. In this case, instead of a two-inch stilt sensation under their feet, you need to deal with a very long stick. You have the sensation of a loose puck on the stick blade at the end of a long shaft, which is a long ways from the hands. It is similar to trying to stand on four-foot stilts for the first time. This is very difficult indeed and, at first, results in loss of control of the stick, therefore loss of control of the puck.

Stick movement is a big part of puck handling. Even with the proper grip, stick length, and good wrist roll, beginners must learn how to move the stick. This is especially important for passing and receiving. Now that we have been concentrating on puck feel, let's talk about stick movement. Here are basic stick-movement considerations to keep in mind while teaching these stick concepts.

> Let the wrists do the work.
> Move the hands with the puck.
> Shoulders should be square to the puck path.
> Arms and shoulders should be relaxed.
> Elbows should be out from the side.
> Keep the blade at right angle to the puck path.
> Turn the toe of the blade in for wide dribbles on each side.

After practicing the drills in books 1 and 2, most of this will become automatic. However, it will take much practice to provide hand, wrist, and forearm strength for good stick control.

Solution

The stick-skill concepts consist of stick manipulation, stick length and reach, and stick blade control. The concepts and drill descriptions follow:

Stick Drill Description

Manipulate—Concept 27

Drill 250E: Dribble diagonal OI HC

The concept of stick manipulation is to maneuver the hockey stick efficiently. Start by standing stationary and dribble the puck diagonally or forty-five degrees on the forehand across in front. Then try doing it diagonal the other way on the backhand side of the stick. Concentrate on arms and shoulder movement, relax the grip, and change grip on lower hand to a finger grip with only thumb and index finger. Continue the drill while skating.

Drill 251E: Dribble square OI HC

Standing stationary move the puck in a square on the ice with the stick blade, move the hands and arms with the puck, then do it while skating.

Drill 252M: Dribble circle OI HC

Standing stationary move the puck in a circle on the ice with the stick blade. Form a half circle, then a full circle with the puck. Move hands and arms with the puck. Make a circle clockwise, then counterclockwise. Continue while skating.

Drill 253M: Dribble back and forth OI HC F

Start while standing stationary, then while skating, move the puck far in front of the skates, straight out in front as far as you can reach, then bring the puck back as close as possible to the toes of the skates. This is very difficult, so try the lower hand with a finger grip when the puck is close in to the body and skates. You can release lower hand at the far end in order to reach as far as you can in front. Continue the drill while skating.

Drill 254M: Run on spot and dribble combo OI F

Run on the spot lifting knees high while dribbling the puck diagonally, then practice dribbling square, and circles as well as, then back and forth (similar to drills 250-253) while still running on the spot. Concentrate on letting the wrists and fingers do the work. Go slow, then fast on the whistle. Then superfast on the next whistle. Then slow again on the next whistle. Effectively you run in three speeds or gears while dribbling and moving the puck in three gears as well.

Drill 255A: Run on spot and dribble eyes closed OI F

This is the ultimate puck-feel drill. While standing stationary, run on the spot with the knees high, while dribbling the puck with eyes closed—concentrate on letting the wrists and fingers do the work. Who can do it the longest without losing the puck? Practice doing it slow, fast, and superfast on the whistle.

Drill 256U: Dribble slalom HC F

Skate slalom drill 70 while dribbling the puck narrow. Remember, most weight is on the heels for the slalom. Skate the slalom in three gears and dribble in three gears as well—slow, fast, and superfast.

Stick Length—Concept 28

Drill 257E: Dribble figure 8 two-handed (moving) HC F

The stick length concept involves getting a better feel for the length of the stick shaft. Start by dribbling the puck while skating crossovers in a figure 8. Start slow then skate fast, then super fast on the whistle.

Drill 258E: Dribble around double pylons F&B

Similar to drill 236 (dribble through single pylons), but instead dribble around a double row of pylons skating with crossovers. The double pylons force kids to dribble the puck wider and forces wider crossovers around the pylons.

This is one of the more important drills in book 2 especially when at a super fast speed with knees high. Start simply by dribbling between double rows of pylons while doing crossovers. Start slowly, then on the whistle move both feet and puck fast, then on the next whistle go superfast (as fast as you can dribble and as fast as you can make short crossovers). Then slow again on the next whistle. Superfast requires much energy, so superfast should last for only a few seconds. This should be practiced backward at all three speeds as well.

Drill 259M: Dribble figure 8 one-handed moving (upper hand) OI HC

Dribble the puck while skating crossovers in a figure 8 with only the upper hand on the stick. This can be done off-ice while running or walking in a figure 8.

Drill 260M: Figure 8 with sharp turns around two pylons
HC P F

Using two pylons, skate a figure 8, making sharp turns around each pylon. No crossovers. Weight on the heels. Lift the toes up to enforce the weight on the heels. Practice with one hand only on the stick, then the other hand. Then use both hands on the stick but drop the lower hand on the stick for better control of the puck as you make the sharp turns. Kids need more speed to make very sharp turns. Start slow then fast then super fast on the whistle.

Drill 261M: Figure 8 transition (facing same way) HC

Dribble while skating in a figure 8, always facing the same direction. You face one direction and skate forward crossovers starting the figure 8, then reverse your direction (pivot) and skate backward crossovers to complete the figure 8, always facing the same direction while continuing to dribble the puck.

Drill 262M: Attacking the triangle (two triangles) OI HC P S

Triangle theory—there are two basic triangles to deal with.

Primary triangle—stick shaft, body (legs), and ice surface.

Secondary triangle—(triangle flat on the ice) left skate, the stick blade, and the right skate. Players must be made aware of both primary and secondary triangles for puck control and passing later.

Attacking the triangle drill—stickhandle through the tripod triangle, with three options: stickhandle through the primary triangle of the tripod on the forehand then on the backhand,. This can be done off-ice with a tripod on any hard surface.

Drill 263M: Dribble stick lift partner on knees OI HC

One player is stationary on the knees holding the stick stationary on the ice, thus making a primary triangle with his stick and body. A second stationary player facing him or her while standing dribbles through the secondary triangle (on the ice) by lifting his or her stick over the primary triangle. After they are comfortable doing it, then the first stationary player who is still on the knees, and up to this point holding the stick stationary, this first player now starts moving the stick back and forth slowly to the left and right, thus making it more difficult to dribble over the primary triangle. They both take turns each getting an opportunity to dribble by lifting their stick over the triangle. This can be done off-ice on a hard surface.

Drill 264M: Dribble stick lift partner standing OI HC

Similar to the previous drill 263 but instead of being on the knees, the first stationary player is standing and holding his stick stationary with stick blade flat on the ice, making a primary triangle with his stick and body. The second player who is facing him or her is also standing while facing each other, then dribbles by lifting the stick over the primary triangle. After they are comfortable doing it, the first player who is still standing and holding the stick stationary moves the stick back and forth to the left and right, making it more difficult to dribble through the triangle. Both take turns each getting an opportunity to dribble over the primary triangle. This can be done off-ice on a hard surface.

Dribble 265A Dribble around body in triangle stationary OI HC

Standing stationary, move the puck in a triangle around the body. Move the puck with only three stickhandling moves around the body in a triangle. This is difficult but can be done with practice. This can be done off-ice on a hard surface.

Drill 266A: Dribble around body in triangle moving. OI HC

Similar to the previous drill 265 but dribble while skating. Move the puck in a triangle around the body while skating. Move the puck with only three stickhandling moves around the body. This can be done off-ice while walking on any hard surface.

Drill 267A: Dribble around body side to side HC

While standing stationary, move the puck around behind the body from one side to the other. Bring the puck behind the outside and move the puck with only two moves behind from one side to the other side, then back to the front. Do it in both directions. Try doing it moving.

Drill 268A: Dribble body opposite OI HC

Dribble narrow while leaning the body to the opposite side of where the puck is being dribbled. Dribble on the left side leaning the body right, then dribble on the right side leaning left. This can be done off-ice on a hard surface.

Drill 269A: Dribble MFB—middle, front, backhand through single line of pucks HC

Make a straight line or single row of pucks and dribble through them without touching them. First, skate over the top of the line of pucks while dribbling through the row of pucks, then skate on the forehand side of the pucks dribbling through the row of pucks. Then skate on the backhand side of the pucks while dribbling through the row of pucks. This requires a great deal of dexterity with the stick shaft, so it will take a good deal of practice to achieve this completely. Don't expect too much success at first, but keep coming back to this drill. Kids will eventually figure out how to do it.

Drill 270A: Dribble through legs from back

Reach to one side and with the body leaning opposite, dribble through legs from the back to front through the legs by reaching from behind the body. In other words, reach behind and bring the puck up to the front through the legs. Practice from both sides.

Drill 271A: Dribble around body stationary (five zones) OI HC

Dribble short narrow dribbles in each zone—front, forehand, backhand, rear, and skate zones—while standing stationary. This can be started with shadow dribbling (no pucks). Skates remain in the same position, pointed to the front and the eyes remain looking up and towards the front. Moving the puck clockwise, dribble in each zone, but keep the puck moving with narrow dribbles while completely moving the puck around the body. The skate zone is dribbling from both sides of the stick blade back to the inside of the skate blade and back to the stick blade. When the puck is in the rear zone, leave the puck behind momentarily and swing the stick all the way back around the front, then back around the other side and reach back to the rear zone again. Practice this clockwise and counterclockwise. This can be done off-ice on any hard surface.

Drill 272U: Dribble around body moving (five zones) HC

Similar to drill 271 but do it while skating. Dribble short or narrow dribbles in each zone—front, forehand, backhand, rear, and skate zones—while skating. This can be started with shadow dribbling. Keep facing the front, and dribble in each of the five zones. The backhand zone is difficult—therefore, the weak zone—and needs lots of practice.

The skate zone is dribbling from both sides of the stick blade back to the inside of the skate blade. Rear zone—while holding the stick forehand stretch all the way around behind and dribble. This is needed later for advanced moves.

Stick Reach—Concept 29

Drill 273E: Dribble figure 8 stick blade flat stationary on ice
OI P HC

The stick-reach concept is to get used to the full reach capability of the stick. Start by placing two obstacles, one in front of each other, vertically in front, one foot apart, and within reach of the player's stick blade. Then while keeping the stick blade flat on the ice, form a figure 8 on the ice with the stick blade by moving the blade around the two obstacles in a figure 8. Use shadow dribbling first, then do it with the puck by moving the puck in a figure 8. Practice with upper hand only, then lower hand only, and finally with both hands on the stick. The two obstacles could be pucks, pylons, the player's gloves, etc. This drill will reinforce the grip. Concentrate on letting the wrists do the work, and let the grip on the lower hand slide up and down as needed. Try griping the stick with the thumb and index finger only, for a better feel and more finesse. Make the figure 8 on the ice clockwise and counterclockwise.

Drill 274E: Puck carry two hand continuous OI HC F&B

This drill is opposite to dribbling, now you keep the puck on the stick blade all the time instead of dribbling. Skate across the rink (or the length of rink) and carry the puck all the way to the other end with both hands on the stick. However, do it with the puck continuously (continuously touching the stick blade) on the inside to the stick blade (backhand side) only. After that carry the puck on the outside of the stick blade (forehand side) only. Practice it skating backward.

Drill 275M: Puck carry one hand upper continuous OI F&B HC

Similar to drill 274 but now hold the stick with one hand, the upper hand only. Skate across the rink or end to end (length of the rink) and carry the puck all the way to the other end with only the upper hand on the stick. Hold the puck continuously (continuously touching the stick blade) on the inside of the stick blade (backhand side). After that carry the puck all the way on the outside of the stick blade (forehand side), again with the upper hand only. Practice it skating backward.

Drill 276M: Puck carry breakaway one hand upper combo OI HC

Similar to drill 275 except now you bump the puck ahead (like on a breakaway) instead of carrying the puck continuously on the stick blade. Skate end to end or across the rink and carry puck on inside of the stick blade, for part of the way, then bump the puck ahead and carry the puck on the outside of stick blade for part of the way with the upper hand on the stick only. This is a combination of alternating the use the inside and outside of the stick blade. Practice by pushing or bumping the puck ahead a short ways at a time (alternating on the inside and then the outside of the stick blade). Pump arms forward with one hand on the stick, moving the stick with an arm pump

Drill 277M: Puck carry breakaway two hand combo S

Similar to drill 276 you bump the puck ahead but now instead you keep both hands on the stick. While skating fast, bump the puck ahead on the inside and outside of stick blade as if on a breakaway. This is a combination of alternating the use the inside and outside of the stick blade. Start in a low body profile and go into full stride as soon as possible. Pump arms forward with two hands on the stick moving stick shaft through a loose grip of the lower hand.

Drill 278A: Forward wave with crossovers HC F

Skate crossovers forward (to the left and right) while dribbling the puck. Follow the instructor, who waves a stick to the left and right, while you skate crossovers to the left and right following the instructors wave of his/her stick. When the instructor drops stick blade on the ice (thus pointing towards one corner), the skater pivots and breaks for that corner, skating forward. Practice three speeds by going fast on the whistle.

Drill 279U: Hound dog S

Similar to breakaway drills 276 and 277, but now do it with a back checker. Skate end to end (length of rink) or across the rink using the breakaway drill (bumping the puck ahead on the inside and outside of stick blade) with one checker chasing.

Stick Blade—Concept 30

Drill 280E: Stick blade pressure OI

The stick-blade concept involves using all the parts of the stick blade. Start by developing more strength in the arms and wrists. Arrange two players who both shoot left on one side of the rink and two players who shoot right on the other side of the rink facing each other across the rink (i.e., start standing near the boards and skate along the blue line). The idea is for one player to skate across the ice carrying a puck toward the other player who is standing stationary on the other side of the rink. As the skater with the puck approaches the stationary skater by moving the puck directly into the stationary player's stick blade, so both stick blades should meet square, blade to blade. Both players should put as much pressure as possible on the blade of the stick to obtain possession of the puck. The player with the most pressure will end up with the puck. The player who is standing stationary is essentially a checker and will check by taking the puck away by simply stopping the moving player's stick blade and puck with the pressure of his stick blade.

Then the stationary player takes the puck and does the same thing, carrying the puck in the other direction across to the other side of the rink, to another stationary player who is waiting at the other side of the rink. This is the beginning of game situations where you start putting body weight into the stick blade.

Drill 281E: Stick toe-heel OI HC

While skating, move the puck ahead on the forehand, and catch the puck with the toe of the stick blade and bring it backward toward the skates, then catch it with the heel of the stick—that is, from toe to heel. Turn the stick a full 180 degrees to catch the puck with the toe of the stick. Practice this standing stationary, then while skating as well.

Drill 282E: Stick toe dribble HC

Using both sides of the toe of the stick blade, dribble the puck side to side and from front to back, back and forth using the toe of the stick only.

Drill 283M: Stick toe drag stationary HC

Toe drag is when you reach out with the puck on the stick then draw the puck back. Reach out in front and quickly draw the puck back as far as you can with the toe of the stick blade and receive it with the middle of the blade or the heel of the stick. This is basically faking the puck outward with the stick blade and the puck, then a quick draw back away from the opponent.

The toe drag can be done in three ways:

1. Vertical—reach out in front than drag the puck back with the toe of the stick back as far away from the opponent as possible.
2. Horizontal—fake a horizontal forehand pass, then drag the puck back laterally back across in front and close to the skates. The backhand is done the same way but is much more difficult.
3. Combo (favorite)—make both moves out front vertically then laterally.

Drill 284M: Dribble toe drag side moving HC

Dribble the puck with a toe drag from the toe to the middle or heel of the stick blade on forehand side while skating.

Drill 285A: Dribble toe drag side and front moving HC

Dribble the puck with a toe drag from toe to the middle of the blade or heel of the stick from the side to the front while skating.

Drill 286A: Dribble toe drag backhand moving S

Dribble the puck with a toe drag, toe to heel or middle of the stick blade from backhand side across to the front while skating.

Drill 287U: Toe drag combo tripod S

Dribble the puck with a toe drag, toe to the middle or the heel of the stick blade. Do a toe drag three ways through or around the tripod, forehand (front), side to side, and backhand.

5—Puck-Control Balance Concepts

Problem

All aspects of skating require balance. Balance involves everything in hockey and is even more important for puck control. Even though we have been doing balances since drill 1, we need to work on balance specifically needed when there is a puck on the stick. The problem is we need more balance during puck movement and control.

Analysis

Up to this point, all the drills involve balance of one type or other. You can see as we progress further that the drills become more difficult. This is the reason concepts in *The Hockey Method* are arranged in a specific order. When all drills are completed successfully, beginners should be progressing toward the end of the beginner stage. Each skill concept has been used to build the next concept. Now beginners are ready to continue the progression to more complex puck-control balance drills.

Solution

The puck-control balance concept is actually balance using the body weight more where more agility is required. Balance concept drill descriptions follow:

Puck-Control Balance Drill Description

Puck-Control Balance—Concept 31

Drill 288E: Stationary fakes OI

The puck-control balance concept starts with an introduction to fakes. While dribbling the puck in a stationary position, practice making a fake motion in one direction, then quickly move the puck in the opposite direction. In a stationary position, practice making dekes or fakes in several ways:

- Hands
- Head
- Shoulder
- Stick

Fake with the hands by simply dropping the hands a couple of inches, without touching the puck with the stick blade. Then shoot or pass.

Head fake is to quickly move the head down or to one side without moving the puck.

Shoulder fake is to drop the shoulder without touching the puck, then shoot or pass.

Stick fake is to move the stick blade quickly in one direction then back to the original position without touching the puck, then make a quick pass or shot.

Practice making fakes (or dekes) in all three stickhandling zones (forehand, front, backhand) while in a stationary position. This can be done off-ice on any hard surface.

Drill 289M: Dekes while skating—repeat drills

When you think a beginner is ready and is seems appropriate, go back and repeat as many drills as possible in book 2 testing all of the various stationary fakes (or dekes) in drill 288 while moving (skating).

Drill 290A: Protected dribbling with shoulder turn

In order to keep the puck away from an opponent during a game, you need to dribble the puck by turning the shoulder, keeping the body between the puck and the checker. Turn the body completely around 360 degrees if necessary in order to keep the puck away from a checker. Practice this anywhere on the ice. It can also be done off-ice on a floor. The instructor or another player can be the checker.

Drill 291A: 360 spin with puck on stick with sharp turns
HC F&B

Similar to drill 181 (spin pivot forward and backward) but now spin 360 degrees with a puck on the stick by making only sharp turns instead of pivoting. Make a 360 degree turn while skating forward by making a sharp turn and short crossovers. Practice stationary first, make 360 degrees turns to the left and after that to the right. Then practice doing it while keeping the puck on the stick. Some refer to this as the Savard turn or move.

Drill 292A: Circle body keep-away P S

This is a tandem drill with two players going around a circle. One player skates around the circle and keeps the puck outside the circle and away from the other player using his body to protect the puck. The other player, the checker, stays inside the circle and tries to take the puck away from the puck carrier skating around inside on the circle.

Drill 293U: Puck straddle HC

Arrange two lines or rows of pucks then carry a puck by dribbling in and out. Start by skating with the body over the top or middle of the double row of pucks and dribble across and outside both sides of the two rows of pucks. Do not touch the pucks. After you can do this, repeat but this time skate outside the rows of pucks and dribble on the forehand. Then repeat again skating on the other side of the rows of pucks but this time dribbling on the backhand. So you are skating firstly, over the top or middle of the rows of pucks, secondly by skating on one side of the rows of pucks and finally you are skating on the other side of the rows of pucks. Of course it doesn't matter whether you hold your stick left or right.

Special Combination drills with the Puck

These are the same two combination drills used in book 1, but now we should be able to do them while keeping a puck on the stick.

Combo 5 (with pucks)

This is a special combination of drills from book 1 to introduce forward stride fundamentals while carrying a puck. This covers as many forward stride fundamentals as possible in the shortest period of time, but now with a puck on the stick. This is preparation for the forward stride. These drills should be done consecutively in this sequence, skating end to end or across the rink. The instructor should monitor and observe the fundamentals of each drill. The skaters must focus on doing each drill correctly. Once kids get to know the sequence of drills, they should be able to do all of them within only two or three minutes.

1. Knee drag toes out (50E)
2. Short steps fast on whistle (13U)
3. Gliding arm pump fast (22E)
4. Full stance long strides with tap (60U)
5. Put it all together doing all of these drills at the time into a forward stride

This sequence of drills can be used periodically as review of the introduction to the forward stride.

Use a different kid to demonstrate and lead each drill. They can become specialists of their specific drill.

Magic 6 (with pucks)

This is another special combination of drills from book 1 to cover the greatest number of agility skating fundamentals within the shortest period of time while carrying the puck. These drills should be done at one end of the rink, across the ice, and around the face-off circles, in this sequence. The instructor should monitor and observe the fundamentals of each drill.

The skaters must focus on doing each drill correctly. Once kids get to know the sequence of drills, they should be able to do all of them within only two or three minutes. In order to reduce boredom, from time to time the first two balances may be replaced with different balances of your choosing.

1. Sit-down balance (113A)
2. Edges forward (68E)
3. Crossovers circles forward (108E)
4. Crossovers circles backward (117U)
5. Two crossovers forward and backward (131A&134U)
6. Sharp turns (88M) two each way (left and right)

This sequence of drills can be used periodically as a quick review of basic agility skating skills.

Use a different kid to demonstrate and lead each of the six drills. They can become specialists for their specific drill.

> **Instructor tip:** Remember, there is no magic list of drills. The approximately three hundred drills listed here have been offered as a base guide. The key is to watch your young skaters carefully and to determine what they are capable (and not capable) of accomplishing. Don't hesitate to be creative and break skills down to their simplest components and start there. Practice the individual movements first, then slowly combine techniques as they develop the overall skill. You may be surprised to find out just how much many youngsters enjoy the graduated approach to learning, progressively getting better as the practice gets a little more complex.

Book 2:
Beginner Puck-Control Drills (Book 2)

Hands Concepts
Grip—Concept 20
200E Stick grip OI
201E Stick length OI

Wrist—Concept 21
202E Wrist roll OI
203M Find the puck OI
204M Balance puck on both sides of stick OI
205U Bounce puck on stick blade OI HC

Puck Repeat—Concept 22
206M Repeat book 1 drills with a puck on the stick.

Eyes Concepts
Dribble—Concept 23
207E Puck feel (eyes off the puck) OI
208E Dribble narrow (short) stationary OI HC F
209E Dribble wide (long) stationary OI HC F
210E Dribble slow stationary arms extended OI
211E Dribble fast stationary OI F
212M Dribble narrow and wide combo moving HC F
213M Dribble 3 zones stationary OI F
214A Dribble eyes closed stationary OI F
215A Dribble super fast stationary OI F
216A Knob drill (narrow-wide-fast) OI S F
217A Dribble rotation (puck spin) (on a string) HC
218A Shadow dribbling no pucks HC F F&B
219A Long wide stride inside edges dribble narrow S
220U Dribble wide through double rows of pylons while skating HC

Balance—Concept 24
221E Dribble one leg (stationary and moving) OI HC F F&B
222E Dribble one hand (upper) (stationary and moving) OI HC F&B F
223E Dribble one hand (lower) (stationary and moving) OI HC F&B F
224M Dribble hands together (stationary and moving) OI HC F&B F
225M Dribble hands wide (stationary and moving) OI HC F&B F
226U Dribble one leg 3 zones while moving (stationary and moving) F&B HC F

Puck Concepts
Soft Hands—Concept 25
227E Switch hands OI HC
228M Dribble inside edge control one leg OI
229M Dribble thru legs stationary OI HC
230M Dribble through the legs moving
231A Puck Scoops stationary and moving HC
232A Pick up puck and stick off the ice with glove OI
233A Control stick flat on ice OI
234A Dribble silent OI F
235U Dribble puck outside on backhand side, and back between skates (then opposite) HC

Agility—Concept 26
236E Dribble through single pylons P HC F F&B
237M Dribble 2 pucks F&B HC When stationary dribble one puck at a time
238M 1 on 1 in corner
239M 1 on 1 in the corner teams
240M 2 on 1 in corner
241M 2 on 1 in corner & chase
242A Dribble 3 pucks
243A 3 man keep away in front to net
244A Russian dribble
245A Dribble two pucks feet HC
246A Heel-to-heel half circle each side S
247A Heel-to-heel half circle 1 on 1 P S
248A Puck catch S
249U Dribble one puck with stick and feet while moving

Stick Concepts
Manipulate—Concept 27
250E Dribble diagonal OI HC
251E Dribble square OI HC
252M Dribble circle OI F
253M Dribble back and forth OI HC F
254M Run on spot and dribble combo OI F
255A Run on spot and dribble eyes closed OI
256U Dribble Slalom HC F

Stick Length—Concept 28
257E Dribble figure 8 two handed (moving) HC F
258E Dribble around two parallel pylons F&B
259M Dribble figure 8 one handed moving (upper hand) OI HC
260M Figure 8 with sharp turns around 2 pylons HC P F
261M Figure 8 transition (facing the same way) HC P
262M Attacking the triangle—2 triangles OI HC P S
263M Dribble stick lift partner on knees (stationary stick) OI HC
264M Dribble stick lift partner standing—both dribble, standing player lift stick over OI HC
265A Dribble around body in triangle stationary OI HC
266A Dribble around body in triangle moving OI HC
267A Dribble round body side to side HC
268A Dribble body opposite—body leans to opposite side of puck OI HC
269A Dribble MFB—middle front backhand thru line of pucks HC
270A Dribble thru legs from back
271A Dribble around body stationary (5 zones) OI HC
272U Dribble around body moving (5 zones) HC

Stick Reach—Concept 29
273E Dribble Figure 8 stick blade flat stationary on the ice OI P HC
274E Puck carry two hand continuous OI HC F&B
275M Puck carry one hand upper continuous OI F&B HC
276M Puck carry breakaway one hand upper combo OI HC
277M Puck carry breakaway two hand combo S
278A Forward wave with crossovers HC F
279U Hound dog—one checker chases drill S

Stick Blade—Concept 30
280E Stick blade pressure OI
281E Stick toe-heel—move the puck ahead with the toe catch it with the heel HC
282E Toe dribble—toe of blade only HC
283M Toe drag stationary HC
284M Dribble toe drag side (forehand out) moving HC
285A Dribble toe drag side & front moving HC
286A Dribble toe drag backhand moving S
287U Toe drag Combo—tripod S

Puck-Control Balance Concepts
Puck Control—Concept 31
288E Stationary Fakes—Hands, stick, head, shoulder OI
289M Dekes (Repeat most drills in book 2 with dekes when appropriate)
290A Protected dribbling with shoulder turn
291A 360 spin with puck on stick and sharp turns (in circle) HC F&B
292A Circle body keep away P S
293U Puck straddle (two line of pucks and go in and out) HC

Special Combination Drills
Combo 5
Combo 5 (50E toe drag, 13U short fast steps, 22E fast arm pump, 60U long stride, all together stride) P
Magic 6
Magic 6—113A sit down balance, 68E edges, 108E circles forward, 117U circles backward, 134U 2 crossovers fwd & bkwd, 88M sharp turns

Conclusion

Basic skating, passing and shooting is the foundation of hockey development. However, since every hockey player was a beginner once, beginner hockey is the footing underneath supporting this foundation. Today's beginners are tomorrow's hockey players. AA, AAA, Junior A, College and NHL players are a direct reflection of the level of skills initially learnt at the very beginning. The final level of the skills achieved by all players, is a direct result of how strong this foundation and the footing underneath it, is built. The higher the level of the skills initially developed, the stronger the final skills will be. The weaker this foundation is, the weaker the ultimate skill level will be.

North American players are behind Europeans in hockey skills today because this foundation is weak, and the footing underneath (beginner hockey) is completely overlooked. The 31 concepts (levels) in book 1 and book 2, should have been completed by the time a player reaches the atom age (9 years old). Instead, most pee wee and bantams can't do them. Even some midget players can't do them. This is because winning and team skills are introduced too early, consequently, these levels of basic skills are sacrificed for more complex team drills that kids are not prepared for. Proof is kids can't do most drills at practices today. There needs to be a better *transition* from the first time a player puts on a pair of skates to when he/she is ready to play that first hockey game. The objective of this book is to fill in this missing gap in beginner hockey development, and build a more solid foundation with this transition phase for beginners.

The Hockey Method is a methodology to teach anyone how to skate and play hockey, starting at the beginner level and progressing on to an elite skill level. This is an analytical approach to hockey skill development. It provides a progressive path of simple drills to follow, identifies the fundamental problems, analyzes them, then provides solutions in the form of skill concepts and drills. It prepares kids early by giving them the confidence needed to successfully complete difficult hockey team drills later. *The Hockey Method* is a progressive path of drills that can be followed easily by parents and other instructors. It may be considered an instructor aid or guide. In fact it is a practice plan for beginners.

There is a virtual line between beginner skating and regular skating. It is an imaginary line intertwined somewhere within the elementary (E) drills, medium (M) drills, and advanced (A) drills described in volume 1. Below that line is the *transition phase* from a first-time skater to a skater ready for team play. Unfortunately, to make the problem even more complicated, this virtual line is different for each individual. Consequently, grading and recording skills is even more critical for beginners. The problem is, many of these elementary concepts are being missed in hockey development today because team play is implemented too soon. Often these skills are not only overlooked, but many become forgotten and are not taught in hockey programs at all. It all starts with beginner development. This book ensures basic skills are not forgotten and are taught as early as possible.

Once the beginner concepts (31 levels) and drills in book 1 and book 2 have been completed, the beginner is no longer a beginner. At that point he or she will be well prepared to move forward and learn to fully enjoy the great game of hockey. Kids will be able to face complex drills involving skating, passing, shooting, and team systems with confidence. Coaches will be supported by records of players' grades and, therefore, will have confidence that their players are ready to move right into team play. Team drills will no longer be too difficult for kids to achieve. They will be well prepared to continue on to the next stage of learning how to play the great game of hockey. Basic skating, passing and shooting is covered in the next volume, *The Hockey Method* volume 2.

Epilogue

Body Contact

Body Contact for Kids

A Rick Hanson Institute report in 2013 indicates that "7% of hockey parents surveyed believe that their child has the potential to play professional hockey . . . One out of 3,000 kids makes it."

One in 3,000 is only 0.03 percent. That means only (.03% divided by 7%) about 4% of the parents who believed their kids could play professional were right. Too many parents believe their kids have a chance to make the big money in hockey. Unfortunately, sometimes parents sacrifice their kids' well-being for that slim chance to making it big time. When does it make sense for kids to take the risk of playing body contact and risk serious injury?

How can we reduce the risk of concussions, and when should body contact take place in minor hockey? The great game of hockey is the fastest body-contact team sport in the world. Most blue-blooded Canadian hockey players of all ages enjoy using the body during the game. In fact, they love it. Fans enjoy it even more. Body contact can be fun, but there is a correct way and a wrong way to use the body in hockey. The proper way to hit can be taught. It is covered under checking in book 3. Body contact means checking an opponent with your body while moving aggressively against the opponent's body—that is, body against body, not stick against body.

Common sense tells us there must be some limit to hitting in hockey. It doesn't mean any part of your body is allowed to hit any part of the opponent's body. Common sense should tell you to never hit any vulnerable part of the body, like the knee, the neck, the head, or slew-footing the skates from behind. The game should allow you to make body contact against less vulnerable parts of the body, like the shoulders and hips, and then only from a low body profile, not jumping up in the air and hitting high. It all comes down to self-discipline, some may call it hockey IQ, others think of it simply as maturity.

With hockey being a fast-moving sport, there always have been rules to prevent injury. Those rules are common-sense rules developed over many years. The rules have changed very little over time. The game has changed; it is faster, the players are bigger, and they possess more skills. Today the rules are somewhat lagged behind the changes in the game. However, the rules alone are not the major reason for the increase in the number of concussions. One problem is that current rules are not enforced by referees.

In order to put a kid's well-being on the line, there must be some justification to do it, in the first place. When you put your body on the line for potential financial benefit, hockey changes from a sport to a business. So body contact actually turns hockey into a business. Even at the midget or junior A level, with all the travel involved, in effect it is really a business. When should kids use body contact? The answer is, when body contact is safe enough and worth the risk of injury, for kids to do so.

When kids start out as beginners and don't know how to stop, they use body contact all the time by accidently running into each other on the ice. When should kids start being allowed to purposely use body contact as part of the game? When should kids start doing what most of them love doing, using the body to stop an opponent on the ice? This is a decision for both parents and minor hockey programs to decide. However, keep in mind, even when body contact is not allowed, there is going to be a certain amount of body contact anyway. Some body contact happens all the time, accidently. So when you say body contact is not allowed, you mean body contact is not allowed to occur on purpose. So in answering this question, one must remember that a certain amount of body contact will happen just by the nature of the game of hockey.

There is enough accidental body contact in the game for kids, especially beginners, without allowing more body contact on purpose. I believe it makes sense to start allowing proper body contact (body contact that is taught) after the peewee age—that is, starting at the bantam age of thirteen. The difference in the size of kids up to the age of twelve, is usually too great, and it makes no sense to allow body contact before that.

Hit-Line Proposal

To reduce concussions, we must enforce current and new rules, redesign hockey equipment, and learn how to keep the head up at an early age. However, we also need to become proactive and more innovative. We should "blue sky" as to what else we can do to reduce concussions while improving the game of hockey.

Here is an example of a blue-sky proposal. To my knowledge this proposal has not been tried; therefore, it has not been tested or proven in ice hockey. Recently I heard where this has been used in ball hockey. Although there is no proven merit for it at this time, it is still something to consider. My proposal, similar to the blue and the red lines painted on the rink, is to add a third line completely around the rink. Paint a hit line on the ice, say, about six feet from the boards all around the rink. At a certain age, allow body contact in the middle of the rink within this so-called hit line, thus in the middle of the ice. Do not allow any body contact outside the hit line.

This hit line could be moved in and out for different age groups. If the hit line is not painted on the ice, then a virtual line (defined by the rule book) could be considered by referees, to use as a reference, to help call body contact infractions. Several scenarios could be tested. No body contact anywhere on the ice for novice and atoms, as is done now in most jurisdictions. Then implement an eight-foot hit line from the boards for peewee, six-foot hit line from the boards for bantam, four-foot hit line from the boards for midgets, and so on. Paint one hit line, say, six feet from the boards, then the referee can use it as a reference line for body contact calls by, say, one or two feet on each side of the hit line for the younger and older players as appropriate.

This hit line could be tested during exhibition games as a trial. What would happen if there was a one-foot hit line from the boards for junior hockey? I don't know. This would mean defenders would have to be in front of the player being checked along the boards before making a hit to the body. No diagonal hit directly into the boards would be allowed. In junior hockey, would it be terrible for a puck carrier to find a defender standing waiting along the boards blocking an allowed one-foot path along the boards? What would the offensive player do? How about making a fake to the boards, then going inside? Would this open up the game to too much offense? I don't think so. Perhaps someday this could be tested in minor hockey during early season exhibition games.

Of course, as I said, this hit line is just blue skying. While this hit line idea may not make sense, we do need to be creative with more experimentation in order to decrease concussions in the game our kids love to play. This suggestion may be out of this world; however, new innovative ideas like this should be tested. I am sure the game of hockey will come up with many more innovative ideas or concepts like this to further reduce concussions and to help keep our kids safe while playing this fun body-contact sport.

Troubleshooting Skill Problems

Skill Problem Solving—Troubleshooting and Correcting Skill Problems

Once a problem has been identified, *The Hockey Method* can be used as a tool to troubleshoot hockey skill problems. When a player can't complete a drill correctly, what do you do? How do you analyze and identify or define the reason for the problem? This is where *The Hockey Method* works well because it has drilled the concepts down into simple, identifiable elementary parts that make up most complex drills. It is designed to assist you in identifying the problem, then provides drills to correct the problem. In other words, this is a method of troubleshooting hockey skill problems. *The Hockey Method* is a hockey problem-solving tool, which will assist the coach solve skill problems. A software version for this coaching aid will be available on this book's website soon. Here are three examples of advanced skills or drills (not beginner drills) that players often can't do properly. Usually it is because they haven't been properly prepared. An analysis and troubleshooting method is explained for these three examples. There are an unlimited number of such examples in the game of hockey.

During the course of the season, once you identified a skill problem, you must then solve the problem. Remember, mistakes become habits you don't want and they are very difficult to correct later. After a mistake has become a bad habit, sometimes it can never be corrected. Some NHL players are hindered with bad habits acquired at a young age. An example is a bad stride that may stay with a skater for the rest of his or her life. Some professional players still don't take a full stride. They can't skate as fast they could. Some NHL'ers can't make a backhand pass—they need to switch to their forehand.

When a player has a problem completing a drill correctly, there is a reason for it. He or she is missing some basic concept of the mechanical movement, manipulation, or balance needed. It is up to the coach to identify the problem and to instruct the player how to correct the problem. Don't ignore it and then continue repeating the mistake every time you practice doing the same drill.

A good coach must be able to recognize the problem and identify what part of the skill is preventing the player from completing it correctly. Then stop the drill. Analyze and correct the mistakes immediately. If you can't stop immediately, then do so as soon as possible. If you can't correct the problem immediately during the practice, make a list of the problems to work on for the next practice. This is why practice plans are made. Design drills (from this book or create your own drills) to correct the problem and add them to your next practice plan.

This is where good assistant coaches could be important. Instead of standing around with nothing to do, assistant coaches should take the players with problems aside and show them how to correct their problems, one-on-one. When a player can't do a drill properly, it doesn't mean the drill is bad or the player doesn't have the ability; it just means the player can't do some small basic part or fundamental of the drill or skill. When the player follows the drill progression listed in this book and successfully completes all the drills in sequence, he or she will be well prepared to attempt any regular hockey drill, including agility, forward, and backward skating while carrying the puck.

The examples of *The Hockey Method* for troubleshooting skill problems are the following:

>Example 1—Crossovers
>>Problem/analysis/solution
>
>Example 2—Stopping
>>Problem/analysis/solution
>
>Example 3—Weak Stride
>>Problem/analysis/solution

Example 1—Crossovers

Problem—Crossovers (Agility skating problem—book 3)

When players are directed to form a line and each player takes a turn skating crossovers around the face-off circle, often several skaters can't do it. Some fall down trying. If this is the case, there is obviously a problem. This is not as simple as it may seem. First, identify the problem. When a beginner cannot complete this crossover circle drill properly, stop the drill and solve the problem immediately or at least move to a different drill and come back and resolve the problem as soon as possible. Don't continue to practice drills being done improperly. The coach should ask, Why is this drill being done incorrectly? Is the player lifting his knees high enough to cross over? Can he or she bend knees high enough? Is there a lack of balance? Are the skates too small or too big? Does the skater's equipment impede movement? There may be numerous reasons causing the player to struggle, in fact, usually there are multiple reasons for failure of difficult drills. Regardless, the problem in this case is that the player can't do crossovers around a circle properly.

Analysis—Crossovers

Analyze the crossover weaknesses or mistakes. How do you analyze the mistake? It's not simply that he can't cross over. There are many parts to this skill as you skate around a circle crossing your feet over and over. You must break the drill down into numerous parts. Ask the question, what part of the drill can he or she not complete? Using the list of drills in book 1 as a reference, you must decide. Is it balance, knee movement, actual leg crossover? Is the circle too big for short legs? You will probably find that the taller kids can cross over better. This is a clue! Probably this means the kids who are smaller may possess legs too short for the size of the circle you are using. In this case, make a smaller circle. You must be decisive and determine what the basic problem is. Once you decide what is not done properly, then you need to come up with a solution.

Solution—Crossovers

Through your analysis of the mechanics involved, you should have a good idea of which basic parts of the drill are not being done properly. The question becomes, what is the solution? This is where this book comes in. Go through the list of drills in volume 1 for ideas. Books 1 and 2 have approximately three hundred solutions in the form of drills. So the question is, which drill do you use to solve this problem? The three hundred drills are arranged in a progressive order, starting with drill 1. Normally you do drill 1, then 2, then 3 until eventually all the drills are successfully completed. Once you completed volume 1 (book 1, beginner skating, and book 2, beginner puck control), you are ready to start volume 2 (skating, passing, and shooting). Crossovers are part of agility skating in book 3 in volume 2. This is another clue to the problem! The crossover drill is probably too difficult for beginners at this stage. They are not properly prepared for difficult and complex drills.

Although this is a problem covered later in book 3, it is a good example of what happens with skill problem solving later. I will discuss it now. Here is the scenario. First, you stop practicing the failed crossover drill. Then you must teach the player to correct his or her weaknesses or mistakes with smaller parts of the skill. Go back to book 1, starting with drill 1, and review the drill list (back of the book). Check each skill concept to see if he or she can do them properly. If lucky, you will have graded the players previously, then you could look for skill weaknesses in the graded records. Maybe some M or A drills were not mastered with an excellent rating. If there are no grading records, then consider all the drills on the drill list. Pick out the drills you think could be part of what is needed to do crossovers. Decide which basic or elementary drills are specific to or in any way related to that skill. How do you know which ones? Simply try each of the selected drills. If you can't do it, it probably is part of the problem.

For starters and after scanning the drill list in book 1, I would consider all drills involving all concepts. After considering all the drills involving crossovers, I would try drills 10, 11, 36, 68, 104, 106, 107, 112, 123, and 129. You may choose others. They involve concepts walk, jump, edges, knee, knee extension, and lateral. I would make certain the player can master all of these simple drills. You may choose a different combination of drills or decide to design new drills of your own that you feel would help. All of these simple drills make up the smaller parts of the more difficult crossover drill. Make sure each player can to do all of these drills and practice them in the sequence of the drill numbers from 10 up to 129. If you can't demonstrate the drill, just explain the drill clearly, then let one of the better skaters do the demonstrating. Once players, with practice, can successfully complete these suggested drills they should be prepared with the basics required to do crossovers around a circle. Then your job should be done regarding preparation for the circle crossover drill.

Now go back to the crossover drill and see how it works out. If the player can't do it correctly, he/she probably needs further practice and time to master the simpler parts of this complex drill. Or you may need a different set of drills. As mentioned earlier, book 3 covers crossovers under the topic agility skating.

While we are discussing this book 3 drill, I would like to describe how this circle crossover drill is handled in book 3. When I start teaching crossover drills around a circle, I start with a small circle. In fact, I start with the dot on the face-off circle. I begin by asking the beginner to walk around the dot in the middle of the face-off circle with knees high, then I ask them to run on the spot, then turn 360 degrees around, spinning on the dot while lifting their knees high and running on the spot. Then I try to introduce them to running around the dot in a very small circle making very small crossovers with knees higher and higher. After that, make the circle larger and larger while asking them to run faster, lifting their knees while doing crossovers. After a lot of practice, you will be able to utilize the full circle. Again this is covered in book 3.

The conclusion is, many complex drills are too difficult for beginners at first. Do all the basic drills in volume 1 before wasting too much time and effort practicing these more difficult drills, which only cause drill failure. Do not underestimate the ability of the player. All kids have the ability to do this drill well, provided they were prepared one step at a time.

Example 2—Stopping

Another example of skill problem solving is when a coach arranges the players to line across the blue line then asks them to skate and stop on the next line and several fall down. This drill is repeated every practice, and after numerous practices, several players are continuing to fall down when they stop. The coach has been practicing mistakes all this time. Again, as stated in example 1, these mistakes become bad habits and end up to be very difficult to correct later. After the bad habit has been formed, the mistake becomes automatic.

Stopping is not simple for the beginner. When a player cannot do a drill like stopping, there is a reason. When you see eight or nine beginners out of ten falling, stop the drill. Analyze, then correct the mistake as soon as possible. Do not practice the mistakes any longer. Again, the fact that most of the players are falling is a clue! They are not ready to attempt to stop on skates. They must be missing something. Stopping on skates, if you think about it, is a very complex maneuver for a beginner. If the players had followed the progression of book 1 drills, in all likelihood they would have been ready to attempt the complexity of stopping on skates.

Problem—Stopping (Agility skating problem—book 3)

The problem is simple. The player cannot stop without falling on the ice.

Analysis—Stopping

What is involved in stopping? What are the mechanical parts of the human body that involve the stop motion? Here is what you are asking a beginner to do.

1. Start skating.
2. Put your feet together.
3. Bend your knees.
4. Keeping feet together, jump sideways (at ninety degrees) without falling. This is not simple or easy for a beginner.

Solution—Stopping

Through your analysis, you should have a good idea of which basic parts of the drill are not done properly. The question then again becomes, what is the solution? This again is where this book comes in.

As I said in the previous example, approximately three hundred drills are arranged progressively starting with drill 1. Stopping on skates is part of agility skating in book 3. This is a clue to the problem! The stopping drill is too difficult for most beginners at this point. They are not properly prepared and do not have the fundamentals needed to accomplish the difficult stopping drill.

First, stop doing the stopping drill incorrectly. Teach the player to correct his or her weaknesses or mistakes. Go back through volume 1 by reviewing all the drills at the back of the book, starting with drill 1. Consider all the skill concepts, then select the parts or basic skills involving the stopping process. Pick the drills you think would be part of what is needed to do the stopping drill. Decide which drills are specific to stopping. How do you know which ones? If you do not have record of the grades from book 1, then try each appropriate drill once and see which of these drills fail.

After considering all drills, I would try drills 21, 29, 30, 35, 36, 111, 112, and 161. You may choose others. However, as I indicated earlier, there is no magic list of drills. You may choose a different combination of drills from this book, or you may decide to create a new drill of your own. Try all the selected drills that make up parts the stopping drill. Make sure each player can do all of these basic drills by practicing them in the sequence of the drill numbers. Once players can successfully complete these suggested drills, they should be prepared with the basics required for the stopping drill. Then your job should be done regarding preparation for the stopping drill. If this did not work, select a different set of drills and try again.

As mentioned earlier, book 3 later covers stopping on skates. In book 3 the stopping drill would follow these steps that were previously identified in the above analysis part of this topic. To accomplish the difficult skill of stopping, skaters must do these elementary skills in sequence.

1. Take a running start.
2. Put both feet together.
3. Bend both knees.
4. Jump sideways (at ninety degrees) without falling.

Most regular skating drills are too difficult for beginners to complete at first. Go back and do the basics in book 1 and book 2 first, and make sure all the basic drills have been mastered.

Example 3—Weak Stride

This is another example of a typical skating problem covered in book 3. How do you correct a weak forward stride? That is, when a player is skating with a lot of extra effort and energy but is in fact skating slower than he or she should or could be skating. The skater obviously has improper technique with the basic stride. The problem is compounded by a coach who continues to practice the incorrect stride until the mistakes become a habit. This poor skating stride could last for the rest of his or her hockey life. Some NHL players have weaknesses with their stride and still succeed in pro hockey. However, they would be able to skate even faster if they eliminated those weaknesses. So stop the drill as soon as you can and go back to the basics.

Problems—Weak Stride (Forward skating problem—book 3)

After close observation of the player's skating stride, it may be apparent there is more than one problem contributing to this weak skating stride. Depending on the situation, after analysis, you may decide that one or more of these are the problems:

1. There is no midline return (returning the pushing skate back adjacent to the supporting skate under the middle of the torso or body).
2. There is no full push or extension of the leg (not pushing back far enough with toes out).
3. The skates are lifted too far off the ice; consequently, he has all his weight on one skate for too long, resulting in loss of balance, and falls down too often.
4. Not pushing back hard enough into the ice.

Analysis—Weak Stride

Hypothetically, in this case the skater is not getting any power in the skating stride and the skater is falling down far too often. The strides are short and the skates are too far apart. He could straddle a twelve-inch-wide piece of lumber and his skates would never touch the piece of lumber.

Solution—Weak Stride

The forward stride is another topic covered in book 3. However, for the purpose of indicating the importance of these beginner drills, this is how I would solve these specific problems if they became evident during forward skating in book 3. I would go back and select specific basic drills in book 1 that make up part of the forward stride. I would review all the skill concepts involved. You may choose any drill or create a new drill for the specific weakness. You may consider all the drills in book 1 or just the combo 5 drill with its combination of five drills. I would try the following drills depending on the problem:

Problem 1—No midline return. During skate recovery time, you must return the pushing skate all the way back to the middle, adjacent to the supporting skate.
>Drills 58, 59, 157, 158

Problem 2—No full extension by the pushing skate. You must bend and stretch the knee and leg fully.
>Drills 52, 58, 59, 118, 121, 191, 195

Problem 3—Skate recovery is too high off the ice. Essentially keep the skate close to the ice during recovery.
>Drills 59, 60, 70, 88, 93, 157, 196, 199

Problem 4—Not pushing hard enough. Must bend the knee more and push harder.
>Drills 48, 51, 52, 53, 85, 88, 189, 191, 195

If this doesn't work, try a different set of drills. These drills are developed progressively because they build upon each other and progress from the very first muscular movement needed during the skating process. Progression means doing drills in a planned order or sequence, starting with the simplest drill first, then using each drill as blocks to build more difficult and complex skills or drills.

The number of drills in volume 1 may seem overwhelming for beginners, but remember that these drills make up all the basic concepts involved in skating. Most complex drills are made up of some combination of these elementary concepts and simple drills. Volume 1 is an introduction to and is in preparation for the bigger picture—team hockey skills.

Acknowledgments

The Hockey Method grew from my hockey school in the 1970s, de la Salle School of Hockey Basics. I still have the lists and descriptions of the original drills from those years, all in my wife Marie's handwriting. I thank her for all her years of support. I also thank my children who unknowingly were the guinea pigs, the first ones to test these ideas and drills and also my grandchildren, who today are still testing versions of those original drills.

I am grateful to my children—Mitch, Gerald, and Laura—for all their input, many times, over and over. This book could not be written as it is without Mitch's analytical knowledge of hockey, Gerald's documentation structure and technical input, and Laura's teaching advice and ideas. I owe thanks to my grandchildren Julie and Chantal Cohen and Erin and Lucas de la Salle for demonstrating most of the drills in this book.

I would like to express my gratitude to Ian Archibald, Don Byers, Bill Marvin, and Art Young, who spent hours critiquing the first draft of the manuscript.

I also would like to thank the Trafford Copyediting Team at Trafford Publishing.

Bibliography

Drill Sources and References

de la Salle School of Hockey Basics—1975

Howie Meeker's Hockey Basics—Howie Meeker, Prentice-Hall Canada 1973

Hockey Canada Skills Development Program
    DVDs at www.hockeycanada.ca

Outliers—Malcolm Gladwell, Little Brown & Co. 2008

Outliers: The Story of Success, Back Bay Books June 2011 ISBN 0316017922 Malcolm Gladwell

Steve Serdachny Power Skating and Hockey—Elite Hockey Training Camps
    DVDs at www.elitepowerskating.com

The Hockey Handbook—Lloyd Percival, Copp Clark 1960, McClelland & Stewart 1992

The Myth of Ability: Nurturing Mathematical Talent in Every Child Walker 2004, ISBN 0802777074

The Myth of Ability—John Mighton, House of Anansi Press 2003 (Harper Collins Canada)

Appendices

Appendix A
Concept List (31 Levels)

Beginner Skating Concepts (Levels)

    Skate Feel Concepts
        Walk—Concept 1
        Run—Concept 2
        Glide—Concept 3
        Jump—Concept 4
        Rock—Concept 5
    Toe-Heel Concepts
        Toes out—Concept 6
        Toes in—Concept 7
        Edges—Concept 8
        Heel—Concept 9
    Knee Concepts
        Knee bend—Concept 10
        Knee extension—Concept 11
        Lateral—Concept 12
        Drop—Concept 13
        Kick—Concept 14
        Advanced jump—Concept 15
    Balance Concepts
        Agility—Concept 16
        Flexibility—Concept 17
        Pivot—Concept 18
        Power—Concept 19

Beginner Puck-Control Concepts (Levels)

Hands Concepts
    Grip—Concept 20
    Wrist—Concept 21
    Puck repeat—Concept 22
Eyes Concepts
    Dribble—Concept 23
    Balance—Concept 24
Puck Concepts
    Soft hands—Concept 25
    Agility—Concept 26
Stick Concepts
    Manipulate—Concept 27
    Stick length—Concept 28
    Stick reach—Concept 29
    Stick blade—Concept 30
Puck-Control Balance Concepts
    Puck control—Concept 31

Appendix B
Elementary (E) Drill List

Book 1—Beginner Skating
Skate-Feel Concepts
Walk—Concept 1
1E Short steps forward OI P
2E Giant steps forward OI P
3E Down and up (get up off the ice) OI P HC
4E Beginners stance OI HC
5E Walk sideways OI P L&R
6E Walk forward on toes OI P

Run—Concept 2
14E Run on spot slow OI P
15E Run on the spot fast on whistle OI P F
16E Run then spin on the spot OI P L&R

Glide—Concept 3
20E Glide two foot P HC F&B
21E Glide two foot sitting F&B
22E Glide fast arm pump F HC
23E Glide two foot and swerve P F&B
24E Glide two foot sit and swerve P F&B

Jump—Concept 4
29E Jump stationary OI P F
30E Jump lines P F
31E Jump high on boards OI
32E Jump high over blue line/floor OI P
33E Balance one foot stationary OI P HC

Rock—Concept 5
38E Rock on boards on skates OI
39E Rock on boards running OI F

Toe-Heel Concepts
Toes Out—Concept 6
44E Toes out 90° sitting on ice OI
45E Toes out 90° standing on ice OI
46E Toes out 90° moving on ice
47E Toes out against the boards OI
48E Push boards (C-cuts forward) on whistle OI S
49E Carry puck in skates OI P HC
50E Knee drag with toes out HC P

Toes In—Concept 7
61E Toes in sitting and against the boards OI
62E Toes in stationary (on ice) OI
63E Toes in toes out stationary and moving on the ice OI P
64E Toes out toes in semicircle on ice HC
65E Backward C-cuts on the boards (toes in then out)

Edges—Concept 8
68E Edges forward (foot in front) P
69E Edges forward (foot behind) P HC
70E Slalom forward parallel P HC F
71E Push and slide S

Heel—Concept 9
Knee Concepts
Knee Bend—Concept 10
102E Bend knees 90 degrees on the boards OI
103E Balance one skate other knee high OI P
104E Run on spot knees high OI P F
105E Run backward and spin backward OI P
106E Mini crossovers circles P F F&B
107E Crossover stability—circles stick horiz on shoulders with crossunders HC F&B
108E Crossovers circles forward on whistle F P
109E Run across rink on toes then balls of feet knees high OI P F

Knee Extension—Concept 11
118E Knee drag P
119E Three Knee Motion glide (25-45-90) then horiz side to side P F&B
120E Single stick stepovers forward and backward S F&B

Lateral—Concept 12
Drop—Concept 13
135E Drop to one knee while stationary and moving OI P F&B
136E Drop to both knees while moving and continue P F&B
137E Drop to stomach while stationary OI P

Kick—Concept 14
142E Rotate skate in circle in air OI P F
143E Side kicks OI P F
144E Front kicks OI P F

Advanced Jump—Concept 15
Balance Concepts
Agility—Concept 16
154E Touch ups & touch backs OI S F
155E Touch combo OI S
156E Single stepover forward tap S
157E Multitap with other skate (while skating) (toe, side heel) OI P
158E Tap skate with stick (by instructor or another player) OI P
159E Walk and run with stick up OI F F&B
160E Horizontal stick touch toes then shoulder roll F&B OI

Flexibility—Concept 17
166E Automobile (OI stationary)
167E Airplane (OI stationary)
168E Ride on stick (OI stationary)

Pivot—Concept 18
176E Mohawk turn OI P HC

Power—Concept 19
189E Power Outside 8s—stationary power arc 180 around each skate S
190E Gauntlet (skate, stick, shaft, shoulder, combo) P OI
191E Isolation Push—stick horiz behind, multi and alternating leg push S

Book 2—Introduction to Puck Control
Hands Concepts
Grip—Concept 20
200E Stick grip OI
201E Stick length OI

Wrist—Concept 21
202E Wrist roll OI

Puck Repeat—Concept 22
Eyes Concepts
Dribble—Concept 23
207E Puck feel (eyes off the puck) OI
208E Dribble narrow (short) stationary OI HC F
209E Dribble wide (long) stationary OI HC F
210E Dribble slow stationary arms extended OI
211E Dribble fast stationary OI F

Balance—Concept 24
221E Dribble one leg (stationary and moving) OI HC F F&B
222E Dribble one hand (upper) (stationary and moving) OI HC F&B F
223E Dribble one hand (lower) (stationary and moving) OI HC F&B F

Puck Concepts
Soft Hands—Concept 25
227E Switch hands OI HC

Agility—Concept 26
236E Dribble through single pylons P HC F F&B

Stick Concepts
Manipulate—Concept 27
250E Dribble diagonal OI HC
251E Dribble square OI HC

Stick Length—Concept 28
257E Dribble figure 8 two handed (moving) HC
258E Dribble around two parallel pylons F&B

Stick Reach—Concept 29
273E Dribble Figure 8 stick blade flat stationary on the ice OI P HC
274E Puck carry two hand continuous OI HC

Stick Blade—Concept 30
280E Stick blade pressure OI
281E Stick toe heel—move the puck ahead with the toe catch it with the heel OI HC
282E Toe dribble—toe of blade only HC

Puck-Control Balance Concepts
Puck Control—Concept 31
288E Stationary Fakes—Hands, stick, head, shoulder OI

Appendix C

Medium (M) Drill List

Book 1—Beginner Skating
Skate-Feel Concepts
Walk—Concept 1
7M Walk forward on heels OI P
8M Walk backward on toes OI P
9M Walk skates loose OI
10M Lateral one side step then stop on whistle OI P L&R
11M Lateral side steps fast on whistle across blue line OI P F L&R

Run—Concept 2
17M Run on toes forward across the ice OI P F
18M Run lateral side steps knees high fast on whistle across blue line OI P F L&R

Glide—Concept 3
25M Glide one foot forward P HC
26M Glide one foot forward with supporting knee bend P HC
27M Glide toe on puck P HC

Jump—Concept 4
34M Hop one foot stationary OI P HC F
35M Jump One Foot OI P HC F&B

Rock—Concept 5
40M Rock stationary on skate blade one foot OI P
41M Rock stationary on skate blades two feet OI P F

Toe-Heel Concepts
Toes Out—Concept 6
51M Power one leg (C-cuts forward) toes out multi push P

52M Power one leg (C-cuts forward) toes out single push P
53M Push heavy objects OI HC
54M Pull heavy objects OI P HC

Toes In—Concept 7
Edges—Concept 8
72M Edges backward (foot beside then behind) P HC
73M Slalom forward leading one skate P HC F
74M Slalom forward leading double pylons P HC F
75M Short C-cuts two skates alternating backward P HC F
76M Long fast C-cuts two skates alternating backward P HC F
77M Pull partner short C-cuts backward HC
78M Pull partner long C-cuts backward HC
79M Pull heavy objects backward P HC
80M Dribble puck between skates P HC
81M Figure 8 inside edges P HC

Heel—Concept 9
87M Walk on heels then jump on heels OI
88M C-cuts forward with heels only P HC F
89M Sharp Turns on dots or gloves P F
90M Power turns stick horizontal or vertical S
91M Quad turns 4 pylons P S F
92M Stick (lying on ice) sharp turns S
93M Sculling (snake) P HC S F
94M Crossover sculls P S
95M Flat foot skating P S

Knee Concepts
Knee Bend—Concept 10
110M Rocking crossovers in circle on whistle P F
111M Jump and turn toes 90 degrees out in parallel stationary OI P
112M Squat (OI Stationary on ice) F&B

Knee Extension—Concept 11
121M Forward scissors wide on outside edges P HC
122M Forward scissors narrow on outside edges fast P HC F

Lateral—Concept 12
128M Lateral crossovers on blue line, stop and fast on the whistle OI P HC F L&R
129M Double stick stepovers forward and backward (over sticks lying on ice) HC F F&B
130M Double stick stepover pivots forward and backward S

Drop—Concept 13
138M Drop to stomach while moving P
139M Drop to stomach and roll OI P S

Kick—Concept 14
145M Back kicks OI P F

Advanced Jump—Concept 15
148M Crossover tripod jump S

Balance Concepts
Agility—Concept 16
161M Jump 90° while skating (beginning of the stop) OI P L&R
162M Stick mirror speed drill S

Flexibility—Concept 17
169M Push puck off the line (inside outside blade) P
170M Squat Jump OI F P S F&B
171M Shumpka jumps (high jumps touching skates behind) OI S

Pivot—Concept 18
177M Partner pivots holding sticks OI P HC S
178M Straight line pivot on blue line stick horizontal HC

Power—Concept 19
192M Acceleration circle drive—circle in front of the net crossovers to accelerate then shoot S
193M Acceleration turn—sharp turn with two crossovers S
194M Steeple—backward and forward with stick horiz & glide S
195M Power Push—2 players hold stick and try to push against each other OI S
196M Stick pull backward—2 players hold stick and pull OI S

Special Combination Drills
Combo 5 (50E toe drag, 13U short fast steps, 22E fast arm pump, 60U long stride, all together stride) P
Magic 6—113A sit down balance, 68E edges, 108E circles forward, 117U circles backward, 134U 2 crossovers fwd & bkwd, 88M sharp turns

Book 2—Introduction to Puck Control
Hands Concepts
Grip—Concept 20
Wrist—Concept 21
Puck Repeat—Concept 22
203M Find the puck OI
204M Balance puck on both sides of stick OI
206M Repeat book 1 drills with a puck on the stick.

Eyes Concepts
Dribble—Concept 23
212M Dribble narrow and wide combo moving HC F
213M Dribble 3 zones stationary OI F

Balance—Concept 24
224M Dribble hands together (stationary and moving) OI HC F&B F
225M Dribble hands wide (stationary and moving) OI HC F&B F

Puck Concepts
Soft Hands—Concept 25
228M Dribble inside edge control one leg OI
229M Dribble thru legs stationary OI HC
230M Dribble through the legs moving

Agility—Concept 26
237M Dribble 2 pucks F&B HC When stationary dribble one puck at a time
238M 1 on 1 in corner
239M 1 on 1 in the corner teams
240M 2 on 1 in corner
241M 2 on 1 in corner & chase

Stick Concepts
Manipulate—Concept 27
252M Dribble circle OI HC
253M Dribble back and forth OI HC F
254M Run on spot and dribble combo OI F

Stick Length—Concept 28
259M Dribble figure 8 one handed moving (upper hand) OI HC
260M Figure 8 with sharp turns around 2 pylons HC P F
261M Figure 8 transition (facing the same way) HC P F
262M Attacking the triangle—2 triangles OI HC P S
263M Dribble stick lift partner on knees (stationary stick) OI HC
264M Dribble stick lift partner standing—both dribble, standing player lift stick over OI HC

Stick Reach—Concept 29
275M Puck carry one hand upper continuous OI F&B HC
276M Puck carry breakaway one hand upper combo OI HC
277M Puck carry breakaway two hand combo S

Stick Blade—Concept 30
283M Toe drag stationary HC
284M Dribble toe drag side (forehand out) moving HC

Puck-Control Balance Concepts
Puck Control—Concept 31
289M Dekes (Repeat most drills in book 2 with dekes when appropriate)

Special Combination Drills
Combo 5 (50E toe drag, 13U short fast steps, 22E fast arm pump, 60U long stride, all together stride) P
Magic 6—113A sit down balance, 68E edges, 108E circles forward, 117U circles backward, 134U 2 crossovers fwd & bkwd, 88M sharp turns

Appendix D

Advanced (A) Drill List

Book 1—Beginner Skating
Skate-Feel Concepts
Walk—Concept 1
12A Walk backward on heels OI P

Run—Concept 2
Glide—Concept 3
Jump—Concept 4
36A Jump legs crossed OI P L&R

Rock—Concept 5
42A Touch toes with horizontal stick then rock OI

Toe-Heel Concepts
Toes Out—Concept 6
55A Penguin walk forward heel-to-heel OI
56A Heel-to-heel on the boards OI
57A Heel-to-heel one skate straight line HC
58A Full skating stance and hold OI
59A Full stance push alternating long strides P S

Toes In—Concept 7
66A Walk toes in OI

Edges—Concept 8
82A Figure 8 outside edges P HC
83A Ankles L&R
84A Slalom backward parallel P
85A Half moon (half figure 8s) inside edges wide multi P HC

Heel—Concept 9
96A Scull Jump P S F&B
97A Euro shuffle both feet on the ice weight on heels P S
98A Heel-to-heel through single pylons P S
99A Heel-to-heel two feet straight line P HC
100A Heel-to-heel sit down OI

Knee Concepts
Knee Bend—Concept 10
113A Sit down balance F&B OI HC
114A Elbow balance OI
115A Step over and under stick (over and under twirl) F&B OI S
116A Step over and under stick jump (over and under twirl) F&B OI S

Knee Extension—Concept 11
123A Forward scissors wide outside edge jump lateral P HC
124A Backward scissors wide on outside edges P
125A Backward scissors narrow on outside edges fast P S F
126A Backward crossovers with tight 360 turn S

Lateral—Concept 12
131A Forward crossovers 3-2-1 P
132A Forward crossovers three speeds P F
133A Backward wave with crossovers P F

Drop—Concept 13
140A Drop to knees and do 360 degree spin on knees P S

Kick—Concept 14
146A Balance (stick horizontal) trio kicks OI F

Advanced Jump—Concept 15
149A Forward 2 foot tripod jump P S
150A Forward 1 foot tripod jump P S
151A Hurdler—high jump with one skate and land with the other P S
152A Forward to backward transition jump P S

Balance Concepts
Agility—Concept 16
163A Partner stepover mirror faster and faster F S
164A Heel-to-heel turn through double pylons P

Flexibility—Concept 17
172A Russian jump—lateral jump off inside edge of outside skate laterally OI P S
173A Edge Extreme drill—thru pylons stretch to inside edges extreme S
174A Stick behind horizontal down to skate heels OI S

Pivot—Concept 18
179A Slalom pivot—forward then pivot backward (feet together) S
180A Stick chases (two sticks lying on ice) S
181A Spin forward (360 degrees) P HC L&R
182A Spin backward (360 degrees) L&R
183A Circle pivot P S
184A Backward crossover pivot 90 degree P S
185A Pivot drive—accelerate toward net then pivot backward shoot S P
186A Starbust—pivots around ice continuously doing 360s like dancing S
187A Bart Simpson—pylons in 2 rows and pivot thru them facing one direction P S

Power—Concept 19
197A Stick battle (backward) OI S
198A Own the stick—2 players one stick push and pull stick OI S

Book 2—Introduction to Puck Control
Hands Concepts
Grip—Concept 20
Wrist—Concept 21
Puck Repeat—Concept 22
Eyes Concepts
Dribble—Concept 23
214A Dribble eyes closed stationary OI F
215A Dribble super fast stationary OI F
216A Knob drill (narrow-wide-fast) OI S F

217A Dribble rotation (puck spin) (on a string) HC
218A Shadow dribbling no pucks HC F F&B
219A Long wide stride inside edges dribble narrow S F

Balance—Concept 24
Puck Concepts
Soft Hands—Concept 25
231A Puck Scoops stationary and moving HC
232A Pick up puck and stick off the ice with glove OI
233A Control stick flat on ice OI
234A Dribble silent OI F

Agility—Concept 26
242A Dribble 3 pucks
243A 3 man keep away in front to net
244A Russian Dribble
245A Dribble two pucks feet HC
246A Heel-to-heel half circle each side S
247A Heel-to-heel half circle 1 on 1 P S
248A Puck catch S

Stick Concepts
Manipulate—Concept 27
255A Run on spot and dribble eyes closed OI

Stick Length—Concept 28
265A Dribble around body in triangle stationary OI HC
266A Dribble around body in triangle moving OI HC
267A Dribble round body side to side HC
268A Dribble body opposite—body leans to opposite side of puck OI HC
269A Dribble MFB—middle front backhand thru line of pucks HC
270A Dribble thru legs from back
271A Dribble around body stationary (5 zones) OI HC

Stick Reach—Concept 29
278A Forward wave with crossovers HC F

Stick Blade—Concept 30
285A Dribble toe drag side & front moving HC

286A Dribble toe drag backhand moving S

Puck-Control Balance Concepts
Puck Control—Concept 31
290A Protected dribbling with shoulder turn
291A 360 spin with puck on stick and sharp turns (in circle) HC P F&B
292A Circle body keep away P S

Appendix E
Ultimate (U) Drill List

Book 1—Beginner Skating
Skate-Feel Concepts
Walk—Concept 1
13U Short steps forward fast on whistle P F S

Run—Concept 2
19U Run on toes backward across the ice OI P

Glide—Concept 3
28U Glide one foot and swerve pylons P

Jump—Concept 4
37U High jumps moving P S F&B

Rock—Concept 5
43U Rock on skate blades while running OI P

Toe-Heel Concepts
Toes Out—Concept 6
60U Full stance push alternating long strides tap P S

Toes In—Concept 7
67U Power backward slow long C-cuts alternating skates P HC

Edges—Concept 8
86U Half moon (half figure 8s) outside edge wide multi P HC

Heel—Concept 9
101U Surfer—heel-to-heel straight line horizontal waist high S

Knee Concepts
Knee Bend—Concept 10
117U Crossovers circles backward on whistle F P

Knee Extension—Concept 11
127U Outside inside & under scull (snake) P S F&B

Lateral—Concept 12
134U Backward crossovers 3-2-1 P F

Drop—Concept 13
141U Russian knee drop OI P S F

Kick—Concept 14
147U Kicks skating backward P F

Advanced Jump—Concept 15
153U Jump 360 from forward to forward P S

Balance Concepts
Agility—Concept 16
165U Lateral crossover touches S

Flexibility—Concept 17
175U Serdachny Shuffle—sit down jump F&B OI P S F&B

Pivot—Concept 18
188U Skiing one foot edges and pivot and go other direction on same foot P

Power—Concept 19
199U Alternating long stride forward stick vertical in front then glide HC

Book 2—Introduction to Puck Control
Hands Concepts
Grip—Concept 20
Wrist—Concept 21
205U Bounce puck on stick blade OI HC

Puck Repeat—Concept 22
Eyes Concepts
Dribble—Concept 23
220U Dribble wide through double rows of pylons while skating HC

Balance—Concept 24
226U Dribble one leg 3 zones while moving (stationary and moving) F&B HC F

Puck Concepts
Soft Hands—Concept 25
235U Dribble puck outside on backhand side, and back between skates (then opposite) HC

Agility—Concept 26
249U Dribble one puck with stick and feet while moving

Stick Concepts
Manipulate—Concept 27
256U Dribble Slalom HC F

Stick Length—Concept 28
272U Dribble around body moving (5 zones) HC

Stick Reach—Concept 29
279U Hound dog—one checker chases drill S

Stick Blade—Concept 30
287U Toe drag Combo—tripod S

Puck-Control Balance Concepts
Puck Control—Concept 31
293U Puck straddle (two line of pucks and go in and out) HC

Appendix F
Fun Drill List

Ideas for Fun Drills

F1 The most important fun game in hockey is shinny. It can be played across the ice with up to three games at one time or on the whole rink end to end. No rules. Let the kids choose the teams. Many variations can be created.

F2 British Bull Dog

F3 Dodge ball (one or two balls)

F4 Race end to end to see who is the fastest

• **F5** Race end to end with sticks up

F6 Relay race end to end on half of the group versus the other half of the group

F7 Circle pass keep-away with and then without sticks. One person in the middle and the others around the circle, only one puck is required. Play keep-away by passing the puck around with the skate until the player in the middle intercepts the puck. Then that player goes on the circle while the other players remain on the outside. A supervisor is required at all time. You can use all the circles on the ice at the same time.

F8 Tandem race, one partner in the sit down position and the other partner pushes. Now race end to end against other groups.

F9 Shinny no sticks

F10 Shinny volleyball

F11 Two man tug of war across the blue line

F12 Two man push across the blue line

F13 Race by seeing who can go the farthest by pushing once with one leg then kick behind in the air with the other leg to keep the momentum going. Remain on one skate for the full race.

F14 Two against one keep-away

F15 Two against two keep-away

F16 Three against one keep-away

F17 Three-on-three keep in one end

F18 Three-on-three at each end of the rink or use the whole rink (make a mini tournament)

F19 Five on two (very good to reinforce passing)

F20 Shinny on knees to score

F21 Shinny wrong way (left shooters hold the stick right and right shooters hold the stick left).

F22 Shinny one arm (one hand on the stick only, left then right)

F23 Partner stepovers—mirror image of each other stepping over the sticks with crossovers

F24 Stick chase—face each other and chase around sticks with heel to heel S

F25 Checker figure 8 chasing puck carrier

F26 Three-man keep-away in front of net

Appendix G

Grading Checklist
E and M drills

Grading Checklist—Elementary (E) Drills

Ratings: NI (Needs Improvement)—still practicing and needs improvement
G (Good)—when appropriate do while skating backward
E (Excellent)—when appropriate do backward while carrying a puck

Name _____

Date _____ _____ _____

Drill	Grade	Grade	Grade

Book 1—Beginner Skating

Skate-Feel Concepts
Walk
1E Short steps forward OI P _____ _____ _____
2E Giant steps forward OI P _____ _____ _____
3E Down and up OI P HC _____ _____ _____
4E Beginners stance OI HC _____ _____ _____
5E Walk sideways OI P L&R _____ _____ _____
6E Walk forward on toes OI P _____ _____ _____
Run

14E Run on spot slow OI P
15E Run on the spot on whistle OI P F
16E Run then spin on spot OI P L&R

Glide
20E Glide two feet P HC
21E Glide two feet sitting F&B
22E Gliding arm pump fast F HC
23E Glide two feet and swerve P F&B
24E Glide two feet sit and swerve P F&B

Jump
29E Jump stationary OI P F
30E Jump lines P F
31E Jump high on boards OI
32E Jump high over blue line OI P
33E Balance one foot OI P HC

Rock
38E Rock on boards on skates OI
39E Rock on boards running OI F

Toe-Heel Concepts
Toes Out
44E Toes out 90° sitting on ice OI
45E Toes out 90° standing on ice OI
46E Toes out 90° moving on ice
47E Toes out against the boards OI
48E Push boards on whistle OI S
49E Carry puck in skates OI P HC
50E Knee drag with toes out HC P

Toes In
61E Toes in sitting & against boards OI
62E Toes in stationary (on ice) OI
63E Toes in toes out on the ice OI P

64E Toes out toes in semicircle ice HC _____ _____ _____
65E Backward C-cuts on the boards _____ _____ _____

Edges

68E Edges forward (foot in front) P _____ _____ _____
69E Edges forward (foot behind) P HC _____ _____ _____
70E Slalom forward parallel P HC F _____ _____ _____
71E Push and slide S _____ _____ _____

Heel

Knee Concepts

Knee Bend

102E Bend knees 90 degrees on boards OI _____ _____ _____
103E Balance one skate other knee high OI P _____ _____ _____
104E Run on spot knees high OI P F _____ _____ _____
105E Run backward and spin backward OI P _____ _____ _____
106E Mini crossovers circles P F F&B _____ _____ _____
107E Crossover stability—circles HC F&B _____ _____ _____
108E Crossovers circles forward F P _____ _____ _____
109E Run on toes balls of feet knees high OI P F _____ _____ _____

Knee Extension

118E Knee drag P _____ _____ _____
119E Three Knee Motion glide P F&B _____ _____ _____
120E Single stick stopovers fwd bckwd F F&B _____ _____ _____

Lateral

Drop

135E Drop one knee while stationary moving OI P F&B _____ _____ _____
136E Drop to both knees while moving P F&B _____ _____ _____

137E Drop to stomach while stationary OI P

Kick

142E Rotate skate in circle in air OI P F

143E Side kicks OI P F

144E Front kicks OI P F

Advanced Jump

Balance Concepts

Agility

154E Touch ups & touch backs OI S F

155E Touch combo OI S

1156E Single stepover forward tap S

157E Multi tap skates (toe, side heel) OI P

158E Tap skate with stick OI P

159E Walk and run with stick up OI F F&B

160E Horiz stick touch toes roll shoulder OI F&B

Flexibility

166E Automobile (OI stationary)

167E Airplane (OI stationary)

168E Ride on stick (OI stationary)

Pivot

176E Mohawk turn OI P HC

Power

189E Power outside 8s S

190E Gauntlet OI P

191E Isolation push stick horiz behind S

Book 2—Beginner Puck Control

Hands Concepts
Grip
200E Stick grip OI
201E Stick length OI
Wrist
202E Wrist Roll OI
Puck Repeat
Eyes Concepts
Dribble
207E Puck feel (eyes off the puck) OI
208E Dribble narrow stationary
   OI HC F
209E Dribble wide stationary OI HC F
210E Dribble slow stationary OI
211E Dribble fast stationary OI F
Balance
221E Dribble one leg OI F HC F&B
222E Dribble one hand OI F HC F&B
223E Dribble one hand OI F HC F&B

Puck Concepts (Puck Feel)
Soft Hands
227E Switch hands OI HC
Agility
236E Dribble through single pylons
   P HC F

Stick Concepts
Manipulate
250E Dribble diagonal OI HC
251E Dribble square OI HC
Stick Length
257E Dribble figure 8 two
   handed HC F

258E Dribble around double pylons F&B ___ ___ ___

Stick Reach

273E Dribble Figure 8 stick on the ice OI P HC ___ ___ ___

274E Puck carry two hand continuous OI HC F&B ___ ___ ___

Stick Blade

280E Stick blade pressure OI ___ ___ ___

281E Stick Toe-Heel OI HC ___ ___ ___

282E Stick toe dribble—toe of blade only HC ___ ___ ___

Puck-Control Balance Concepts
Puck Control

288E Stationary Fakes OI ___ ___ ___

Grading Checklist—Medium (M) Drills

Ratings: NI (Needs Improvement)—still practicing and needs improvement
G (Good)—when appropriate do while skating backward
E (Excellent)—when appropriate do backward while carrying a puck

Name _____

Date _____ _____ _____

Drill	Grade	Grade	Grade

Book 1—Beginner Skating

Skate-Feel Concepts
Walk
7M Walk forward on heels OI P
8M Walk backward on toes OI P
9M Walk skates loose OI
10M Lateral one side step whistle OI P L&R
11M Lateral side steps fast whistle OI P F L&R

Run
17M Run on toes forward OI P F
18M Lateral high side steps whistle OI P F L&R

Glide
25M Glide one foot forward P HC
26M Glide one foot forward knee bend P HC
27M Glide toe on puck P HC

Jump

34M Hop one foot stationary OI P
HC F

35M Jump One Foot OI P HC F F&B

Rock

40M Rock stationary one foot OI P

41M Rock two foot while skating
OI P F

Toe-Heel Concepts

Toes Out

51M Power one leg toes out multi
push P

52M Power one leg toes out single
push P

53M Push heavy objects OI HC

54M Pull heavy objects OI P HC

Toes In

Edges

72M Edges backward (foot behind)
P HC

73M Slalom forward leading skate P
HC F

74M Slalom forward leading pylons P
HC F

75M Short C-cuts alternating
backward P HC F

76M Long C-cuts alternating
backward P HC F

77M Pull partner short C-cuts
backward HC

78M Pull partner long C-cuts
backward HC

79M Pull heavy objects backward
P HC

80M Dribble puck between skates P HC

81M Figure 8 inside edges P HC

Heel

87M Walk on heels then jump on heels OI

88M C-cuts forward with heels only P HC F

89M Sharp Turns on dots or gloves P F

90M Power turns stick horiz or vertical S

91M Quad turns 4 pylons P S F

92M Stick (lying on ice) sharp turns S

93M Sculling (snake) P HC S F

94M Crossover skulls P S

95M Flat foot skating P S

Knee Concepts

Knee Bend

110M Rocking crossovers circle whistle P F

111M Jump and turn 90 degrees stationary OI P

112M Squat (OI Stationary on ice) F&B

Knee Extension

121M Forward scissors wide outside edge P HC

122M Forward scissors narrow outside edge F P HC

Lateral

128M Lateral crossovers whistle OI P HC F L&R

129M Double stick stepover HC F F&B

130M Double stepover pivots S _____ _____ _____

Drop
138M Drop to stomach while moving P _____ _____ _____
139M Drop to Stomach and roll OI P S _____ _____ _____

Kick
145M Back kicks OI P F _____ _____ _____

Advanced Jump
148M Crossover tripod jump S _____ _____ _____

Balance Concepts

Agility
161M Jump 90° while skating OI P L&R _____ _____ _____
162M Stick mirror speed drill S _____ _____ _____

Flexibility
169M Push puck off the line P _____ _____ _____
170M Squat Jump OI F P S F&B _____ _____ _____
171M Shumpka Jumps OI P S _____ _____ _____

Pivot
177M Partner pivots holding sticks OI HC S _____ _____ _____
178M Straight line pivot blue line horiz HC _____ _____ _____

Power
192M Acceleration circle drive S _____ _____ _____
193M Acceleration turn 2 crossovers S _____ _____ _____
194M Steeple backward horiz & glide S _____ _____ _____
195M Power Push OI S _____ _____ _____
196M Stick pull backward OI S _____ _____ _____

Book 2—Beginner Puck Control

Hands Concepts
Grip
Wrist
Puck Repeat
203M Find the puck OI
204M Balance Puck on both sides of stick OI
206M Repeat Book 1 drills with puck

Eyes Concepts
Dribble
212M Dribble combo moving HC F
213M Dribble 3 zones stationary OI F
Balance
224M Dribble hands together OI HC F&B F
225M Dribble hands wide OI HC F F&B F

Puck Concepts (Puck Feel)
Soft Hands
228M Dribble inside skate edge one leg OI
229M Dribble thru legs stationary OI HC
230M Dribble through the legs moving
Agility
237M Dribble 2 pucks F&B HC
238M one-on-one in corner
239M one-on-one in the corner teams
240M 2 on 1 in corner
241M 2 on 1 in corner & chase

Stick Concepts

Beginner Puck Control

Manipulate

252M Dribble circle OI HC _____ _____ _____

253M Dribble back and forth OI HC F _____ _____ _____

254M Run on spot and dribble combo OI F _____ _____ _____

Stick Length

259M Dribble figure 8 one hand OI HC _____ _____ _____

260M Figure 8 with sharp turns 2 pylons HC P F _____ _____ _____

261M Figure 8 transition HC _____ _____ _____

262M Attacking the triangle OI HC P S _____ _____ _____

263M Dribble stick lift partner on knees OI HC _____ _____ _____

264M Dribble stick lift partner standing OI HC _____ _____ _____

Stick Reach

275M Puck carry one hand continuous OI F&B HC _____ _____ _____

276M Puck carry breakaway one hand OI HC _____ _____ _____

277M Puck carry breakaway two hand S _____ _____ _____

Stick Blade

283M Stick toe drag stationary HC _____ _____ _____

284M Dribble toe drag side moving HC _____ _____ _____

Puck-Control Balance Concepts

Puck Control

289M Dekes (Repeat most drills in book 2) _____ _____ _____

Appendix H

Grading Checklist—Skill Concepts (Concepts/Levels 1-31)

Ratings: NI (Needs Improvement)—still practicing and needs improvement
G (Good)—can do more than half of the drills involving the concept while skating backward
E (Excellent)—can do 75 percent of the drills involving the concept while skating backward while carrying a puck

Book 1: Beginner Skating Concepts/Levels

Name _____

Date _____ _____ _____

Basic Skills	Grade	Grade	Grade
Skate-Feel Concepts			
1 Walk	____	____	____
2 Run	____	____	____
2 Glide	____	____	____
4 Jump	____	____	____
5 Rock	____	____	____
Toe-Heel Concepts			
6 Toes Out	____	____	____
7 Toes In	____	____	____
8 Edges	____	____	____
9 Heel	____	____	____

Knee Concepts
    10 Knee Bend
    11 Knee Drag
    12 Lateral
    13 Drop
    14 Kick
    15 Adv Jump

Balance Concepts
    16 Agility
    17 Flexibility
    18 Pivot
    19 Power

Book 2: Beginner Puck-Control Levels

Hands Concepts
    20 Grip
    21 Wrist
    22 Puck Repeat

Eyes Concepts
    23 Dribble
    24 Balance

Puck Concepts
    25 Soft Hands
    26 Agility

Stick Concepts
    27 Manipulate
    28 Stick Length
    29 Stick Reach
    30 Stick Blade

Puck-Control Balance Concepts
    31 Puck Control

Appendix I

General Contents Volume 2

Content Summary Volume 2—*The Hockey Method* Books 3-5
Book 3—Skating
    Introduction
    Instructing
    Basic Skills
    Skating
        1. Basic Stop Process
        2. Forward Skating
            Timing
            Video
            Stride
            Sprint
            Acceleration
        3. Backward Skating
        4. Agility Skating
            1. Starts
            2. Stops
            3. Crossovers
            4. Turns
            5. Pivots

Book 4—Passing
    Puck Control
    Forehand or Wrist
    Sweep
    Backhand
    Flip
    Flat
    Snap

Relay

Book 5—Shooting
Flip
Wrist
Backhand
Slap
Snap

Book 6—Coaching
Planning Process
    Strategy
    Yearly Practice Plan
    Daily Practice Plan
Team Play
    Offensive
    Defensive
Goaltending
Fun Drills